New Edition

Longman

Chemistry

11–14

Iain Brand | Richard Grime

Contents

Contents

Contents

How to use this book

Introduction: Each topic starts with a question. The question should help you to think about what you are going to study. You should be able to answer this question by the time you finish the topic.

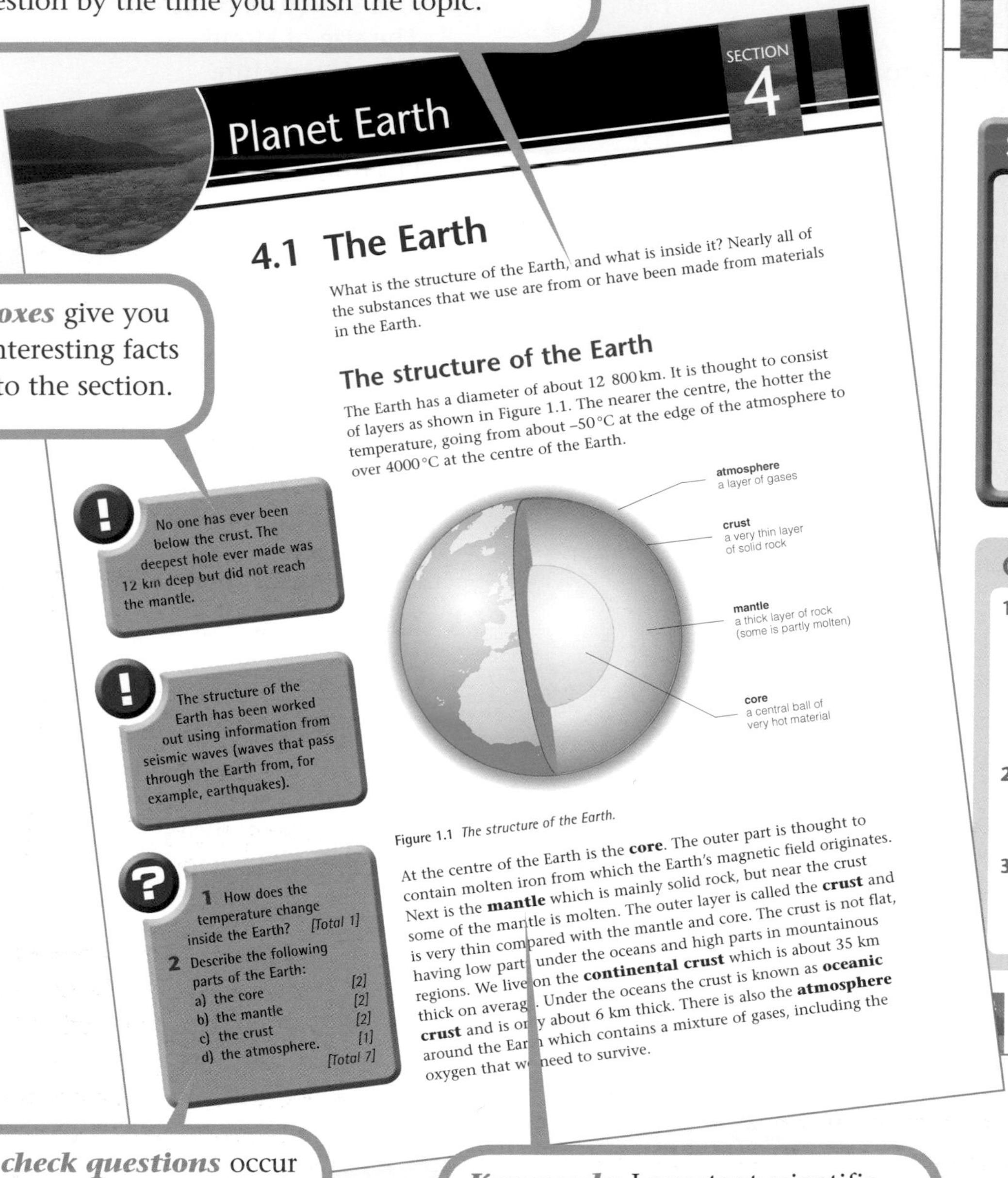

Planet Earth

SECTION
4

4.1 The Earth

What is the structure of the Earth, and what is inside it? Nearly all of the substances that we use are from or have been made from materials in the Earth.

The structure of the Earth

The Earth has a diameter of about 12 800 km. It is thought to consist of layers as shown in Figure 1.1. The nearer the centre, the hotter the temperature, going from about –50°C at the edge of the atmosphere to over 4000°C at the centre of the Earth.

Fact boxes give you some interesting facts linked to the section.

! No one has ever been below the crust. The deepest hole ever made was 12 km deep but did not reach the mantle.

! The structure of the Earth has been worked out using information from seismic waves (waves that pass through the Earth from, for example, earthquakes).

? 1 How does the temperature change inside the Earth? [Total 1]

2 Describe the following parts of the Earth:
a) the core [2]
b) the mantle [2]
c) the crust [2]
d) the atmosphere. [1]
[Total 7]

atmosphere
a layer of gases

crust
a very thin layer of solid rock

mantle
a thick layer of rock (some is partly molten)

core
a central ball of very hot material

Figure 1.1 *The structure of the Earth.*

At the centre of the Earth is the **core**. The outer part is thought to contain molten iron from which the Earth's magnetic field originates. Next is the **mantle** which is mainly solid rock, but near the crust some of the mantle is molten. The outer layer is called the **crust** and is very thin compared with the mantle and core. The crust is not flat, having low parts under the oceans and high parts in mountainous regions. We live on the **continental crust** which is about 35 km thick on average. Under the oceans the crust is known as **oceanic crust** and is only about 6 km thick. There is also the **atmosphere** around the Earth which contains a mixture of gases, including the oxygen that we need to survive.

Quick check questions occur throughout the topic. These will help you and your teacher to check you have understood the material so far.

Key words: Important scientific words are in bold the first time that they appear in a section. You will also find a glossary at the back of the book. The glossary has a definition of each of these words.

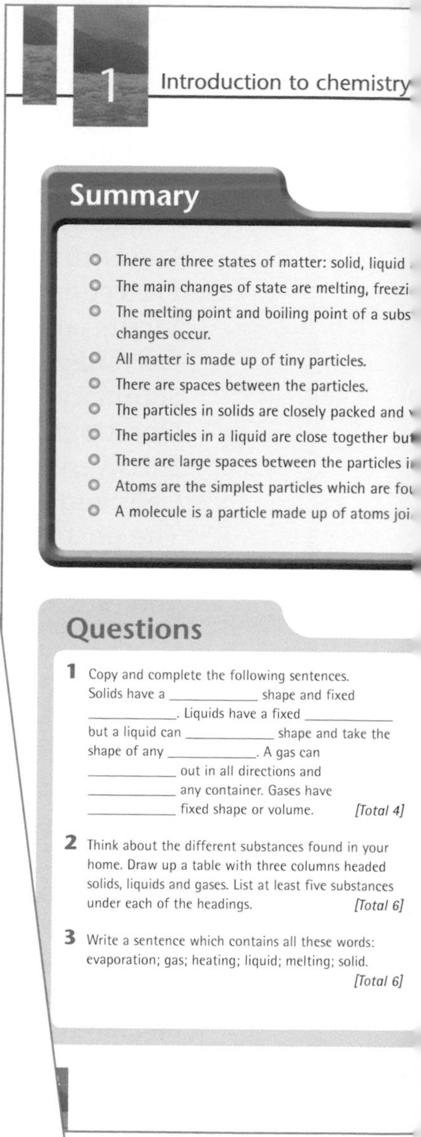

---

1 Introduction to chemistry

Summary

- There are three states of matter: solid, liquid
- The main changes of state are melting, freezi
- The melting point and boiling point of a subs changes occur.
- All matter is made up of tiny particles.
- There are spaces between the particles.
- The particles in solids are closely packed and
- The particles in a liquid are close together but
- There are large spaces between the particles i
- Atoms are the simplest particles which are fou
- A molecule is a particle made up of atoms joi

Questions

1 Copy and complete the following sentences. Solids have a _____ shape and fixed _____. Liquids have a fixed _____ but a liquid can _____ shape and take the shape of any _____. A gas can _____ out in all directions and _____ any container. Gases have _____ fixed shape or volume. [Total 4]

2 Think about the different substances found in your home. Draw up a table with three columns headed solids, liquids and gases. List at least five substances under each of the headings. [Total 6]

3 Write a sentence which contains all these words: evaporation; gas; heating; liquid; melting; solid. [Total 6]

Summary boxes: Each topic ends with a summary which will help you to draw together what you have just read. They will also help you to revise.

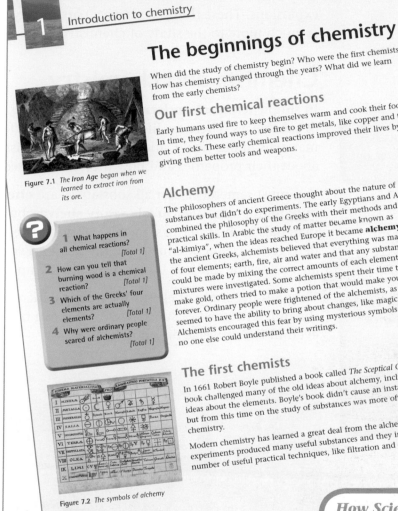

1 Introduction to chemistry

The beginnings of chemistry

When did the study of chemistry begin? Who were the first chemists? How has chemistry changed through the years? What did we learn from the early chemists?

Our first chemical reactions

Early humans used fire to keep themselves warm and cook their food. In time, they found ways to use fire to get metals, like copper and tin, out of rocks. These early chemical reactions improved their lives by giving them better tools and weapons.

Figure 7.1 *The Iron Age began when we learned to extract iron from its ore.*

?

1 What happens in all chemical reactions?
[Total 1]

2 How can you tell that burning wood is a chemical reaction?
[Total 1]

3 Which of the Greeks' four elements are actually elements?
[Total 1]

4 Why were ordinary people scared of alchemists?
[Total 1]

Alchemy

The philosophers of ancient Greece thought about the nature of substances but didn't do experiments. The early Egyptians and Arabs combined the philosophy of the Greeks with their methods and practical skills. In Arabic the study of matter became known as "al-kimiya", when the ideas reached Europe it became **alchemy**. Like the ancient Greeks, alchemists believed that everything was made up of four elements; earth, fire, air and water and that any substance could be made by mixing the correct amounts of each element. Many mixtures were investigated. Some alchemists spent their time trying to make gold, others tried to make a potion that would make you live forever. Ordinary people were frightened of the alchemists, as they seemed to have the ability to bring about changes, like magic. Alchemists encouraged this fear by using mysterious symbols so that no one else could understand their writings.

The first chemists

In 1661 Robert Boyle published a book called *The Sceptical Chymist*. The book challenged many of the old ideas about alchemy, including the ideas about the elements. Boyle's book didn't cause an instant change, but from this time on the study of substances was more often called chemistry.

Modern chemistry has learned a great deal from the alchemists. Their experiments produced many useful substances and they invented a number of useful practical techniques, like filtration and distillation.

Figure 7.2 *The symbols of alchemy*

36

boiling and condensation.
~xed temperatures at which those

~nd each other.
particles move in all directions.
~r.

~e the changes of state described here.
~Molten iron cooling and solidifying. [1]
~Vax dripping down a candle. [1]
~he bathroom window misting up. [1]
~ainted fence drying in the sun. [1]
[Total 4]

~natter is made up of tiny particles.
~Vhat are the three states of matter? [1]
~n which state are the particles
~ furthest apart
~) closest together? [2]
~escribe the difference between the particles in a
~olid and the particles in a liquid. [2]
[Total 5]

How Science Works pages: At the end of each section there are pages that look at How Science Works. Each topic on these pages is linked to part of the work in the section you have just read.

Question boxes: There are question boxes at the end of each topic. The questions towards the end of each box may be a little harder, to help you to see how well you have understood the work.

Some questions have an **R** next to them. These are research questions. You will need to use other books or the Internet to write a full answer to these questions.

In the end of section questions some questions have a **P** next to them. These questions can be used to help you plan practical investigations.

Introduction to chemistry

1.1 What is chemistry?

What is chemistry and what do chemists do? Some people think that chemistry is all about strange coloured liquids, smelly gases and violent explosions. These things do have a part to play in the subject, but there is much more to the study of chemistry.

Chemists and chemistry

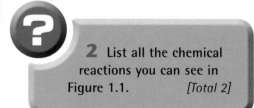

1 What do chemists try to find out? *[Total 1]*

In simple terms, **chemistry** is the study of the structure and properties of substances. There are literally millions of different substances and materials in our world, and by studying chemistry we can find out about their properties and how they can be used.

You must remember that all substances are **chemicals**. They are not only found in bottles on laboratory shelves, but include everyday materials such as plastics, metals, fabrics, adhesives, paints, dyes, detergents, cosmetics, fuels and medicines. Even the food we eat, the air we breathe and our bodies are all made up of chemicals.

Through the study of chemistry we have increased our knowledge of the different types of substances which can be found in our world, and even in the universe beyond.

Most foods are mixtures of naturally occurring chemicals. For example chocolate, probably one of the most complex foods, contains over 300 different chemicals.

2 List all the chemical reactions you can see in Figure 1.1. *[Total 2]*

Figure 1.1 Chemical reactions in everyday life.

Chemistry has undoubtedly helped us gain a better understanding of ourselves and our environment. In particular, we have learned how one substance can be changed into another. These changes, which are called **chemical reactions**, are very important in chemistry. Chemical reactions always involve the formation of one or more new substances. They occur all around us: fuels burning, foods cooking, plants growing and cars rusting are all examples of chemical reactions in everyday life. The study of chemical reactions, and how to make new substances is the basis of the chemical industry. An understanding of chemical reactions can also be used to explain many of the complex changes that occur in nature and the home.

? **3** What is a chemical reaction? [Total 1]

What do chemists do?

Many people think that a chemist is someone who works in a chemist's shop, making up prescriptions and selling cosmetics. This type of chemist is called a **pharmacist** but there are many other kinds of chemist.

? **4** What is the difference between a chemist and a pharmacist? [Total 1]

Since chemistry is the study of all substances, chemists can be found working in a large number of different industries and occupations. Any activity that involves materials or the use or production of substances must require some knowledge of chemistry. In fact anyone who understands something about the nature of substances and chemical reactions could be called a chemist.

Here are a few examples of some jobs and activities that require a knowledge of chemistry.

Figure **1.2** *Jobs in chemistry.*

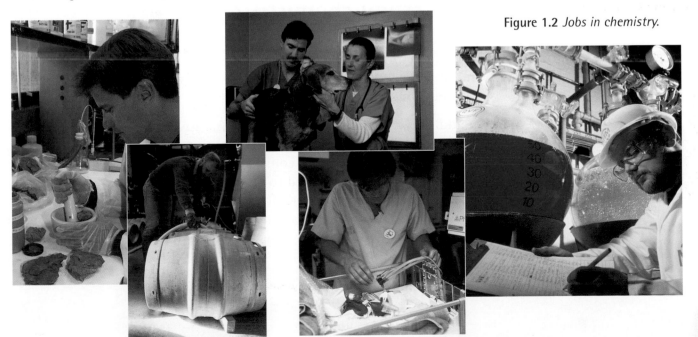

Figure 1.3 *A chemical plant that produces petrochemicals.*

Figure 1.4 *Made from salt.*

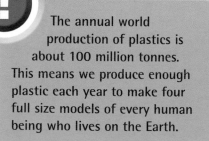

The annual world production of plastics is about 100 million tonnes. This means we produce enough plastic each year to make four full size models of every human being who lives on the Earth.

The chemical industry in the United Kingdom

The **chemical industry** makes a major contribution to the wealth of our country and the quality of our lives. The purpose of this industry is to make a profit by manufacturing useful products from **raw materials**. The main raw materials used in the chemical industry are **coal**, **crude oil**, **natural gas**, **metal ores**, other **minerals**, **air** and **water**.

The chemical industry is responsible for the manufacture of a vast range of useful products. These new materials have helped to improve our health and our standard of living. Can you imagine a world without medicines, plastics, soaps, detergents, textiles, cosmetics, paints, food additives, fertilisers, solvents, pesticides and all the other products of the chemical industry?

Since the age of the Industrial Revolution and the large scale production of chemicals such as bleaches, dyes, acids and alkalis, the chemical industry has been very important to our economy. The chemical industry is the fourth largest manufacturing industry in the United Kingdom and brings billions of pounds into the country every year.

Consider some of the uses of common salt, which we obtain from the raw material called rock salt. We all know that we put salt on our food and spread it on icy roads. However, salt and its products are also used in many chemical industries.

Why study chemistry?

There are many reasons why we should study chemistry. Everything around us is made up of chemicals. Indeed everything we can see, feel and touch is made up of chemicals. We need a knowledge of chemistry to understand all these substances and to use them properly.

In addition, many of the most important advances in science and technology have been made possible by the production of new chemicals. From the silicon computer chip to the nose cone of a space rocket, we are indebted to chemists and chemistry for the specialised materials required. To continue to develop our civilised world we will need more new materials, with new properties and new uses. We will therefore always need people who understand chemistry and chemical reactions.

Finally, take a look around you at all the different substances we use to improve our lives.

Unfortunately we misuse them sometimes, causing pollution, damaging our health and wasting resources. Serious problems like these cannot be solved unless we all understand our material world. We cannot leave everything to the experts, and common sense is not always enough. Everyone needs some chemical sense, and this can only be gained by studying chemistry.

Figure 1.5 *Chemistry can tell us the causes and cures of pollution.*

 The chemical industry is the only major manufacturing industry in the UK to export more than it imports. This is very important to the UK.

 5 Name five products made from salt. *[Total 2]*

6 Why should we study chemistry? *[Total 1]*

Summary

- Chemistry is the study of the structure and properties of substances.
- All substances are chemicals.
- Chemical reactions involve the formation of new substances.
- The chemical industry changes raw materials into more useful products.
- The main raw materials are coal, crude oil, natural gas, metal ores, minerals, air and water.
- A knowledge of chemistry is necessary to understand our material world.

Questions

1 a) Copy and complete the following sentences.
Chemistry is the study of the _____
and _____ of _____. People
who study chemistry are called
_____. The chemical industry makes
useful _____ from _____
materials. [3]

b) Copy and complete Table 1.1 by listing five
more activities or occupations which involve
chemistry, and state why you think that
they are important. [10]

Table 1.1

Activity or occupation involving chemistry	Importance
Pharmacy	To supply medicines and understand their use in the treatment of illnesses.

[Total 13]

2 a) What happens in all chemical reactions? [1]

b) Describe three everyday chemical reactions. [3]

[Total 4]

3 The chemical industry is very important to our
economy and our everyday life.

a) List four raw materials used in the chemical
industry. [4]

b) Name four useful products made by the
chemical industry. [2]

c) Table 1.2 shows the annual (2007) world
production of some of our major chemical
products that are not derived from oil.
Draw a **bar chart** to show all this information
clearly. (Remember to give a title to your chart
as well as labelling each axis and giving
any units.) [4]

d) Use the bar chart to answer the following
questions.
i) Which *two* chemicals are produced in greatest
quantities?
ii) Compare the production of ammonia and
chlorine gas. How much more ammonia is
produced each year? [2]

Table 1.2

Chemical product	Annual world production (million tonnes) in 2007
ammonia	124
chlorine	55
sulphuric acid	157
phosphoric acid	34
sodium hydroxide	46

[Total 12]

4 Imagine that a friend has asked you why you need
to study chemistry. Write a short passage (about
100 words) to explain why an understanding of
chemistry is both useful and important. [Total 5]

5 Read the following passage to help you answer
the questions below.
Industrial, agricultural and domestic waste are all
possible sources of pollution to our environment.
Gases produced by burning fuels pollute the air.
The rivers and lakes are polluted by waste from
factories. Rubbish pollutes the land. These waste
materials pose a threat to all life forms, including
ourselves. It is therefore essential that we
understand problems of pollution and are willing
to take action to solve them.

a) Suggest a suitable title for this passage. [1]

b) Describe three ways that our environment can
be polluted. [3]

c) Describe one example of pollution and briefly
explain how it poses a threat to life. [2]

[Total 6]

1.2 Experiments in chemistry

What kinds of equipment and skills do chemists need to carry out experiments? Chemists find out about the nature of substances by carrying out **experiments** in a **laboratory**. Knowledge and understanding of the apparatus and skills required for these **practical investigations** is an important aspect of chemistry.

? **1** List as many pieces of apparatus used in chemistry as you can.

[Total 2]

Apparatus in chemistry

The equipment used in a chemistry laboratory is called **apparatus**. When describing an experiment, the apparatus is usually drawn as an outline diagram. Not only is this easier than drawing a picture of the apparatus, it also gives a clearer description of how the experiment was carried out. Examples of outline diagrams are shown in Figure 2.1, alongside a photograph of the apparatus.

! Glass is made from sand (chemical name, silicon dioxide). Different types of glass can be made by adding different substances to the sand. Adding soda-lime makes a cheap glass used for windows and bottles. Pyrex, which is used for beakers and test tubes, has boric oxide added.

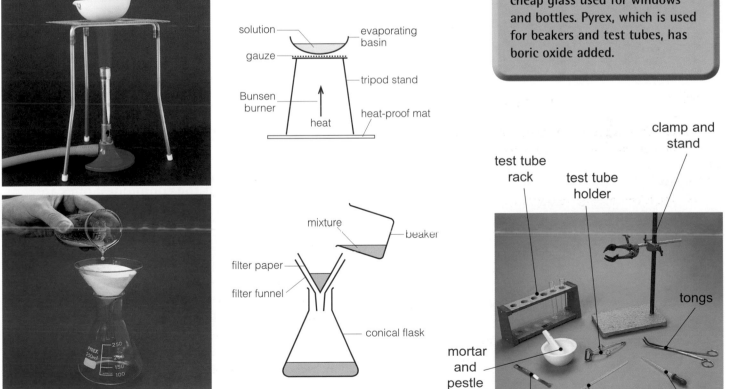

Figure 2.1 *Common lab apparatus.*

There are many other pieces of apparatus which are used by chemists. Often they will not be included in diagrams. More examples of pieces of apparatus are shown in Figure 2.2.

Figure 2.2 *More apparatus used in chemistry.*

Figure 2.3 *The Bunsen burner.*

The Bunsen burner

The **Bunsen burner** is the main source of heat used in the laboratory. It is safe and easy to use if you remember the following rules.

- The air hole should be closed before lighting.
- Have a flame ready to light the Bunsen burner before turning on the gas.
- If you are *not using* the Bunsen burner, close the air hole to give a *yellow flame* or turn it off (Figure 2.3, top).
- To *heat gently*, half open the air hole to give a *blue flame* (Figure 2.3, middle).
- To heat strongly, open the air hole wide to give a roaring flame (Figure 2.3, bottom).

The gas flow can also be adjusted to change the size of the flame.

The hottest part of the Bunsen burner flame is at the top of the central cone, which is formed when the air hole is wide open. The temperature at this point can be as high as 1800 °C.

Measurement in chemistry

In many experiments we have to measure quantities such as mass, volume, temperature and time. The ability to use measuring devices, read scales and apply the correct units is an essential skill in chemistry and all science subjects.

Measuring mass

A **balance** can be used to measure the **mass** of a substance. There are many different types of balances, but the commonest ones are **electronic balances**.

The correct units for measuring mass are grams (g) and kilograms (kg).

- 1 kilogram = 1000 grams
- or 1 kg   = 1000 g

A sensitive electronic balance is an expensive piece of apparatus. Balances should always be used carefully. Never pour chemicals directly on to the weighing-pan, but place them in a beaker or other suitable container. The weight of the substance in the container is found by subtraction. For example:

- mass of beaker + substance = 156.70 g
- mass of beaker   = 125.50 g
- mass of substance   =   31.20 g

Some balances have a 'tare facility' that sets the reading back to zero. This simplifies weighing chemicals, by automatically taking away the mass of the container.

Measuring volume

The **volume** of a liquid is a measure of how much space it takes up. There are several pieces of apparatus that can be used for measuring volumes. The most suitable measuring device depends on the volumes to be measured and the accuracy required. The measuring cylinder is the simplest to use and can measure fairly large volumes. However, burettes and pipettes are more accurate, and droppers can be used to measure small volumes of liquid.

Figure 2.4 *The correct way to read a measuring cylinder.*

The correct units for measuring the volume of a liquid are litres (l) and cubic centimetres (cm^3).

- 1 litre = 1000 cubic centimetres
- or 1 l = 1000 cm^3

The scales on most measuring cylinders, burettes and pipettes show the volume in cubic centimetres (cm^3) although some use millilitres (ml). These units have the same value, that is, 1 cm^3 = 1 ml.

In all volume measuring devices, the surface of the liquid curves upwards at the edges and forms a **meniscus**. When reading the scale on a measuring cylinder you should:

- place the cylinder on a flat surface
- make sure your eye is level with the surface of the liquid
- read the scale at the bottom of the meniscus.

How would you measure the volume of 1 drop of water? Add 100 drops of water to a measuring cylinder and measure the volume. Divide this volume by 100 and you have the volume of one drop. Easy!

Figure 2.4 shows the correct way to use a measuring cylinder. The volume of liquid in this cylinder is 42 cm^3.

Measuring temperature

A **thermometer** can be used to measure **temperature**. There are several different types of thermometer. The ones most commonly used in the chemistry laboratory are the alcohol in glass thermometer, as shown in Figure 2.5, and the mercury in glass thermometer.

Temperature is measured using the **Celsius scale**, which is based on the temperatures at which water freezes and boils. The correct units for measuring temperature are degrees Celsius (°C), i.e.

- boiling point of water = 100 °C
- freezing point of water = 0 °C

Figure 2.5 *Measuring the temperature of a liquid using an alcohol in glass thermometer.*

The German chemist Christian Schonbein (1799–1868) discovered a type of explosive when he accidentally spilled a mixture of sulphuric and nitric acid on his kitchen table. He wiped up the spill with his wife's apron and left it near the fire to dry. His attempts to cover up his accident were exposed, however, when the apron suddenly exploded. His wife wasn't amused, but Schonbein had discovered nitro-cellulose, an explosive fabric. Similar methods were later used to produce other explosives like nitroglycerine (dynamite) and trinitrotoluene (TNT).

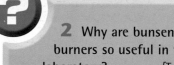

2 Why are bunsen burners so useful in the laboratory? *[Total 1]*

3 Name four measuring instruments used by chemists. *[Total 1]*

4 Choose one safety rule and explain why it is important. *[Total 1]*

To measure the temperature of a liquid correctly, totally immerse the bulb of the thermometer and leave it for a minute or two before reading the scale. Do not take the thermometer out of the liquid to read the scale.

Measuring time

A stop clock can be used to measure the time passed. The correct units for measuring time are hours (hr), minutes (min) and seconds (s).

- 1 hour = 60 minutes
- 1 minute = 60 seconds

Laboratory safety rules

Chemistry laboratories are safe places to work in as long as everyone obeys the safety rules.

Here is a set of laboratory safety rules. Make sure you understand and obey them.

- Do not enter the laboratory unless a teacher gives you permission.
- Never run or fool around in the laboratory.
- Never eat or drink in the laboratory.
- Never carry out experiments without your teacher's approval.
- Before starting an experiment put all bags, jackets and stools out of the way, and tie back loose hair and clothing.
- Make sure you understand all instructions before you start an experiment.
- Wear eye protection during all experiments involving heat or chemicals.
- Always use small amounts of chemicals.
- When heating a test tube point it away from people.
- Report all accidents and breakages immediately.
- Take your time: if you are not sure what to do, ASK!
- Clean and clear up all apparatus and leave the laboratory as you found it.

The safety rules are only common sense. A chemistry laboratory should be a tidy and orderly environment. A place to work and learn, not a place to play. Ignoring safety rules is not only stupid and dangerous, it is also unscientific.

Figure 2.6 *What safety rules?*

Hazard symbols

The substances used in a chemistry laboratory are safe if used properly. However, certain chemicals can cause particular problems, so they are labelled with **hazard symbols**.

Table 2.1 shows the meanings of some of the standard hazard symbols.

The terms 'flammable' and 'inflammable' are similar. Both describe a substance that can catch fire. A substance that is not flammable is called non-flammable.

Table 2.1

Label	Hazard	Label	Hazard
	Corrosive: Substances which can burn and destroy living tissue.		Toxic: Substances which represent a serious risk of causing death by poisoning.
	Explosive: Substances which may explode if heated, exposed to a flame or knocked.		Harmful: Substances which represent a moderate risk to health.
	Flammable: Substances which, if in contact with air, may catch fire easily.		Irritant: Substances which can cause inflammation of the skin.

The ancient Greeks, including Aristotle and Democritus, were the first to consider the structure of materials. They didn't do experiments, however, but tried to find answers to questions by reasoned argument alone. They were philosophers, not scientists, and it wasn't until we learned to use experiments and practical investigations that we could properly explain the nature of substances.

Writing up experiments

Chemists should always plan their experiments and investigations carefully. They must use scientific methods to solve problems in chemistry. Most experiments will involve a series of steps and these should be explained when writing up the experiment.

- The **aim** describes what you are trying to find out.
- The **method** describes how the experiment is to be carried out.
- The **results** of the experiments should be recorded in a suitable form.
- The **conclusion** describes what you have found out.

Practical investigations are special types of experiments which are essential to the study of all science subjects including chemistry. They are dealt with in more detail in Section 7.

Summary

- Chemists study substances by doing experiments and practical investigations.
- The equipment used in chemistry is called apparatus.
- Measuring cylinders, burettes, pipettes and droppers are used to measure volumes of liquids.
- Volume is measured in litres (l) or cubic centimetres (cm^3).
- Mass is measured in grams (g) or kilograms (kg).
- Temperature is measured in degrees Celsius (°C).
- Time is measured in hours (h), minutes (min) and seconds (s).
- When doing experiments you must always follow the laboratory safety rules.
- The main stages in any experiment are: aim, method, results, conclusions.

Questions

1 Copy and complete the following sentences.
Chemists work in a _____ using
equipment which is usually called _____.
Beakers, _____ and _____ are all
glass containers used to hold liquids.   *[Total 2]*

2 Draw an outline diagram of the following pieces
of apparatus:
a) beaker   *[1]*   b) Bunsen burner *[1]*
c) tripod stand *[1]*   d) test tube   *[1]*
e) conical flask *[1]*   f) filter funnel.   *[1]*
                                              [Total 6]

3 Briefly describe what each of the following pieces
of apparatus is used for:
a) tongs   *[1]*   b) spatula *[1]*
c) conical flask *[1]*   d) dropper. *[1]*
                                              [Total 4]

4 Here is a list of measuring devices:
measuring cylinder   stop clock
electronic balance   thermometer
a) Which device is most likely to be used by each
   of the following people?
   i) doctor   ii) athletics coach
   iii) gold merchant   iv) pharmacist.   *[4]*
b) Briefly describe how the measuring device
   might be used in each occupation.   *[4]*
                                              [Total 8]

5 A pupil was asked to heat 100 cm³ of water in a
beaker by using a Bunsen burner, and to measure
the temperature of the water with a thermometer
every 2 minutes. Draw a labelled outline diagram
of the apparatus for this experiment.   *[Total 2]*

6 Calculate the following conversions of units:
a) 3400 cm³ to litres   *[1]*
b) 3.8 litres to cm³   *[1]*
c) 0.55 kilograms to grams   *[1]*
d) 2400 grams to kilograms   *[1]*

e) $4\frac{1}{2}$ minutes to seconds   *[1]*
f) 1220 seconds to minutes and seconds.   *[1]*
                                              [Total 6]

7 Using Figure 2.6 on page 11, list all the hazards and
broken rules you can see in the picture. (Hint: there
are at least 12 examples of bad laboratory practice in
the drawing.)   *[Total 6]*

8 Draw hazard symbols that could be used to remind
pupils of the following safety rules.
a) Never run in the laboratory.
b) Wear eye protection during experiments.
c) When heating a test tube point it away
   from people.   *[Total 3]*

9 Write a sentence for each of the following words to
explain what each means:
a) corrosive   *[1]*
b) flammable   *[1]*
c) toxic   *[1]*
d) irritant.   *[1]*
                                              [Total 4]

10 Class 1M1 of St Margaret's High School have
been investigating freezing and melting. They
now want to find out if salt speeds up the rate at
which an ice cube melts. They have decided that
this could be achieved by measuring the volume
of water produced by a melting ice cube over a
certain time interval. They have been given the
following pieces of apparatus:

tray of ice cubes   bottle of salt
measuring cylinder   filter funnel   stop clock

a) Write down the aim of this investigation.   *[1]*
b) Draw a labelled diagram of how the apparatus
   should be set up to measure the volume of
   water produced in a certain time.   *[3]*
c) Write down a description of the method – that
   is the steps the pupils would need to carry out
   to find out if salt affects the rate of melting. *[3]*
                                              [Total 7]

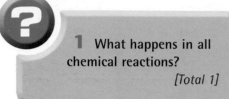

1.3   Chemical and physical change

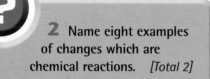

1   What happens in all chemical reactions?

[Total 1]

What is the difference between **chemical** and **physical changes**? Chemistry is all about substances and their properties. The changes which occur to substances are classified as either chemical or physical.

Chemical change

Everything in the universe is changing all of the time. Stars are born and die, mountains change shape, rivers change direction, our bodies grow older and the weather changes from day to day. Chemists are most interested in changes which involve the formation of new substances. These types of changes are called **chemical reactions**.

2   Name eight examples of changes which are chemical reactions.   [Total 2]

Chemical changes occur all around us in the natural world, in industry and in the home. Chemical changes happen anywhere that materials are changed and new substances produced. Cooking food, growing plants, burning fuels, rusting iron and making plastics are all examples of chemical reactions.

Chemical reactions in the laboratory

The chemistry laboratory is an obvious place to find examples of chemical reactions. In many of these reactions we can easily see the new substances formed. In some reactions we may see a gas or a solid being formed, or even a change in colour. In others we may observe an energy change, with heat energy being given out or sometimes taken in.

Effervescence

When a chemical reaction fizzes, it is usually because it is producing a gas. This is called **effervescence**. In Figure 3.1, lumps of **chalk** are reacting with hydrochloric acid. The gas being produced is called carbon dioxide.

Precipitation

Some reactions between solutions produce a solid. This is called a **precipitation** reaction and the solid formed is called a **precipitate**. In Figure 3.2, calcium nitrate solution is reacting with sodium carbonate solution to produce a white precipitate of calcium carbonate.

Figure 3.1 *Effervescence.*

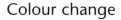

Colour change

In some reactions a colour change indicates the formation of new products. For example, green copper carbonate reacts, when heated, to form black copper oxide and carbon dioxide gas.

Energy changes

Chemical reactions will often involve a noticeable energy change. Many reactions give out heat. They are called **exothermic reactions** and they make the temperature of the surroundings and reaction mixture rise. The **combustion** of a fuel and the use of explosives are obvious examples of exothermic reactions. A fireworks display is the result of many different exothermic reactions, which also give out light and sound energy.

Heat energy can, however, be taken in during some types of chemical reaction. This type of change is called an **endothermic reaction**. These cause the temperature of the surroundings and reaction mixture to go down.

Chemical equations

The substances we start with in a chemical reaction are called the **reactants** and the new substances formed are called the **products**. Chemical reactions are often described using **chemical equations**. In chemical equations an arrow is used to show the direction of chemical change. In a **word equation** the names of the reactants are written on the left of the arrow and the products are written on the right.

A chemical equation shows   reactants $\longrightarrow$ products

Consider the chemical reactions described earlier. Word equations are a useful way of describing these chemical reactions.

When chalk (calcium carbonate) was added to hydrochloric acid, the effervescence was due to the formation of carbon dioxide gas. Water and a solution of calcium chloride were also produced. The word equation for this change is:

$$\text{calcium carbonate} + \text{hydrochloric acid} \rightarrow \text{calcium chloride} + \text{water} + \text{carbon dioxide}$$

When calcium nitrate solution was added to sodium carbonate solution the precipitation reaction produced solid calcium carbonate and a solution of sodium nitrate. The word equation for this change is:

$$\text{calcium nitrate} + \text{sodium carbonate} \rightarrow \text{calcium carbonate} + \text{sodium nitrate}$$

Figure 3.2 *Precipitation.*

Figure 3.3 *Spectacular exothermic reactions.*

? 3 What kinds of energy are given out by fireworks? [Total 1]

! Many chemical reactions need heat energy to start them off. For example when we strike a match, the heat energy produced by friction causes the phosphorus in the match to react with the oxygen in the air.

Reactants

Products

Figure 3.4 *Striking a match.*

Soap was first made by a chemical reaction between pig fat and wood ash. It was probably invented by accident when someone's cooking went wrong.

Figure 3.5 *Rusting is an unwanted reaction.*

When green solid copper carbonate was heated a colour change occurred forming carbon dioxide gas and a black solid called copper oxide. The word equation for this change is:

copper carbonate → copper oxide + carbon dioxide

Notice that in many chemical reactions the products are very different from the starting materials. The new substances formed may bear no resemblance to the reactants involved.

At home with chemical reactions

Chemical reactions occur all around us in nature, in industry and in the home. For example many chemical reactions occur in the kitchen, where food is fried, baked, boiled and sometimes even burned. On many occasions it is easy to see the new products formed. Here are some examples of chemical reactions in the home.

If you strike a match, this exothermic reaction produces several products, including carbon dioxide and water (as well as heat and light energy).

Frying an egg produces new substances with different colours and states. Iron corrodes when exposed to air and water. This unwanted reaction costs the country millions of pounds each year. The rust formed by the reaction looks very different from the original iron.

Complex changes occur throughout the lives of all living things. The growth and development of both plants and animals depend on a large number of different chemical reactions.

Photosynthesis is a reaction which occurs in the leaves of green plants. The plant takes in carbon dioxide and water and produces glucose and oxygen. This reaction is essential to life on Earth as it produces food and oxygen for all living things. The process only occurs in sunlight, as the Sun's energy is taken in to make the reaction happen. Photosynthesis is therefore an example of a natural endothermic reaction.

Reversing chemical change

It is often difficult to reverse a chemical reaction to reform the reactants. In each of these examples we can clearly see the products formed. The burned match, the fried egg, the rust and the glucose in the leaf are all very different from the starting materials. We can also see why many chemical reactions are difficult to reverse. For example, can you imagine trying to make a new match from the charred ash and gases formed when it is burned? It would be practically impossible.

Physical change

Physical changes are different from chemical changes in that no new substances are formed during the change. In a physical change the materials may alter state or be mixed together. This type of change is usually easier to reverse.

Mixing substances

Mixing substances can be described as a physical change. If no new substances are produced it is usually quite easy to separate the substances in a mixture.

Salt can dissolve in water forming a salt solution. The salt and water can be separated by **evaporation** of the water. Dissolving and evaporation are physical changes.

Powdered iron and sulphur can be mixed together without reaction. They can be easily separated again by using a magnet.

Other important mixtures include

- **Air**: a mixture of gases including oxygen, nitrogen, argon and carbon dioxide.
- Sea water: a mixture of water, salt and other dissolved substances.
- Soil: a mixture of rock fragments, water, dissolved minerals, air and **humus**.
- Rocks: a mixture of different **minerals**.

The techniques used to separate different types of mixtures are dealt with in more detail in subsection 2.5.

Changes of state

Substances can be **solids**, **liquids** or **gases**. Most substances can exist in all three states. Common changes of state include **melting**, **boiling**, **evaporation**, **condensation** and **freezing**.

Changes from one state to another can be brought about by changes in temperature. Heating a substance, and increasing the temperature, can bring about melting, boiling and evaporation. Cooling a substance, and lowering the temperature, can bring about condensation and freezing.

These changes of state are explained in the next subsection.

reactants
carbon dioxide + water

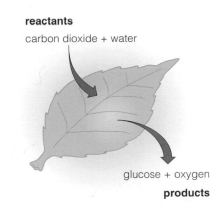

glucose + oxygen
products

Figure 3.6 *Photosynthesis.*

Figure 3.7 *Separating mixtures.*

> Milk is a mixture of many substances but is mainly made up of drops of oil suspended in a watery solution. This type of mixture, where the particles are spread out but not actually dissolved, is called a **colloid**.

Figure 3.8 *Changes of state.*

Summary

- A chemical reaction involves the formation of one or more new substances.
- A precipitation reaction forms a solid from mixing solutions.
- Effervescence occurs when a chemical reaction gives off a gas.
- Most chemical reactions involve an energy change.
- Exothermic reactions give out heat and endothermic reactions take in heat.
- Most chemical changes are difficult to reverse.
- A physical change may involve a change of state – e.g. melting, freezing, boiling, evaporation or condensation.
- A physical change may involve mixing substances together – e.g. dissolving.
- Most physical changes are easy to reverse.

Questions

Questions

1 Copy and complete the following sentences.
A chemical change always involves the formation
of one or more _____ _____.
Examples of physical change include, changes of
_____ like condensation, _____,
_____ and _____.   *[Total 3]*

2 Briefly explain the main difference between a
physical and a chemical change.   *[Total 2]*

3 State which of the following represents a physical
change, and which represents a chemical reaction.
a) The rusting of an iron nail.   *[1]*
b) Condensation of water vapour on a window.   *[1]*
c) Mixing sand and water.   *[1]*
d) Icicles forming in winter.   *[1]*
e) Lump of coal burning.   *[1]*
f) Water boiling in a pan.   *[1]*
g) Frying an egg.   *[1]*
   [Total 7]

4 Describe two examples of chemical reactions and
two examples of physical changes, which are not
listed in question 3.   *[Total 4]*

5 Write a sentence for each of the following words
to explain what each means:
a) exothermic   *[2]*
b) evaporation   *[2]*
c) condensation.   *[2]*
   [Total 6]

6 Write out a word equation for each of the
following descriptions of chemical reactions.
a) Aluminium iodide is produced in the reaction
of iodine with aluminium.   *[2]*
b) When a lump of zinc is added to sulphuric acid
solution, effervescence occurs producing
hydrogen gas and a solution of zinc sulphate.
   [2]

c) Natural gas, chemical name methane, burns by
reacting with oxygen to produce water and
carbon dioxide.   *[2]*
   [Total 6]

7 Suggest a single word to describe each of the
following changes.
a) Puddles drying up on a hot summer day.   *[1]*
b) Bubbles of gas being produced when a metal
is added to a solution.   *[1]*
c) Scrap iron being heated and changing into
liquid iron.   *[1]*
d) A solid being formed when two clear solutions
are added together.   *[1]*
   [Total 4]

8 The temperature of 500 cm³ of water was measured
as it was heated with a Bunsen burner. The results of
these measurements are shown in the table.

Time (min)	0	2	4	6	8	10	12	14
Temperature (°C)	20	48	69	84	95	100	100	100

a) Draw a line graph to show these results.
Remember to give names and units for each
axis and to plot the points carefully.   *[4]*
b) Use the graph to answer the following
questions.
   i) What temperature rise occurred in the first
4 minutes?
   ii) Predict the temperature after 5 minutes.
   iii) If the heating continued, what
temperature would be reached after
20 minutes?
   iv) Briefly explain your answer to question
b) iii).   *[4]*
   [Total 8]

1.4 Particles and the states of matter

What is matter made up of and why are there different states? Substances can exist in one of three states: solid, liquid or gas. The difference between the states must be to do with the basic building blocks of matter.

The states of matter

Matter is the scientific word used to describe all the different types of substances and materials found in our universe. The three **states of matter** are **solid**, **liquid** and **gas**.

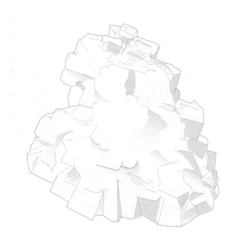

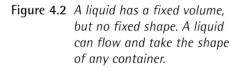

Figure 4.1 *A solid has a fixed shape and a fixed volume. A force must be used to change the shape of a solid.*

Figure 4.2 *A liquid has a fixed volume, but no fixed shape. A liquid can flow and take the shape of any container.*

Figure 4.3 *A gas has no fixed shape or volume. A gas can spread out in all directions and fill any container.*

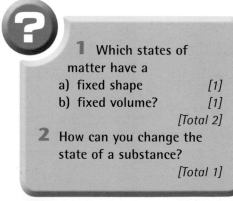

?

1 Which states of matter have a
a) fixed shape [1]
b) fixed volume? [1]
[Total 2]

2 How can you change the state of a substance?
[Total 1]

Changing states

Most substances can exist in all three states. The state of a substance depends on the temperature, and so changes of state are brought about by heating and cooling. When heated, most solids will eventually melt and if the heating continues the liquid formed will boil and then evaporate to produce a gas. Similarly, if a gas is cooled it will eventually condense and if the cooling continues the liquid will freeze to form a solid.

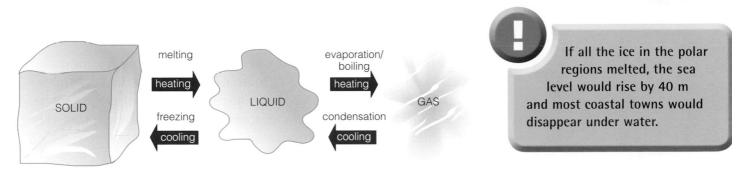

Figure 4.4 *Changing state.*

In a pure substance, changes of state occur at fixed temperatures (except by evaporation). The **boiling point** (b.p.) of a liquid is the temperature at which it rapidly changes into a gas. The **melting point** (m.p.) of a solid is the temperature it changes into a liquid. Some examples of melting and boiling points are shown in Table 4.1.

Table 4.1

Substance	Melting point	Boiling point
helium	– 272 °C	– 269 °C
oxygen	– 218 °C	– 183 °C
water	0 °C	100 °C
aluminium	660 °C	2467 °C
tungsten	3410 °C	5660 °C

If all the ice in the polar regions melted, the sea level would rise by 40 m and most coastal towns would disappear under water.

3 What happens at a substance's
a) melting point [1]
b) freezing point? [1]
[Total 2]

4 Use the data in Table 4.1 to give the state of:
a) oxygen at –200 °C [1]
b) aluminium at 600 °C [1]
c) water at 150 °C. [1]
[Total 3]

The **freezing point** (f.p.) of a substance is the same as its melting point. The temperature at which a solid changes into a liquid is the same as the temperature at which the liquid changes back into the solid.

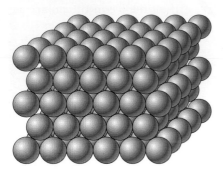

Figure 4.5 *Atoms of iron.*

Atoms are so small that there are over five million, million, million, million atoms in a glass of water.

Figure 4.6 *Water molecules.*

At room temperature the particles in air are moving at a speed of about 1500 km/hr (930 mile/hr). That is faster than a jet aircraft.

Matter and particles

Scientists have been investigating and observing matter for thousands of years and now believe that all matter is made up of tiny particles which are in constant motion. They also believe that there are forces of attraction holding the particles together and that these forces vary in the different states of matter.

This has been called the **particle theory** of matter and it is very important to chemists as it helps us explain the physical and chemical changes which occur around us.

Atoms and molecules

The particles in matter can be arranged in different ways. The simplest particles are called **atoms**. We can imagine that an atom looks like a tiny ball, like the ones shown in Figure 4.5. There are different kinds of atom and they are found in all types of matter.

Remember that the atoms in any state of matter are very small. The largest atoms have a diameter of about 0.000 000 000 5 m. Most atoms are even smaller.

Some substances, whether solid, liquid or gas, are made up of **molecules**. These are groups of two or more atoms which are joined together, like the molecules of water shown in Figure 4.6.

States and particles

The difference between the three states of matter can be explained in terms of particles: their movements, spacing and the forces of attraction between them. The atoms and molecules are too small to see, even with the highest power microscope. However, we need to imagine what they look like to help us understand and explain the nature of matter.

These ideas about the particles in matter are very important. Try to imagine what they look like. Shut your eyes and picture how the particles are spaced out and move about. Try to see the difference between the particles in a solid, a liquid and a gas. You need to be familiar with this particle theory in order to understand the simplest physical change or chemical reaction.

Figure 4.7

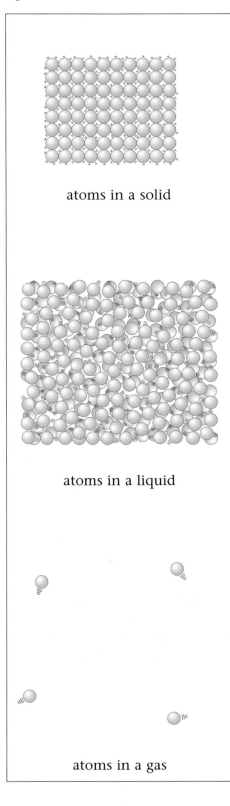

atoms in a solid

atoms in a liquid

atoms in a gas

The atoms or molecules in a solid are held closely together by strong forces of attraction. The particles cannot move over each other but vibrate (wobble) back and forth.

The forces of attraction between the atoms or molecules in a liquid are weaker. The particles are slightly further apart and can move around each other.

There are only weak forces of attraction between the atoms or molecules of a gas. The particles are very far apart and can move about in all directions.

Figure 4.8

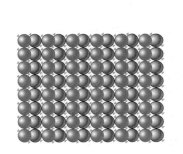

molecules in a solid

molecules in a liquid

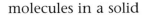

molecules in a gas

Summary

- There are three states of matter: solid, liquid and gas.
- The main changes of state are melting, freezing, evaporation, boiling and condensation.
- The melting point and boiling point of a substance are the fixed temperatures at which those changes occur.
- All matter is made up of tiny particles.
- There are spaces between the particles.
- The particles in solids are closely packed and vibrate.
- The particles in a liquid are close together but can move around each other.
- There are large spaces between the particles in a gas and the particles move in all directions.
- Atoms are the simplest particles which are found in all matter.
- A molecule is a particle made up of atoms joined together.

Questions

1 Copy and complete the following sentences.
Solids have a _____ shape and fixed
_____. Liquids have a fixed _____
but a liquid can _____ shape and take the
shape of any _____. A gas can
_____ out in all directions and
_____ any container. Gases have
_____ fixed shape or volume.   *[Total 4]*

2 Think about the different substances found in your
home. Draw up a table with three columns headed
solids, liquids and gases. List at least five substances
under each of the headings.   *[Total 6]*

3 Write a sentence which contains all these words:
evaporation; gas; heating; liquid; melting; solid.
   [Total 6]

4 Name the changes of state described here.
a) Molten iron cooling and solidifying.   *[1]*
b) Wax dripping down a candle.   *[1]*
c) The bathroom window misting up.   *[1]*
d) Painted fence drying in the sun.   *[1]*
   [Total 4]

5 All matter is made up of tiny particles.
a) What are the three states of matter?   *[1]*
b) In which state are the particles
i) furthest apart
ii) closest together?   *[2]*
c) Describe the difference between the particles in a
solid and the particles in a liquid.   *[2]*
   [Total 5]

1.5 Explaining physical changes

What happens to the particles of a substance during physical changes? Heating, cooling and changes of state affect the arrangement of the particles of a substance. Being able to explain simple physical changes in terms of the particle theory is essential to our understanding of the nature of matter.

Heating and cooling

Altering the temperature of substances by **heating** and **cooling** can bring about changes in state. These changes take place because the temperature of a substance affects the energy, and therefore the speed and movement, of its particles.

The particles in matter change speed as the temperature changes. The higher the temperature the greater the energy of the particles and the faster they move about or vibrate. Temperature is a measure of the movement energy (kinetic energy) in the particles of a substance.

- When a substance is heated the particles have more energy and move faster so the temperature rises.
- When a substance is cooled the particles have less energy and move slower so the temperature falls.

Melting, evaporation and boiling

When a solid is heated, energy is supplied to the particles making them vibrate faster. The speed at which the particles vibrate continues to increase as the temperature rises. If the heating is continued long enough the particles will eventually vibrate fast enough to break free from each other and move about more freely. This is **melting** and a liquid is formed.

> **!** The arrangement of atoms in a substance will alter during chemical and physical changes. However the actual atoms remain the same. Most of the atoms in and around us have been here since the Earth was formed 4500 million years ago.

> **?**
> **1** What is temperature a measure of? *[Total 1]*
> **2** What happens to the particles of a solid when they are heated? *[Total 1]*

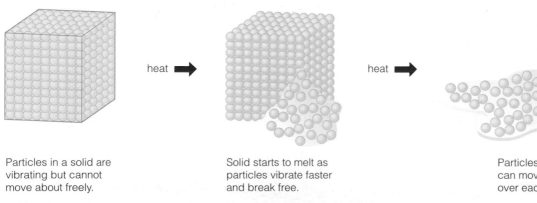

Particles in a solid are vibrating but cannot move about freely.

Solid starts to melt as particles vibrate faster and break free.

Particles in the liquid state can move freely and slide over each other.

Figure 5.1 *How the arrangement of particles changes during melting.*

?

3 How can water evaporate below its boiling point? [Total 1]

4 What is the difference between the melting point and freezing point of a substance? [Total 2]

The particles of a liquid have different energies, so there are always some that move slowly and others that move very quickly. Therefore, even at fairly low temperatures some of the particles at the surface of a liquid are moving fast enough to escape and form a gas. This explains how **evaporation** occurs and why puddles will dry up, even on a cold day.

When a liquid is heated, energy is supplied to the particles making them all move faster. The speed of the particles continues to increase as the temperature rises. If the heating is continued long enough many of the particles throughout the liquid will eventually move fast enough to escape from the liquid. This is how **boiling** occurs.

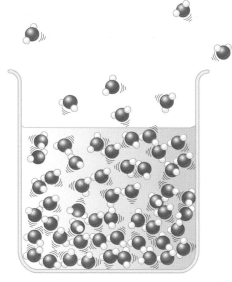

Figure 5.2 *The evaporation of water.*

Condensation and freezing

When a gas is cooled, heat energy is removed from the particles making them move more slowly. The speed of the particles continues to decrease as the temperature falls. If the cooling is continued long enough the particles will eventually lose their freedom of movement. **Condensation** takes place and the gas changes into a liquid.

When mercury is heated strongly, the particles escape from the liquid and the liquid evaporates. Further up the tube the mercury cools and the particles slow down and condense forming beads of liquid mercury.

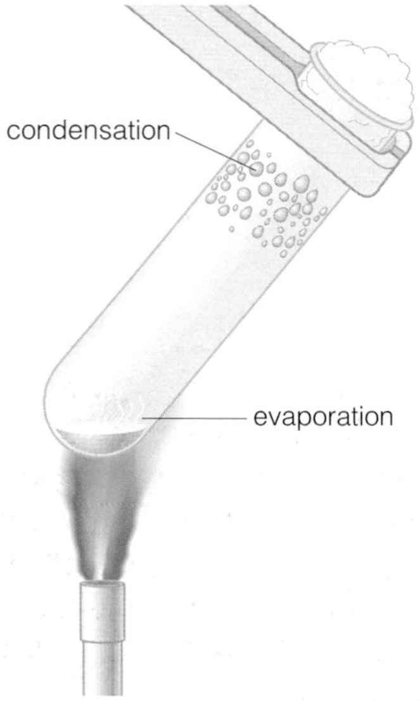

When a liquid is cooled, heat energy is removed from the particles making them move more slowly. The speed of the particles continues to decrease as the temperature falls. If the cooling is continued long enough the particles will eventually not be able to move about. This is called **freezing** and a solid is formed.

condensation

evaporation

Figure 5.3 *Evaporation and condensation of mercury.*

Sublimation

Some substances, like iodine and graphite, do not melt when heated but change straight from a solid into a gas. This change is reversible like melting and evaporation. These unusual changes of state, solid to gas and gas to solid, are both called **sublimation**.

Compressing matter

It is hard to compress (squash) solids and liquids because the particles are so close together they have little space between them. Gases, however, are fairly easy to compress. The particles are far apart in gases and they can be squeezed into a smaller space by forcing the particles closer together. Figure 5.5 shows what happens to the particles in air when they are compressed in a syringe.

Figure 5.4 *Sublimation of iodine.*

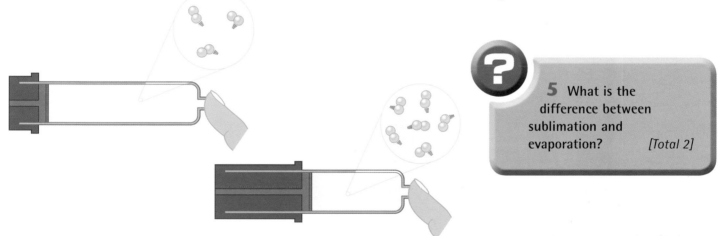

Figure 5.5 *Compressing gases.*

5 What is the difference between sublimation and evaporation? [Total 2]

Diffusion

Diffusion occurs when the particles of one substance spread out and mix with the particles of another substance. Diffusion occurs most rapidly in gases because the particles in gases move fastest and are furthest apart. If two gas jars are placed together and the lid removed, the gas particles rapidly mix together due to the movement of their particles.

It is due to diffusion of gas particles that we are able to smell substances like perfume or food. This happens because the gas particles of the smelly substance are moving about in all directions and

As particles slow down, the temperature of a substance falls. Eventually the particles must stop moving and it cannot get any colder. This is the minimum temperature possible, it occurs at −273.16°C and is called absolute zero.

> The contest for the worst smelling substance in the world is, of course, a matter of choice and debate. However, ethyl mercaptan (C_2H_5SH) must be one of the favourites, with a smell which is described as a combination of garlic, onions, rotting cabbage, burnt toast and sewage gases!

eventually spread out and fill the room, including the space in your nose. (Remember you only smell substances when some of their particles are actually inside your nose. A sobering thought when we think of where some of the smells have come from!)

Diffusion also occurs in liquids. However, the mixing is not as fast as in gases, because the particles are closer together and move more slowly. If a crystal of purple potassium manganate(VII) is placed in water it dissolves and the particles spread out between the water particles. Eventually the purple colour spreads evenly throughout the solution.

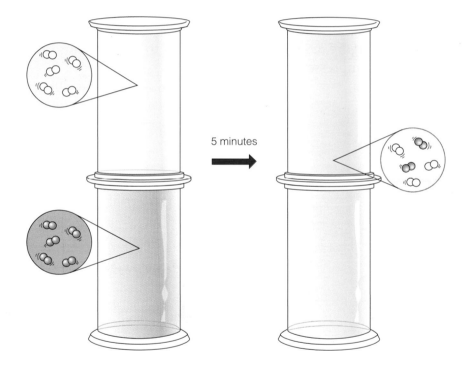

5 minutes

Figure 5.6 *Diffusion of gases.*

Figure 5.7 *Potassium manganate(VII) diffuses through water.*

Summary

○ The state of a substance depends on the temperature.

○ As particles have more energy and move faster, the temperature of a substance increases.

○ Changes of state can be explained by changes in the movement of the particles.

○ The melting point and freezing point of a pure substance is the fixed temperature at which melting or freezing occurs.

○ The boiling point of a liquid is the fixed temperature at which the liquid rapidly changes into a gas.

○ Sublimation is changing from a solid straight to a gas (or gas to a solid).

○ Gases are easily compressed because their particles are furthest apart. (Solids and liquids are not easily compressed.)

○ Diffusion occurs when the particles of a substance mix with the particles of another substance.

Questions

1 Copy and complete the following sentences.
When a solid is heated, its particles get more
_____ and vibrate _____. The
temperature of the solid _____. If the heating
is continued the solid will eventually _____
and form a _____. The particles in a liquid can
move _____ each other.   *[Total 3]*

2 Susan and David were carrying out an experiment to
find out how quickly water cooled down when placed
in a fridge. They placed a glass of water in the fridge
and measured its temperature every 2 minutes. The
results of their experiment are shown below.

Time (min)	0	2	4	6	8	10	12	14	16	18	20
Temperature (°C)	24	18	13	9	6	4	3	3	3	3	3

a) Draw a line graph of temperature against time.
Remember to put labels and units on each axis
and give the graph a title.   *[4]*

b) What was the temperature drop in the first
five minutes?   *[1]*

c) What is the temperature inside the fridge?
Explain your answer.   *[2]*
                                   [Total 7]

3 The particle theory of matter can be used to explain
many physical changes in nature. Use this theory to
answer the following questions.
a) What happens when a solid is heated and its
temperature rises (without melting)?   *[1]*
b) What changes occur when a liquid boils?   *[2]*
c) Why is it more difficult to compress a liquid
than a gas?   *[2]*
                                   [Total 5]

4 Imagine that you are one of the particles in a drop of
water. Describe what happens to you as the drop of
water freezes when the temperature falls.
                                   [Total 3]

1.6 More about properties of matter

What other properties of matter can be explained using particle theory? Changes of state and diffusion can be described in terms of the movement, spacing and energy of the particles. However, the theory can also be used to help explain expansion, contraction, changes in density and air pressure.

Expansion and contraction

When a substance **expands** it gets bigger and takes up more space. When a substance **contracts** it gets smaller and takes up less space. We say that solids and liquids have a fixed volume, but this is only true if the temperature is kept constant. Some experiments are shown in Figure 6.1 which show that solids, liquids and gases all expand when heated and contract when cooled.

The heat from the pupil's hands is enough to make the air in the flask expand. The increased volume of air can be seen as it bubbles out of the tube. If the flask is cooled then the air inside will contract and water will move up the tube to fill the space left.

The heat from the pupil's hand makes the alcohol in the thermometer expand and move up the tube. If the thermometer is cooled the alcohol inside contracts and moves back down the tube.

The ball and ring are made so that the ball fits through the ring at normal temperatures. The heat from the Bunsen burner makes the metal ball expand slightly. The ball does not look any different but it is now too big to fit through the ring. If the ball is cooled it will contract and fit through the ring once more.

These experiments show that

- all matter expands when heated and contracts when cooled
- liquids expand and contract more than solids
- gases expand and contract more than liquids.

Explaining expansion and contraction

We can use the particle theory of matter to explain why substances expand when heated and contract when cooled.

Figure 6.1 *Gases, liquids and solids expand when heated.*

! Water is the only common substance which expands as it freezes. This explains why ice is less dense than water and floats. It also explains why water pipes burst in cold weather. The pipes burst as the water freezes, but we only notice the problem when the ice melts.

Think about the structure of a solid. The particles of a solid are close together but there are small spaces between them. These particles are locked in the structure and vibrate back and forth. If the solid is heated the particles have more energy and vibrate more. When the particles vibrate more they bump into each other and take up more space and so the solid expands. Figure 6.2 shows what happens to the particles in a solid when it is heated.

A similar explanation can be used to explain the expansion and contraction in liquids and gases. The only difference is that the particles in liquids and gases have more freedom of movement and so they expand and contract more than solids.

Expansion and contraction in real life

Temperature changes cause substances to expand and contract all the time. These changes can sometimes cause problems but they can also be useful. Here are some examples of expansion and contraction in real life.

- When telephone wires are put up in the summer they must be left slack. This is because they will contract in the winter and the cables could easily snap.
- Bridges and other large structures are longer in the summer than they are in the winter. To prevent structural damage, gaps called expansion joints are built into the bridge or roadway.
- The metal lid on a jam jar can be difficult to remove. If this happens we can run hot water over it. This causes the metal lid to expand more than the glass jar and makes it easier to remove.

Matter and density

Which is heavier, a kilogram of lead or a kilogram of feathers? This old question can be used to illustrate the property of density. Of course the two things have the same mass, they are both one kilogram. However, the feathers will take up much more space than the lead. We say that the lead has a greater **density** than the feathers. A very dense substance like lead has a large mass in a small **volume**.

The density of a substance is usually taken as the mass of one cubic centimetre of the substance. For example the mass of 1 cm^3 of water is 1 g. Therefore the density of water is 1 g/cm^3. The density of lead is 11.3 g/cm^3 as 1 cm^3 of lead has a mass of 11.3 g.

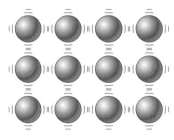

Cold iron atoms

Hot iron atoms

Figure 6.2 *When a piece of iron heats up its atoms take up more space.*

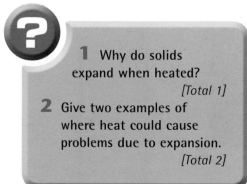

Figure 6.3 *Telephone wires need to be slack in the summer.*

?

1 Why do solids expand when heated?
[Total 1]

2 Give two examples of where heat could cause problems due to expansion.
[Total 2]

We can work out the density of any substance by using the following equation.

$$density = \frac{mass}{volume}$$

where   density is in grams per cubic centimetre (g/cm^3)

mass is in grams (g)

volume is in cubic centimetres (cm^3)

Example 1

A gold bar measures 12 cm × 5 cm × 4 cm and has a mass of 4632 grams. What is the density of gold?

First find the volume of the gold bar

$$volume = length \times width \times height$$
$$= 12 \times 5 \times 4$$
$$= 240\ cm^3$$

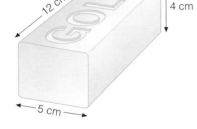

Now use the equation to calculate the density of the gold:

$$density = \frac{mass}{volume}$$
$$density = \frac{4632}{240}$$
$$= 19.3\ g/cm^3$$

The volume of a regular object, like a cube, can be found by calculation. However, to find the volume of an irregular shaped object you can use the displacement of water in a measuring cylinder.

Figure 6.5 shows how to measure the volume of a small stone.

The measurements are:

volume of water with small stone added = 65 cm^3

volume of water at the start   = 50 cm^3

therefore, volume of small stone   = 15 cm^3

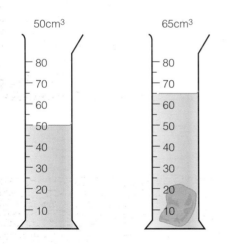

Figure 6.4 *Gold bar.*

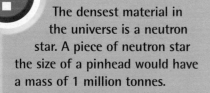

Figure 6.5 *Measuring volume by displacement.*

Explaining density

Gases are much less dense than solids and liquids. This is because the particles in gases are much further apart, and so there are far fewer particles and a smaller mass in the same volume.

When matter is heated, its density usually decreases. This is because matter expands when heated. The particles move faster and get further apart so there are fewer particles in the same volume.

This fact is used in hot air balloons. Hot air is less dense than cold air so hot air rises and a balloon filled with hot air will also rise.

The densest material in the universe is a neutron star. A piece of neutron star the size of a pinhead would have a mass of 1 million tonnes.

Air pressure

The atoms and molecules in air are moving about in all directions. Therefore, air particles are hitting us all the time. We call the force of these particles hitting a surface **air pressure**. We do not usually feel the effect of the air pressure, but it is always there.

A **vacuum** pump can be used to remove the air from inside a container. (The term 'vacuum' means completely empty, that is containing no particles.) If the air is removed from inside a metal can, the air pressure on the outside will crush the can.

> **!** The mass of all the air in a column directly above our head and shoulders is 1000 kg (1 tonne).

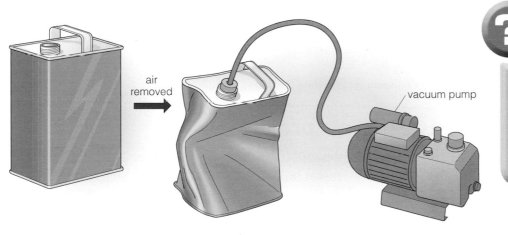

air removed

vacuum pump

> **?**
> **3** Suggest what would happen if you found yourself in space with no air around you. [Total 1]
> **4** Suggest why we use the name 'vacuum cleaner'. [Total 1]

Figure 6.7 *The power of air pressure.*

This is due to the air particles hitting the outside of the can. It is not crushed when there is air in the can because air particles hit both the inside and the outside of the can with equal force.

Changing air pressure

Air pressure can be changed in two ways.

If air or any other gas is heated, the molecules move about faster. This means that its molecules will hit the side of the container more often, and with greater force. Therefore increasing the temperature, without changing the volume, increases air pressure.

If air or any other gas is squeezed into a smaller volume, then there will be more molecules in a smaller space. Therefore its molecules will hit the sides of the container more often. Decreasing a volume increases the air pressure.

Figure 6.6 *Hot air is less dense than cold air.*

5 Suggest two reasons why air pressure is less at the top of high mountains.
[Total 1]

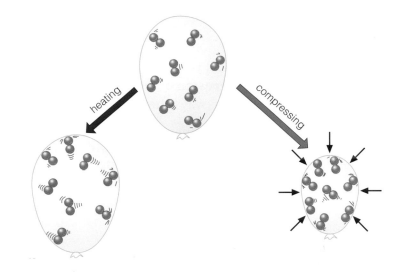

Figure 6.8 *Changing air pressure.*

Measuring air pressure

We can measure air pressure by using a **barometer**. This usually consists of a springy metal box attached through a system of levers to a pointer. As the air pressure around the box changes, the lid of the box moves in or out and the pointer moves. The air pressure can be read by the position of the pointer on a scale. The units used to measure air pressure are **pascals** (Pa).

Barometers can be used to predict the weather. In general, high pressure is associated with settled weather, clear skies and little cloud. Low pressure often means poor, unsettled weather.

Summary

- Most substances expand when heated and contract when cooled.
- Substances expand when heated as their particles move or vibrate faster and move further apart.
- Substances contract when cooled as their particles move more slowly and move closer together.
- Density is a measure of the mass of one cubic centimetre of a substance.
- Density = $\frac{\text{mass}}{\text{volume}}$.
- Gases are less dense than liquids and solids because their particles are further apart.
- As temperature increases, density usually decreases.
- Air pressure is caused by moving air particles hitting things.
- A barometer is used to measure air pressure in pascals (Pa).

Questions

1 Copy and complete the following sentences.
The particles of air _____ about in all
_____ and _____ the sides of a
container causing air _____. Air pressure
is measured using a _____ and the units
are _____.   *[Total 3]*

2 Write a sentence for each of the following words
to explain what each means:
a) expand *[1]*   b) contract *[1]*
c) density. *[1]*   *[Total 3]*

3 Explain, using diagrams of the particles, why any
liquid will expand when heated.
                                              [Total 3]

4 Use your ideas about expansion and contraction
to explain how a thermometer works. You should
try to include all of the following words in your
answer. Underline each of these words in your
answer.
alcohol   expand   cool
temperature heat   contract   *[Total 6]*

5 A blacksmith has been asked to repair a wooden
wagon wheel. He starts by making an new iron tyre
for the wheel, but the tyre he makes is just too
small to fit over the wheel. Explain the following.
a) How can the blacksmith use heat to make the
   tyre fit over the wheel?   *[2]*
b) Why does the blacksmith make the tyre too
   small in the first place?   *[1]*
                                              [Total 3]

Figure 6.9 *The tyre is just
too small to fit over the
wheel!*

6 The densities of some common metals are given
in Table 6.1.

Table 6.1

Metal	Density (g/cm³)
iron	7.9
lead	11.3
silver	10.2
nickel	8.9
magnesium	1.7
aluminium	2.7

a) List these metals in order of increasing density.   *[2]*
b) Draw a bar chart of the densities of these metals,
   in the order you have listed in part a). Remember
   to put labels and units where appropriate, and
   give the chart a title.   *[4]*
                                              [Total 6]

7 The density of a substance can be measured in g/cm³.
a) Which is more dense, a kilogram of iron or a
   kilogram of wood? Briefly explain your answer. *[2]*
b) Calculate the density, in g/cm³, of a gas if
   2500 cm³ of the gas has a mass of 8.0 g. *[1]*
c) If 5 litres of a liquid has a mass of 850 g what is
   the density of the liquid in g/cm³?   *[2]*
d) If a block of wood with each side 5 cm long has a
   density of 2.4 g/cm³, what is the density of a block
   of the same wood with 10 cm long sides?   *[2]*
e) A metal has a density of 12.0 g/cm³. What is the
   mass of a cube of this metal which has sides
   which are 2 cm long?   *[2]*
f) If a sugar solution has a density of 1.2 g/cm³,
   what volume of the solution would have a mass
   of 720 ?   *[1]*
                                              [Total 10]

8 Bicycle tyres are hard because of the pressure of air
inside the tyre.
a) What causes the air pressure inside the tyre? *[1]*
b) Why does the air pressure increase when you
   pump up the tyre?   *[2]*
c) How would the air pressure inside the tyre change
   as the temperature increased on a hot day? *[1]*
d) Briefly explain your answer to part c).   *[2]*
e) Explain why tyres which contain air absorb bumps
   better than solid rubber tyres.   *[2]*
                                              [Total 8]

The beginnings of chemistry

When did the study of chemistry begin? Who were the first chemists? How has chemistry changed through the years? What did we learn from the early chemists?

Our first chemical reactions

Early humans used fire to keep themselves warm and cook their food. In time, they found ways to use fire to get metals, like copper and tin, out of rocks. These early chemical reactions improved their lives by giving them better tools and weapons.

Figure 7.1 *The **Iron Age** began when we learned to extract iron from its ore.*

Alchemy

The philosophers of ancient Greece thought about the nature of substances but didn't do experiments. The early Egyptians and Arabs combined the philosophy of the Greeks with their methods and practical skills. In Arabic the study of matter became known as "al-kimiya", when the ideas reached Europe it became **alchemy**. Like the ancient Greeks, alchemists believed that everything was made up of four elements; earth, fire, air and water and that any substance could be made by mixing the correct amounts of each element. Many mixtures were investigated. Some alchemists spent their time trying to make gold, others tried to make a potion that would make you live forever. Ordinary people were frightened of the alchemists, as they seemed to have the ability to bring about changes, like magic. Alchemists encouraged this fear by using mysterious symbols so that no one else could understand their writings.

1 What happens in all chemical reactions?

[Total 1]

2 How can you tell that burning wood is a chemical reaction?

[Total 1]

3 Which of the Greeks' four elements are actually elements?

[Total 1]

4 Why were ordinary people scared of alchemists?

[Total 1]

The first chemists

In 1661 Robert Boyle published a book called *The Sceptical Chymist*. The book challenged many of the old ideas about alchemy, including the ideas about the elements. Boyle's book didn't cause an instant change, but from this time on the study of substances was more often called chemistry.

Modern chemistry has learned a great deal from the alchemists. Their experiments produced many useful substances and they invented a number of useful practical techniques, like filtration and distillation.

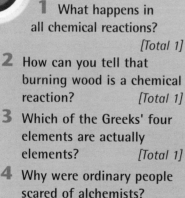

Figure 7.2 *The symbols of alchemy*

The beginnings of chemistry

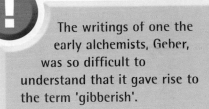

However, modern chemists are much more organised in their experiments than the alchemists. They make careful plans with specific aims and are able to take precise measurements and observations. Most importantly they record their findings clearly, so others can check their work and add their own knowledge and ideas.

> **!** The writings of one the early alchemists, Geber, was so difficult to understand that it gave rise to the term 'gibberish'.

> **?** **5** Name four measuring instruments used by modern chemists that wouldn't have been used by the alchemists. *[Total 1]*

Figure 7.3 *Robert Boyle described an element as a substance that couldn't be broken down into a simpler substance.*

Figure 7.4 *A chemist at work.*

Questions

1 Give two examples of how early man used fire to bring about chemical reactions.
[Total 2]

2 Alchemists, believed that everything was made up of four elements.
a) Where did the word alchemy come from? *[1]*
b) What were the four elements? *[1]*
[Total 2]

3 a) The word chemistry first appeared in the 17th century. Name the title of the book, its author and the year of publication. *[3]*

b) Robert Boyle used a book to challenge the ideas of the early alchemists. How do scientists share their discoveries and challenge others' work today? *[3]*
[Total 6]

4 a) How was alchemy different from the philosophy of the Greeks? *[1]*
b) Describe how modern chemists are different from alchemists. *[3]*
[Total 4]

5 Why do you think the alchemists tried to keep their work secret? *[Total 2]*

End of section questions

1 a) Write down the name of a substance which could
   be found as a solid, liquid or gas in your kitchen.
   Briefly explain where you could find each state of
   the substance. [4]

   b) Figure 1 shows the atoms in a solid and the
   molecules in a solid.

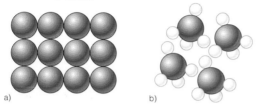

a)   b)

Figure 1 *a) atoms in a solid; b) molecules in a solid.*

Copy the diagrams into your book and draw similar
diagrams to represent:
   i) the atoms in a liquid
   ii) the molecules in a gas.   [4]
                                            [Total 8]

2 There are three states of matter: solid, liquid and gas.
The particles in each of these states have different
energies, speeds and spacing. In which of these states:
   a) do the particles vibrate but not move around
      each other?   [1]
   b) are the spaces between the particles greatest? [1]
   c) do the particles have most movement energy? [1]
                                            [Total 3]

3 Write word equations to fit each of the following
descriptions of chemical reactions.
   a) The alcohol in alcoholic drinks is called ethanol. It is
      formed by the fermentation of glucose, with carbon
      dioxide also being formed as a by-product.   [2]
   b) When hydrochloric acid is added to lime, chemical
      name calcium oxide, the lime appears to dissolve.
      Calcium chloride and water are formed in the
      reaction.   [2]
                                            [Total 4]

4 Chemical reactions are continually happening all
around us. Write a short story (approximately 200
words) about some of the chemical reactions which
occur in your home everyday.   *[Total 8]*

5 Sandra and Christopher were investigating chemical
reactions. Read the following description of the
experiment that they carried out.
   i)   A solution of sodium carbonate was made up in
        25 cm^3 of water in a beaker.
   ii) This solution was transferred into a boiling tube.
   iii) Then 100 cm^3 of copper sulphate solution was made
        up in a conical flask.
   iv) The sodium carbonate solution was colourless and
        the copper sulphate solution was light blue in
        colour.
   v)   Finally the sodium carbonate solution was added to
        the copper sulphate solution and a green precipitate
        was formed in the conical flask.
   a) Draw a labelled diagram showing step v) in this
      experiment.   [3]
   b) What evidence is there that a chemical reaction
      has taken place?   [1]
   c) Name the reactants in the chemical reaction. [1]
   d) What is a precipitate?   [1]
                                            [Total 6]

6 a) Explain, in terms of particle size and spacing, why
      when 50 cm^3 of sand and 50 cm^3 of peas are placed
      in a measuring cylinder and mixed, the total volume
      of the two is less than 100 cm^3.   [2]
   b) In an experiment involving mixing liquids, some
      pupils were surprised to find that when they added
      50 cm^3 of water to 50 cm^3 of alcohol in a
      measuring cylinder the total volume of the two
      liquids together was only 97 cm^3. Explain this
      result in terms of particle size and spacing. [2]
                                            [Total 4]

7 When substances are heated they **expand** and when they are cooled they **contract**.
a) Explain the meaning of these terms. *[2]*
b) Describe one example or use of expansion and contraction in everyday life. *[2]*
[Total 4]

8 a) Write down two different laboratory safety rules. Explain why each of your chosen rules is important. *[2]*
b) The symbol shown in Figure 2 is to remind people to wear eye protection when doing experiments. Design and draw a safety symbol for the following safety rules.

Figure 2

i) Never run or fool around in the laboratory.
ii) Never eat or drink in the laboratory.
iii) When heating a test tube point it away from people.
iv) Clean and clear up all apparatus – leave the laboratory as you found it. *[4]*
[Total 6]

9 a) Explain why gases are always less dense than liquids or solids. *[2]*
b) Calculate the density of a solid block of material which measures 20 cm × 12 cm × 8 cm and has a mass of 2000 g. *[2]*
[Total 4]

10 The densities of some common gases are shown in the table below.

Table 3

Gas	Density (g/cm^3)
chlorine	0.0032
neon	0.0009
krypton	0.0037
helium	0.0002

a) Which is the least dense of these gases? *[1]*
b) If balloons were filled with each of these gases, which of the balloons would float upwards if released in air (air density = 0.0013 g/cm^3)? Briefly explain your answer. *[2]*
c) Try to explain why different gases have different densities. *[1]*
[Total 4]

11
P Bunsen burners are an important source of heat in the chemistry laboratory. What factors could affect how quickly a Bunsen burner heats water in a beaker. For example how would you investigate the effect of the size of the air hole on how quickly water is heated?

12
R Chemists like Antoine Lavoisier, Joseph Priestley and Michael Faraday have contributed to our understanding of chemistry. Find out about one of these chemists and write a short report about their life and works. The report could include the following information: name; nationality; date of birth and death; where they worked; contribution to chemistry and main discoveries/inventions.

13
R Alchemists used symbols so that others couldn't understand what they were writing about. Find out about the symbols used by alchemists and design a poster which describes what some of the symbols mean.

2.1 Properties of substances

Why are different substances used for different jobs? There are millions of different substances, all with very different **properties**. We must know the properties of a substance before we can decide whether it will be suitable for a particular use.

What is a property?

Iron is hard, strong, conducts electricity and heat, has a high melting point and is magnetic. These are some of the properties of iron. The properties of a substance describe what it looks like and what it can do. Different substances have different properties and so have different uses, from copper for making water pipes to silicon for making microchips. The uses a substance has depend on its properties.

There are many different properties that we can investigate:

- strength
- hardness
- **flexibility** – how easily a substance bends without breaking
- colour
- **melting** and **boiling points**
- **solubility** – how well a substance dissolves in different solvents
- **thermal conductivity** – how well heat passes through a substance
- **electrical conductivity** – how well electricity passes through a substance
- magnetism
- **density** – the mass of 1 cm^3 of a substance
- **flammability** – how easily a substance catches fire
- **malleability** – how easily a substance can be hammered into different shapes
- **ductility** – how easily a substance can be stretched out into a wire
- **toxicity** – how harmful the substance is to humans and other living creatures.

Choosing the best substance for a job

When a substance is chosen for a particular job, it is often chosen because its properties are ideal for that job, but its cost is also taken into account. Sometimes an expensive substance has to be used because there is nothing cheaper that is right for the job. At other times there are many cheap materials that are fine for the job.

!
Diamond is the hardest natural substance we know of.

?
1 Steel is malleable, ductile, has a high density and is an electrical conductor. Explain what each of these properties means. *[Total 4]*

2 Benzene is toxic and flammable. Explain what each of these properties means. *[Total 4]*

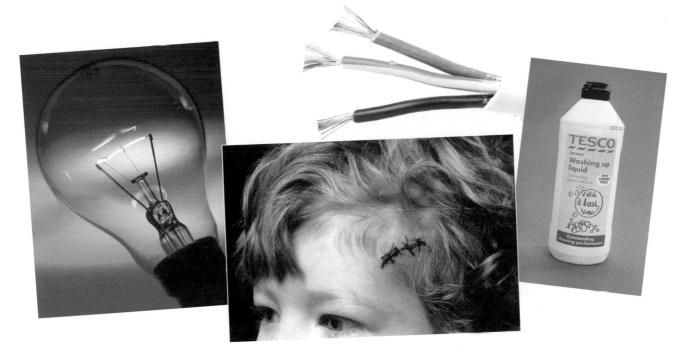

Figure 1.1 *Substances have many very different uses.*

Electrical wires

Electrical wires are made of two materials. In the middle is copper, which is an excellent conductor of electricity. On the outside is plastic which protects us from electric shocks because it does not conduct electricity. Both materials must be flexible so that wires can bend.

Medical stitches

Many people have stitches after an injury or an operation. The material used for stitches has to have certain properties. It must be strong enough so that it does not break, flexible enough so that it can be sewn, non-toxic so that it does harm the person having the stitches, and they must slowly decay away as the wound heals.

The inside of light bulbs

The filament in a light bulb is made of tungsten. When switched on the filament reaches over 2500 °C. At this temperature, oxygen and even nitrogen from the air would react with the tungsten. Argon gas is used to fill the light bulb because it will not react with tungsten, even at this temperature.s

Detergents

Most dirt will not dissolve in water and so cannot be washed away using water. Detergents are added to water to wash away dirt. Detergents are special substances that dissolve dirt as well as dissolving themselves in water.

> **!** The metals that conduct electricity best are silver, copper and gold. Copper is used in wires because it is much cheaper than gold or silver!

Figure 1.2 A space shuttle.

Space shuttle tiles

The space shuttle experiences a wide range of temperatures on a flight. In orbit, the temperature is about –120 °C and on re-entry into the Earth's atmosphere it can be over 3000 °C. The outside of the shuttle must not melt or decompose at these temperatures. Also, it must insulate the inside of the shuttle from these extreme temperatures. Special silica materials are used which are very expensive.

The gas in crisp packets

Many food packets, such as crisps, contain nitrogen rather than air. Crisps would go off if packed in air as they react with the oxygen. Nitrogen is used instead because the crisps do not react with it.

Figure 1.2 A space shuttle.

Summary

- The properties of a substance describe what it is like and what it can do.
- Some of the most important properties include strength, hardness, melting and boiling points, thermal and electrical conductivity.
- A substance must have the right properties for its use.

Questions

1 List some of the properties of each of the following substances:
a) steel [4]
b) glass. [3]
[Total 7]

2 Give two important reasons why the following substances are used for the jobs shown:
a) polystyrene for packaging [2]
b) plastic for making rulers [2]
c) PVC for making window frames [2]
d) methane (natural gas) for burning in gas fires [2]
e) oil on bicycle chains [2]
[Total 10]

3 Write one sentence for each of the following words to explain what each means:
flexible, flammable, toxic, ductile, malleable.
[Total 5]

4 Aluminium has a low density but is not very strong. Copper is strong, but has a higher density. Alloys are mixtures of metals. Aeroplane bodies are made out of an alloy of copper and aluminium called duralumin.
a) Why are aeroplane bodies not made out of aluminium alone? [1]
b) Why are aeroplane bodies not made out of copper alone? [1]
c) What is an alloy? [1]
d) Why are aeroplane bodies made out of an alloy of copper and aluminium? [2]
[Total 5]

2.2 Elements

What is an **element**? There are millions of different substances, but only about 100 of them are elements. They are either metals or non-metals.

What is an element?

An element is a substance that contains only one kind of atom. For example, in the element carbon all the atoms are carbon atoms. Elements cannot be broken down into simpler substances in the laboratory.

Atoms and their symbols

There are about 90 different kinds of atoms that occur naturally on Earth. There are also a few more that can be made by nuclear reactions, making over 100 in total.

Every atom has its own symbol. The symbol for every atom starts with a capital letter. As there are only 26 letters in the alphabet, most atoms have a second letter, which is always a small one. For example, there are 11 atoms whose symbols start with the letter C. Only one can have the symbol C, so the others have a second letter. The elements are:

- C — carbon
- Cl — chlorine
- Ca — calcium
- Cr — chromium
- Co — cobalt
- Cu — copper
- Cd — cadmium
- Cs — caesium
- Ce — cerium
- Cm — curium
- Cf — californium

The symbols for some atoms do not start with the first letter of their name. This is because their symbols often come from much older names in other languages. For example, the symbol for iron atoms is Fe from the old Latin name *ferrum*; the symbol for gold atoms is Au from the old Latin name *aurum*.

The names of elements come from different sources. Some are named after places (e.g. europium after Europe), people (e.g. einsteinium after Einstein), or a property of the element (e.g. chlorine from the Greek word *chloros* meaning pale green).

Formulas of elements

The particles in most elements are individual atoms, but in some elements the particles are molecules. The formula of an element tells us whether it is made up of atoms or molecules, and how many atoms there are in any molecules. Table 2.1 shows the particles of some common elements.

> **!** It is very difficult making new elements by nuclear reactions. One of the newest, element 118, ununoctium (Uuo), was made in 1999. It was made by firing lead atoms at krypton atoms. Just three atoms of ununoctium were made, and they lasted less than a millisecond before breaking apart.

> **!** The names of the elements vary in different languages, but their symbols are always the same. For example, iron is *fer* in French, *eisen* in German, *hierro* in Spanish, *ferro* in Italian, *ijzer* in Dutch and *haearn* in Welsh. However, the symbol is always Fe.

> **!** Four elements have been named after Ytterby in Sweden. They are called yttrium, ytterbium, terbium and erbium. They are just four of the eleven elements first discovered in minerals that were found in Ytterby in 1787.

Table 2.1

Name	Symbol of atoms	Diagram of particles	Formula of particles	Description of particles
argon	Ar		Ar	atoms
iron	Fe		Fe	atoms
oxygen	O		O_2	molecules (each with 2 atoms)
sulphur	S		S_8	molecules (each with 8 atoms)

Metals and non-metals

About three-quarters of the elements are metals and the rest are non-metals. Metals and non-metals have different properties, which are shown in Table 2.2.

Table 2.2

Properties of metals	Properties of non-metals
shiny (when polished)	dull
solids at room temperature (except mercury which is a liquid)	solids, liquids and gases at room temperature
conduct heat	insulator – do not conduct heat (except graphite)
conduct electricity	insulator – do not conduct electricity (except graphite)
three are magnetic (iron, cobalt and nickel) – the rest are not	not magnetic
strong	brittle (break easily)
malleable	not malleable
ductile	not ductile

The Periodic Table

All the elements are listed in the Periodic Table. The elements are shown by the symbol for their atoms (not the formula of their particles). The properties of some well known elements are shown. You do not have to learn the Periodic Table.

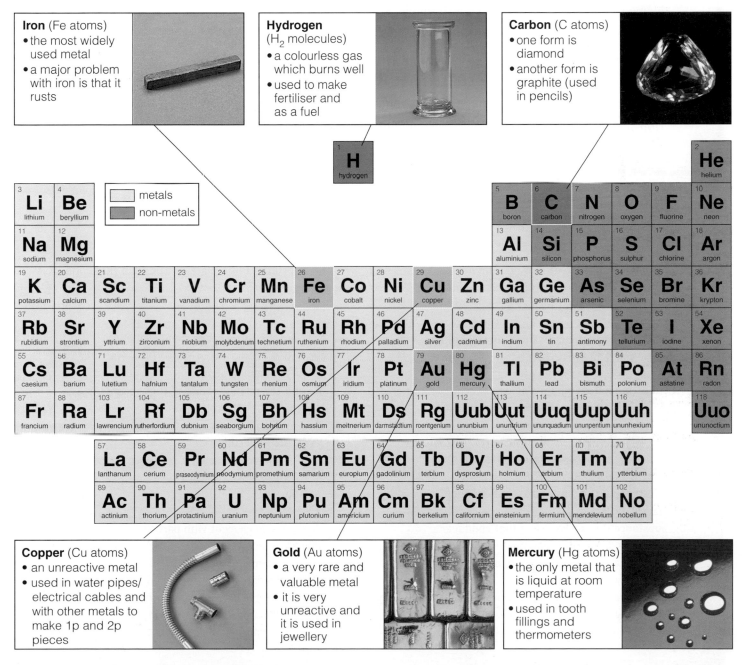

Iron (Fe atoms)
• the most widely used metal
• a major problem with iron is that it rusts

Hydrogen (H₂ molecules)
• a colourless gas which burns well
• used to make fertiliser and as a fuel

Carbon (C atoms)
• one form is diamond
• another form is graphite (used in pencils)

metals
non-metals

Copper (Cu atoms)
• an unreactive metal
• used in water pipes/ electrical cables and with other metals to make 1p and 2p pieces

Gold (Au atoms)
• a very rare and valuable metal
• it is very unreactive and it is used in jewellery

Mercury (Hg atoms)
• the only metal that is liquid at room temperature
• used in tooth fillings and thermometers

Figure 2.1 *Some of the elements in the Periodic Table.*

Summary

○ There are millions of known substances, but only about 100 are elements.

○ An element is a substance that contains only one kind of atom.

○ Elements cannot be broken down into simpler substances.

○ The particles in elements can be atoms or molecules.

○ The elements are all arranged in the Periodic Table.

○ About three-quarters of the elements are metals.

○ Metals are generally shiny when polished, strong and conduct heat and electricity.

○ Non-metals are generally dull, brittle and do not conduct heat and electricity.

Questions

1 Copy and complete the following sentences. Substances that cannot be broken down into simpler substances are called _____. There are about _____ of these substances. The particles in these substances are either _____ or _____. *[Total 2]*

2 Which of the following are elements?
salt   water   lead   bronze   air   carbon   methane   uranium   *[Total 4]*

3 Decide whether each of the following is a metal or a non-metal.
a) Substance **A** is a shiny solid that conducts electricity. *[1]*
b) Substance **B** is a silver solid that conducts electricity and is not magnetic. *[1]*
c) Substance **C** is a gas that does not conduct electricity. *[1]*
d) Substance **D** is a liquid that conducts electricity at room temperature. *[1]*

e) Substance **E** is a black, brittle solid that conducts electricity. *[1]*
[Total 5]

4 Here are the formulas of some elements.
He H_2 P_4 Cu Cl_2 Pt   Na   Fe
a) What is an element? *[1]*
b) Find the name of each of these elements. *[4]*
c) What is a molecule? *[1]*
d) i) Which of these elements have particles that are molecules?
    ii) Which of these elements have particles that are atoms? *[4]*
[Total 10]

5 Mercury is an element with particles of formula Hg. Bromine is an element with particles of formula Br_2. They are both liquids at room temperature, but can be turned into gases on heating or solids on cooling. Draw a series of three diagrams for *both* mercury and bromine to show how their particles are arranged when each one is a solid, a liquid and a gas. *[Total 5]*

2.3 Compounds

What is a compound? Most of the millions of different substances that exist are compounds. There are differences between compounds and elements.

Mixtures and compounds

Hydrogen and oxygen are elements. Hydrogen is a colourless gas that is flammable. Oxygen is a colourless gas in which other substances burn. If you mix hydrogen and oxygen, then you still have the same substances, hydrogen and oxygen. You just have a mixture of the elements.

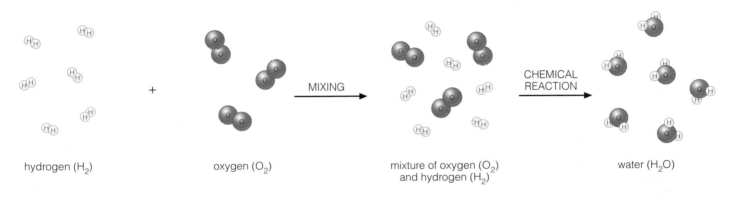

hydrogen (H_2)   oxygen (O_2)   mixture of oxygen (O_2)   water (H_2O)
                                                              and hydrogen (H_2)

Figure 3.1 *The reaction between hydrogen and oxygen.*

If a flame is put near the mixture of hydrogen and oxygen, a chemical reaction takes place. This reaction produces the new substance water. This new substance is very different to both hydrogen and oxygen. It is a colourless liquid that puts fires out. This new substance is a compound.

The word equation for this chemical reaction is:

  hydrogen + oxygen → water

In a mixture of hydrogen and oxygen, the hydrogen and oxygen atoms are not joined to each other, they are just mixed together. In the compound water, the hydrogen and oxygen atoms are joined to each other.

A **compound** is a substance that contains atoms of more than one kind joined together. Compounds can be broken down into simple substances.

Although there are only about 100 elements, there are millions of known compounds.

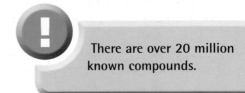

? 1 Explain why water has different properties than hydrogen and oxygen. [Total 1]

! There are over 20 million known compounds.

The properties of each substance in a mixture are the same as before they were mixed. However, the new substance formed when they react, the compound, has properties which are different from the substances in the mixture.

Making more compounds

Compounds are very different to the elements from which they are made. Some more examples of chemical reactions between elements that produce compounds are shown in Figure 3.2.

! Chlorine gas was used to kill soldiers during World War I.

! Common salt is sodium chloride, but there are thousands of other salts.

? **2** Sodium chloride (salt) is made from the elements sodium (a dangerous metal) and chlorine (a toxic gas). Why is salt not like sodium or chlorine? [Total 2]

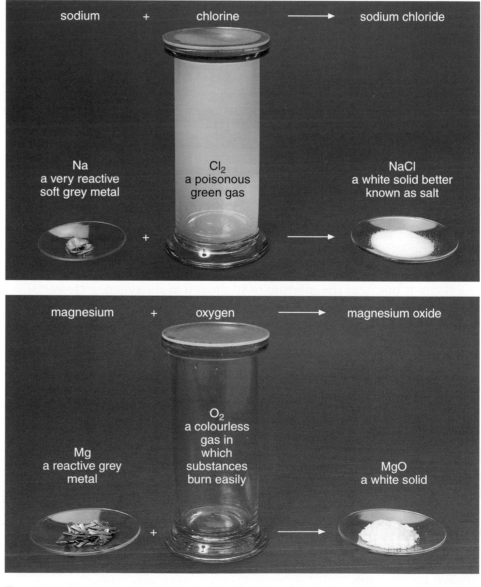

Figure 3.2 *Making compounds from elements.*

The formulas of compounds

In a compound, there is always a fixed number of atoms of each kind. For example, in water there are always two hydrogen atoms and one oxygen atom in each molecule. This gives water the formula H_2O. We do not usually write the formula as H_2O_1, because if the number is a '1' we leave it out. This means that if there is no number in a formula then it is a '1'.

Aspirin and ethanol (alcohol) are both compounds made from carbon, hydrogen and oxygen atoms, but they are very different. In the compound aspirin, there are always nine carbon atoms, eight hydrogen atoms and four oxygen atoms in each molecule. This gives aspirin the formula $C_9H_8O_4$. In the compound ethanol, there are always two carbon atoms, six hydrogen atoms and one oxygen atom in each molecule. This gives ethanol the formula C_2H_6O.

This fixed number of atoms is very different to a mixture, where there can be any amount of the substances mixed together. For example, in a mixture of hydrogen and oxygen, there could be ten times as much hydrogen as oxygen, or three times as much, or half as much, etc.

Note that a formula like CO means a compound made from carbon (C) and oxygen (O). This is very different to Co, which is the element cobalt. This shows why it is important to use capital and small letters correctly.

Naming compounds

The names of many compounds end in the letters -ide. These are made from two elements. If a compound is made from a **metal** and a **non-metal**, the name of the metal comes first, followed by the non-metal. For example:

- sodium chloride is made from sodium and chlorine
- magnesium oxide is made from magnesium and oxygen.

Sometimes, part of the name starts with *mono-*, *di-* or *tri-*. This can help to tell some compounds apart. For example, there are two compounds containing only carbon and oxygen. They are carbon monoxide (CO) and carbon dioxide (CO_2). The *mono-* part of carbon monoxide tells us there is one oxygen for each carbon. The *di-* part of carbon dioxide tells us there are two oxygens. *Tri-* means three, as in sulphur trioxide (SO_3).

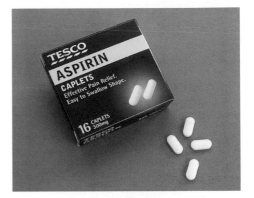

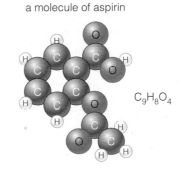

a molecule of aspirin

$C_9H_8O_4$

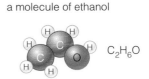

a molecule of ethanol

C_2H_6O

Figure 3.3 *Aspirin and ethanol – two very different compounds, but both made from carbon, hydrogen and oxygen atoms.*

3 Which elements are in
the following compounds?
a) nickel oxide   [1]
b) sodium nitrate   [1]
c) copper sulphide   [1]
d) hydrogen fluoride [1]
e) nitrogen triiodide [1]
                 [Total 5]
4 Name the compounds
containing the following
elements:
a) silver and chlorine   [1]
b) potassium, carbon and
   oxygen   [1]
c) chromium and oxygen [1]
                 [Total 3]

The names of some other compounds end in the letters *-ate*. These are made from three elements, the third one being oxygen. For example:

- copper sulphate is made from copper, sulphur and oxygen
- calcium carbonate is made from calcium, carbon and oxygen.

Breaking up compounds

It is usually easy to separate the substances in a mixture. Methods like distillation, filtration and evaporation are used (see subsection 2.5). These only involve physical changes as the substances are just separated from each other and are not chemically changed into different substances.

To split up a compound into its elements, a chemical reaction is required, and so is much more difficult. Breaking up a compound is called a **decomposition** reaction. It often requires a lot of energy to break up compounds. This is the opposite of when compounds are formed from elements, when energy is usually given out.

A few compounds split into their elements when heated. This is called **thermal decomposition**. For example, when mercury oxide is heated, it splits up into mercury and oxygen (see Figure 3.4).

mercury oxide ⟶ mercury + oxygen

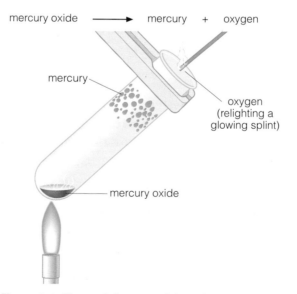

Figure 3.4 *Thermal decomposition of mercury oxide.*

Some compounds split into their elements when electricity is passed through them. This is called electrical decomposition or **electrolysis**. Not all compounds do this, and those that do have to be molten or in solution. For example copper and chlorine are formed when electricity is passed through a solution of copper chloride, (see Figure 3.5).

copper chloride ⟶ copper + chlorine

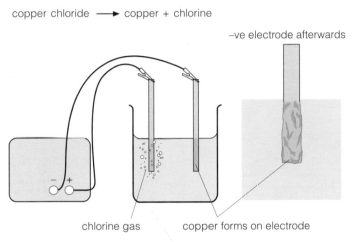

–ve electrode afterwards

chlorine gas   copper forms on electrode

Figure 3.5 *Electrical decomposition of copper chloride.*

?

5 What is a decomposition reaction? *[Total 1]*

6 What is thermal decomposition? *[Total 1]*

7 What is electrolysis? *[Total 1]*

8 Write word equations for the decomposition of the following compounds:
a) silver oxide *[1]*
b) lead bromide *[1]*
c) potassium iodide *[1]*
[Total 3]

Summary

- A mixture contains two or more substances mixed together, but not chemically joined.
- Mixtures can contain any amount of the substances in it.
- The substances in a mixture each behave in the same way as they would on their own.
- It is easier to separate the substances in a mixture because the separate substances are not joined together.
- A compound is a substance that contains more than one kind of atom joined together.
- Compounds contain a fixed number of atoms of each kind.
- Compounds have very different properties to the elements from which they are formed.
- It is often difficult to break compounds up into their elements (because the atoms are joined together).
- Some compounds can be broken up into their elements by a decomposition reaction, which usually requires energy.

Questions

1 Copy and complete the following sentences.
Substances can be elements or compounds. There are
about 100 _____, but there are millions of
_____. Elements can react together to make
compounds. It is _____ to break compounds
up into elements because the atoms are
_____ together. *[Total 2]*

2 a) What is a compound? *[1]*
b) The formulas of some substances are shown.
Which are compounds?
Br_2 PF_3 H_2SO_4 Na N_2 H_2O CO   *[4]*
[Total 5]

3 You may need to use the Periodic Table on page 45
to help you with this question.
a) Which elements do the following compounds
contain?
i) iron sulphide   iv) NH_3
ii) sulphur trioxide   v) Fe_2O_3
iii) magnesium nitrate   vi) $Cu(OH)_2$ *[6]*

b) Give the name of each of the following compounds.
i) CuO   iii) FeS
ii) $MgCO_3$ iv) $FeSO_4$ *[4]*
[Total 10]

4 Look at Figure 3.6. Decide whether each diagram
represents the particles in an element, a compound
or a mixture. *[Total 6]*

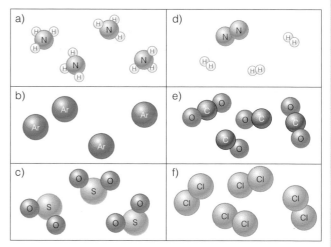

Figure 3.6

2.4 Solutions

Have you ever wondered what happens to sugar when you add it to a cup of tea? Different liquids can dissolve different substances, but some substances will not dissolve in some liquids. Dissolving is a physical change.

What happens when something dissolves?

When sugar dissolves in a cup of tea, you can still taste the sugar. It is still there even though you cannot see it. When sugar dissolves, the moving water particles hit the sugar particles, knocking them into the water. This produces a mixture of water and sugar particles.

Figure 4.1 *Sugar dissolves in water.*

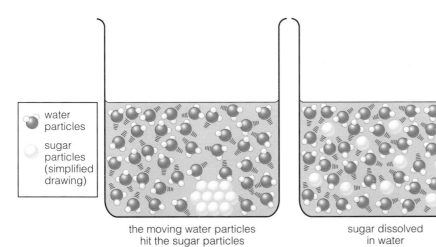

water particles

sugar particles (simplified drawing)

the moving water particles hit the sugar particles

sugar dissolved in water

Figure 4.2 *Sugar dissolving in water.*

The sugar is said to be **soluble** in water because it dissolves in it. The sugar is known as the **solute** (the substance that dissolves) and the water as the **solvent** (the liquid it dissolves in). A **solution** is what you get when a solute dissolves in a solvent. Solutions are transparent (i.e. clear, you can see through them). There are many other solvents besides water, such as ethanol, propanone, turpentine and white spirit.

Mass is conserved when a solution is formed. That is, the total mass of a solution is equal to the mass of the solvent plus the mass of the solute. For example, if 5 g of sugar dissolves in 100 g of water, the mass of the solution would be 105 g.

> **!** You can dissolve about 120 teaspoons of sugar in a tea cup of hot water (if you can keep it hot while you try!).

> **!** There are about 27 g of salt dissolved in one litre of sea water. It contains many other dissolved substances as well.

> **?** 1 Brine is a solution of salt in water.
> a) Name the solute. [1]
> b) Name the solvent. [1]
> [Total 2]
> 2 What is the mass of a solution of brine where 20 g of salt is dissolved in 100 g of water? [Total 1]

> **!** Many bottles of medicine contain an insoluble solid in water. The bottle has to be shaken before use to produce a suspension, so that the solid is spread evenly throughout the bottle and the patient takes the correct amount of the solid.

A substance is **insoluble** if it cannot dissolve in a solvent. For example, sand is insoluble in water. When an insoluble substance is shaken in a liquid, the solid particles can be seen spread throughout the liquid. This is called a **suspension** (you cannot see through a suspension). The solid particles usually settle down to the bottom quite quickly.

To test if a substance is soluble or insoluble in a solvent, you add a small amount of the substance to the solvent and then stir or shake. If the substance cannot be seen it is soluble, but if you can still see the solid then it is insoluble.

When a white substance dissolves, a colourless solution is formed (for example when sugar dissolves in water). When a coloured substance dissolves in water, a coloured solution is formed (for example when copper sulphate crystals dissolve in water).

> **!** Gardeners spray solutions containing copper sulphate onto some plants to protect them from disease.

sugar solution

copper sulphate solution

sugar

copper sulphate

Figure 4.3 *Solutions.*

Is dissolving a chemical or physical change?

Dissolving is a **physical** change. The solute and solvent do not change into different substances, they just mix together. For example, when sugar dissolves in water, the solution is a mixture of sugar and water, the same two substances. If we evaporate the water, the sugar will be left behind.

Some substances react with water producing different substances. This is a **chemical** change and is not the same as dissolving. For example, when sodium is added to water, a reaction takes place producing hydrogen gas and a solution of sodium hydroxide. These are not the same substances as sodium and water.

Figure 4.4 *Sodium reacting with water.*

Speeding up dissolving

There are three things that you can do to make something dissolve faster:

- heat up the solvent
- stir or shake the solvent
- grind the solute up into smaller pieces.

Heating and stirring both make the solute dissolve faster by making the solvent particles move faster, so hitting the solute particles harder and more often. In addition, heating makes the solute particles vibrate faster, helping them to break free more easily.

When a solute dissolves, the particles under the surface cannot dissolve until those above them on the surface have dissolved. When a solute is ground up into small pieces, more of the particles are at the surface, so it dissolves faster.

Different solvents

Water is the most common solvent because it is readily available and cheap, but there are many other solvents. A substance that might dissolve in one solvent may not be soluble in another. For example, salt dissolves in water but not in ethanol (alcohol). Some substances are soluble in more than one solvent. For example, sugar dissolves in both water and ethanol.

Solvents have many uses, some of which are shown in Table 4.1.

Some people think that solvents are glues. This is wrong, but some glues work by having a sticky substance dissolved in a solvent. When the glue is used, the solvent evaporates leaving the sticky substance in place.

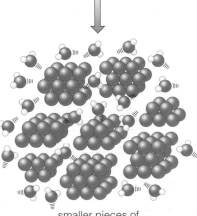

large piece of solid in water

smaller pieces of solid in water

Figure 4.5 *When the solute is broken up, more of its particles are at the surface.*

Table 4.1

Solvent	Use
propanone	nail varnish remover, removing grease
ethanol	some glues, aftershaves, perfumes
tetrachloroethene	dry cleaning clothes, cleaning circuit boards
white spirit	gloss paint, paint brush cleaner
toluene	glue remover (for some glues)

Figure 4.6 *Nail varnish dissolves in propanone.*

3 Name a solvent that disolves:
a) grease [1]
b) gloss paint. [1]
[Total 2]

4 Give three ways in which you could speed up the dissolving of a piece of jelly in water. [Total 3]

5 Use the solubility curves in Figure 4.7 to answer these questions.
a) What is the solubility of potassium bromide in water at 80 °C? [1]
b) At what temperature does 60 g of potassium bromide dissolve in 100 g of water? [1]
[Total 2]

A few solids become less soluble in water as it becomes hotter. One example is calcium hydroxide (limewater is a solution of calcium hydroxide in water).

6 What is a saturated solution? [Total 2]
7 Why do crystals form if a saturated solution is cooled down? [Total 1]

The effect of temperature on the solubility of solids

There is a limit to how much solute can dissolve in a solvent. If you keep adding salt to water, eventually you reach a point when no more salt can dissolve, and any more that is added collects at the bottom. A solution is said to be **saturated** when no more solute can dissolve. If more solute can dissolve in a solution, then it is said to be **unsaturated**.

Usually, the hotter a solvent, the more solid that can dissolve. Figure 4.7 shows how the solubility of some substances in water changes with temperature. These graphs are known as **solubility curves**. The solubility is measured as the maximum mass of the solute that dissolves in 100 g of water.

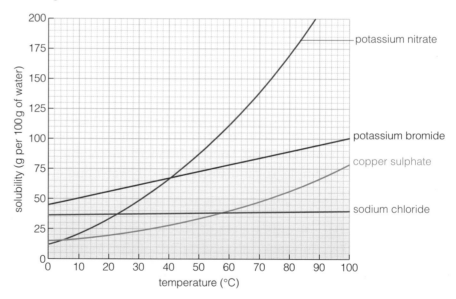

Figure 4.7 *Solubility curves for some solids.*

A **saturated solution** is a solution in which no more solute can dissolve, at that temperature. If a saturated solution is heated then it is no longer saturated because more solute could dissolve. For example, the graphs show that a saturated solution of copper sulphate at 20 °C contains 20 g of dissolved copper sulphate (per 100 g of water). If it is warmed to 80 °C, then a total of 56 g could dissolve, 36 g more than at 20 °C.

If a saturated solution is cooled down then less solute can dissolve, and so some solute crystallises out of the solution. For example, a saturated solution of copper sulphate at 80 °C contains 56 g of copper sulphate. If it is cooled to 20 °C, then only 20 g can stay dissolved, so the other 36 g crystallises out of solution.

The effect of temperature on the solubility of gases

Temperature has the opposite effect on the solubility of gases. The hotter a solvent, the less can dissolve. Figure 4.8 shows how the solubility of oxygen varies with temperature. As the temperature rises, gases become less soluble in water.

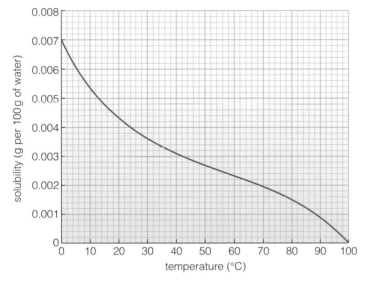

Figure 4.8 *Solubility curve for oxygen.*

! Fish can be killed if hot water is added to rivers because not enough oxygen can dissolve in the water.

?

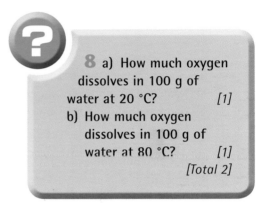

8 a) How much oxygen dissolves in 100 g of water at 20 °C? [1]
b) How much oxygen dissolves in 100 g of water at 80 °C? [1]
[Total 2]

Summary

- A solute dissolves in a solvent to form a solution.
- A solution is a mixture of a solute and a solvent.
- A substance is soluble in a solvent if it dissolves in it, but insoluble if it does not dissolve.
- A saturated solution is one in which no more solute can dissolve at that temperature.
- More solid can dissolve in a solvent at higher temperatures.
- Less gas can dissolve in a solvent at higher temperatures.
- Dissolving a solid can be speeded up by heating, stirring or crushing the solid.
- There are many different solvents. Different substances are soluble in different solvents.

Questions

1 Copy and complete the following sentences.
A solution contains a _____ dissolved in
a _____. A solution in which no more
_____ can be dissolved is a
_____ solution. There are many other
solvents as well as water, such as _____
and _____.

[Total 3]

2 Sea water contains salt dissolved in water.
a) Name the solvent in sea water. [1]
b) Name the solute in sea water. [1]

[Total 2]

3 a) Describe how you can tell if a solid is soluble
in water. [2]
b) Which of the following substances are soluble
in water? [3]

sugar   sand   flour   copper
sulphate   chalk   salt   [Total 5]

4 Deepak wants to dissolve a sugar cube in water.
He put it in a glass of water, but it was dissolving
very slowly. Describe three ways Deepak could
make the sugar cube dissolve faster.

[Total 3]

5 Use Figure 4.7 on page 56 to answer this question.
a) What mass of potassium nitrate dissolves in
100 g of water at 80 °C? [1]
b) What is the mass of a saturated solution of
potassium nitrate in 100 g of water at 80 °C? [1]
c) What is the lowest temperature at which 80 g
of potassium nitrate will dissolve in 100 g
of water? [1]
d) How much potassium nitrate will crystallise
out of solution if a saturated solution of
potassium nitrate in 100 g of water was
cooled from 80 °C to 20 °C? [2]

[Total 5]

6 Use Figure 4.7 on page 56 to answer this question.
a) What mass of copper sulphate dissolves in
100 g of water at 70 °C? [1]
b) What mass of copper sulphate dissolves in
200 g of water at 70°C? [1]
c) At what temperature will 50 g of copper
sulphate dissolve in 100 g of water? [1]
d) At what temperature will 20 g of copper
sulphate dissolve in 50 g of water? [1]

[Total 4]

7 Lauren is painting her bedroom. She paints the walls
with emulsion paint (a water based paint) and the
door with gloss paint (a white spirit based paint). She
used a different brush for each paint. When she had
finished, she tried to clean the brushes by rinsing
them with water. Only one brush was cleaned.
a) Which brush could be cleaned in the water? [1]
b) Why did that brush clean in the water? [1]
c) Why did the other brush not clean in the water? [1]
d) How could you clean the other brush? Explain
why your method works. [2]

[Total 5]

8 a) Describe the relationship between the
temperature and the solubility of gases. [1]
b) Comment on this relationship compared with the
solubility of solids. [2]
c) Fizzy drinks are fizzy due to carbon dioxide
dissolved in the drink. Two glasses of cola were
poured from a new bottle of cola taken straight
out of the fridge. One was left on a table in a
room for five minutes, and the other one kept in
a fridge. Which drink will be fizzier and why? [3]
d) Use ideas about particles to explain the effect of
temperature on the solubility of a gas. [2]

[Total 8]

2.5 Separating mixtures

How can the substances in a mixture be separated? Most of the materials found on this planet are not pure, but are a mixture of substances. For example air, sea water, oil, rocks and food are all mixtures. Many of the substances in mixtures like these are very useful and we need to know how to separate them.

What is a mixture?

A **pure** substance is one in which all the particles are the same (a pure substance can be an element or a compound). For example:

- pure water contains only water particles (H_2O molecules)
- pure iron contains only iron particles (Fe atoms)
- pure oxygen contains only oxygen particles (O_2 molecules).

In a **mixture**, there are different particles. For example:

- in tap water there are other particles as well as water particles, such as oxygen, carbon dioxide, calcium fluoride and aluminium sulphate particles
- in steel there are carbon particles as well as iron particles
- in air, there are many other particles as well as oxygen particles, such as nitrogen, argon, water and carbon dioxide particles.

We often have to separate the different substances in a mixture. There are many ways to separate mixtures, and each one depends on some difference between the substances in the mixture. For example, steel and aluminium drinks cans can be separated using a magnet. This is because steel is magnetic, but aluminium is not.

This subsection describes several different ways to separate mixtures, each one depending on a difference between the substances being separated. All the methods involve physical processes because in each one the substances are separated from each other and are not changed into different substances.

Decanting – separating an insoluble solid from a liquid

Usually an insoluble solid settles to the bottom of a liquid. Sometimes it is possible to carefully pour off the liquid, leaving the solid at the

Figure 5.1 *A magnet being used to separate steel from aluminium.*

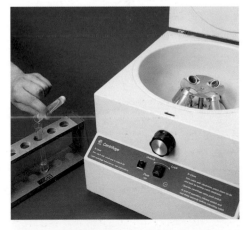

Figure 5.2 *Decanting a liquid from a solid after being centrifuged.*

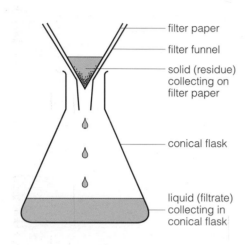

Figure 5.3 *Filtration.*

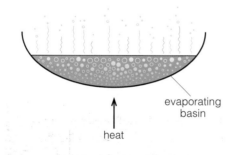

Figure 5.4 *Evaporation.*

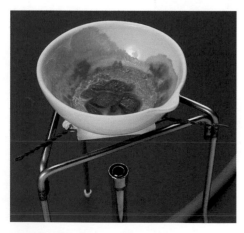

Figure 5.5 *Copper sulphate crystals form as the solution cools.*

bottom. This is called **decanting**, but it is difficult to separate the liquid and solid completely.

The solid can be made to settle at the bottom better by spinning it round very quickly in a centrifuge. However, it is still difficult to separate the solid and liquid completely.

Filtration – separating an insoluble solid from a liquid

A better way to separate an insoluble solid is to pour the mixture onto filter paper in a filter funnel. The filter paper has many very small holes, though they are too small to see. The liquid can go through the holes in the filter, but the solid cannot and stays on the filter. The filter paper acts like a tiny sieve.

During filtration, the solid left on the filter paper is called the **residue**. The liquid that passes through the filter is called the **filtrate**.

Evaporation – separating a soluble solid from a solution

A solid dissolved in a solution can be separated by evaporating the solvent. This works because the solvent escapes leaving the solid behind.

The solution is placed in an evaporating basin and either left alone for the solvent to evaporate, or evaporated more quickly by heating.

If the solvent is flammable, like ethanol for example, then instead of heating directly with a Bunsen burner, the solution is heated with a water bath to avoid it catching fire.

Crystallisation – separating a soluble solid from a solution

Rather than completely evaporating the solvent, some solids can be separated from a solution by evaporating some of the solvent and then letting the solute slowly **crystallise**. This works because as the saturated solution cools, solute that can no longer stay dissolved crystallises.

The solution is usually heated until crystals start to form and then left to cool. The crystals can be separated from the remaining solvent by filtration.

Distillation – separating a solvent from a solution

A solvent can be separated from a solution by evaporating and then condensing the solvent. This is called **distillation**. This works because the solvent evaporates and boils, but the solute does not. It uses the same process as evaporation, but this time the solvent is collected, not the solute.

The solution is heated and the solvent evaporates and boils. Instead of letting the **vapour** escape into the air, it is directed into a cold tube in which it condenses (turns back to a liquid). The cold tube is called a water-cooled condenser. It has a central tube which is surrounded by a second tube through which cold water runs.

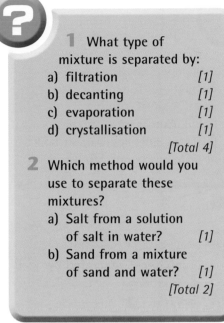

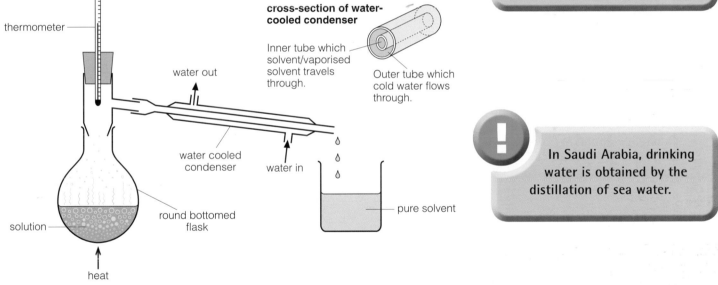

Figure 5.6 *Distillation.*

Fractional distillation – separating two liquids that are mixed together

Some liquids mix together, like ethanol and water. Liquids that mix together are called **miscible**. The fact that the liquids have different boiling points is used to separate them.

The mixture is heated, and the liquid with the lowest boiling point will boil first. This liquid vaporises and condenses in the water-cooled condenser before the other liquid boils. The long fractionating column

---

?

1 What type of mixture is separated by:
a) filtration   [1]
b) decanting   [1]
c) evaporation   [1]
d) crystallisation   [1]
                    [Total 4]

2 Which method would you use to separate these mixtures?
a) Salt from a solution of salt in water?   [1]
b) Sand from a mixture of sand and water?   [1]
                    [Total 2]

! In Saudi Arabia, drinking water is obtained by the distillation of sea water.

! Some alcoholic drinks, such as brandy, are made from other alcoholic drinks, such as wine, by distillation.

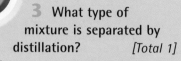

The gases in air are separated using low-temperature fractional distillation. The air is cooled to about –200 °C turning it into a liquid. As it warms up, the different substances in air boil at different temperatures.

3 What type of mixture is separated by distillation? *[Total 1]*

4 What type of mixture is separated by fractional distillation? *[Total 1]*

5 What type of mixture is separated with a separating funnel? *[Total 1]*

6 What is the difference between miscible and immiscible liquids? *[Total 1]*

helps to make sure that the second liquid does not get into the condenser until all of the first one has.

Fractional distillation is different to simple distillation because the long fractionating column allows liquids that boil at similar temperatures to be separated.

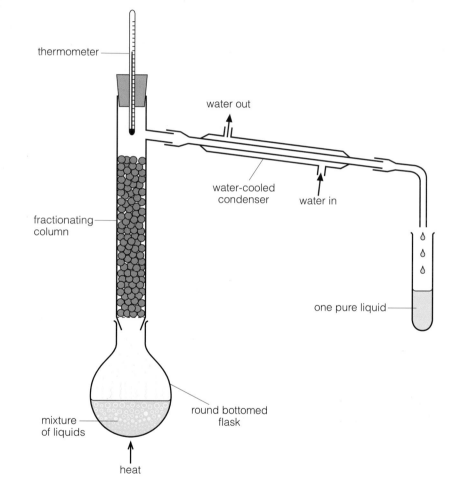

Figure 5.7 *Fractional distillation.*

Separating funnel – separating two liquids that do not mix together

Some liquids cannot mix together, like oil and water. Liquids that do not mix together are called **immiscible**. The fact that they do not mix is used to separate them.

The liquids are placed into a separating funnel where they form two layers, with the most dense liquid at the bottom. The bottom layer is run off through a tap.

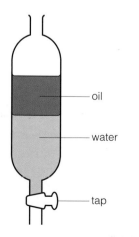

Figure 5.8 *Separating funnel.*

Chromatography – separating soluble substances

Chromatography can be used to separate mixtures of soluble substances, like inks or dyes. It depends on substances having different solubilities in a solvent.

A sample of the mixture is placed on a piece of chromatography paper, and then a solvent is allowed to soak up the paper. The most soluble substance in the mixture travels furthest up the paper, and the least soluble the shortest distance.

Chromatography can be done on a larger scale using a column of silica or alumina. This allows substances to be separated and collected (even if they are colourless).

Figure 5.9 *Chromatography on a larger scale.*

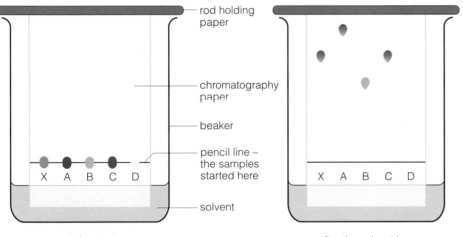

rod holding paper

chromatography paper

beaker

pencil line – the samples started here

solvent

X A B C D

at the start

X A B C D

after the solvent has soaked up the paper

Figure 5.10 *Analysing a mixture using chromatography.*

Chromatography is often used to analyse mixtures. Figure 5.10 compares an unknown mixture of dyes, X, to four known dyes, A, B, C and D. The experiment shows that X is a mixture of two dyes, C and D.

Summary

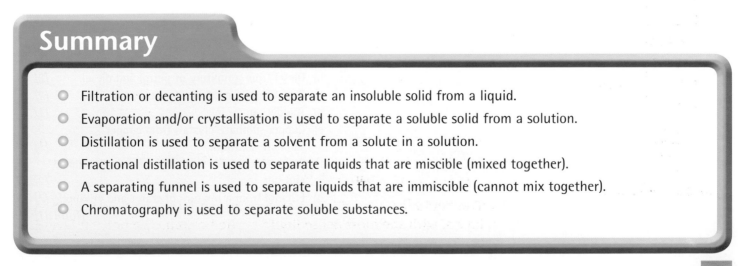

- Filtration or decanting is used to separate an insoluble solid from a liquid.
- Evaporation and/or crystallisation is used to separate a soluble solid from a solution.
- Distillation is used to separate a solvent from a solute in a solution.
- Fractional distillation is used to separate liquids that are miscible (mixed together).
- A separating funnel is used to separate liquids that are immiscible (cannot mix together).
- Chromatography is used to separate soluble substances.

Questions

1 Copy and complete the following sentences. Most natural materials are not _____ substances, they are mixtures. The particles of each substance in a mixture are not _____ to each other and so the substances can often be separated. There are several ways of separating the substances in a mixture, such as _____ and _____. *[Total 2]*

2 Decide whether each of the following is a pure substance or a mixture of substances:
a) mineral water *[1]*
b) air *[1]*
c) table salt *[1]*
d) sugar *[1]*
e) fresh orange juice *[1]*
f) sea water *[1]*
[Total 6]

3 Write a paragraph to explain how distillation works. *[Total 4]*

4 A sample of water was taken from the sea. The sea water was dirty, having sand in it. Sea water contains dissolved salt. Describe how you could separate the water, sand and salt, ending up with all three separate substances. *[Total 2]*

5 Daniel has dropped two glass jars containing sugar and salt as he tried to get them down from the kitchen cupboard. He now has a mixture of glass, sugar and salt. Describe in detail how he could separate the three substances. Sugar and salt are both soluble in water, but only sugar is soluble in ethanol (remember that ethanol is flammable and should not be heated directly). *[Total 7]*

6 Rosie did an experiment to compare the dyes in each colour of Smarties. She compared some colour from the different coloured Smarties with the dyes mentioned on the tube. The results are shown in Figure 5.11.

E104 E110 E120 E122 E133 | orange green brown blue yellow violet pink

Figure 5.11

a) What is this method of separation called? *[1]*
b) Which colours of Smartie contain more than one dye? *[1]*
c) Which dyes are in the following coloured Smarties:
   i) orange ii) green
   iii) yellow iv) violet? *[4]*
d) i) How many of the dyes mentioned on the tube do the brown Smarties contain?
   ii) Which dyes are they? *[2]*
[Total 8]

7 Outline how you would obtain the substance stated from the mixtures a) to g). Try to use the easiest method in each case. Some information that you may need is given first.
• Petrol boils at lower temperatures than diesel.
• Petrol and diesel are miscible.
• Petrol and water are immiscible.
• Water is denser than petrol.
• Benzoic acid is soluble in hot water, but not cold water.
• Ethanol and water are miscible.
• Ethanol boils at a lower temperature than water.
a) Sugar from a solution of sugar in water. *[1]*
b) Diesel from a mixture of petrol and diesel. *[2]*
c) Petrol from a mixture of water and petrol. *[2]*
d) The dyes in an ink. *[1]*
e) Copper sulphate crystals from copper sulphate solution. *[1]*
f) Benzoic acid from a mixture of benzoic acid and salt. *[2]*
g) Ethanol from a mixture of water and ethanol. *[2]*
[Total 11]

Food additives

The food we buy has to be prepared and transported to the shop before we buy it. We often keep it for a few more days before eating it. **Additives** called **preservatives** can be added to food to help to keep it fresh until we eat it. Additives can also be added to food to improve its taste or appearance. Some additives are natural but some are artificial. For example, salt has been used as a preservative in meat and fish for hundreds of years.

Additives have been given **E numbers** by the European Food Safety Authority. For an additive to be given an E number, it must first pass safety checks.

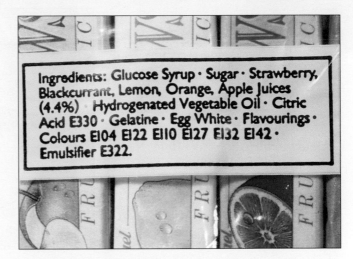

Ingredients: Glucose Syrup · Sugar · Strawberry, Blackcurrant, Lemon, Orange, Apple Juices (4.4%) Hydrogenated Vegetable Oil · Citric Acid E330 · Gelatine · Egg White · Flavourings · Colours E104 E122 E110 E127 E132 E142 · Emulsifier E322.

Figure 6.1 *Food label showing additives.*

Additive	What it does	Examples
preservatives	prevent the growth of microbes and stop us getting food poisoning	E234 nisin (found in milk and cheese) E280 propanoic acid
antioxidants	food reacts with oxygen in the air and goes off – antioxidants slow down the reaction with oxygen making the food last longer	E300 vitamin C E306 vitamin E
emulsifiers	allow water and oils to mix in foods such as salad dressings, ice cream and margarine	E322 lecithin (from egg yolks) E471 mono- or diglycerides of fatty acids
colours	sometimes added to food to improve the appearance	E150a caramel (brown from heating sugar) E160a beta carotene (orange from carrots)
flavourings	sometimes added to food to improve the taste	most flavourings do not have E numbers because they are controlled by different laws
sweeteners	make food taste sweeter – some have very low energy content and are used in slimming (low calorie) foods	E951 aspartame E954 saccharin

Table 6.1 *Examples of some types of food additives.*

2 Elements, compounds and mixtures

?

1 Why are preservatives added to foods? *[Total 1]*

2 What do emulsifiers do? *[Total 1]*

3 Who gives additives E numbers? *[Total 1]*

Figure 6.2 *Food goes off.*

?

4 What is hyperactivity? *[Total 2]*

Figure 6.3 *Some drinks contain colourings.*

There is a lot of debate about food additives. Some studies suggest that certain food additives can cause **allergies**. For example, there is evidence that the preservative sodium sulphite (E221) can trigger asthma attacks. There are very few other examples where the evidence is clear.

In the 1970s people started to think there may be a connection between child behaviour and eating food containing additives. Some experts now believe that there is enough evidence to show that some food additives can cause **hyperactivity** in children – an example of this is the colouring tartrazine (E102). Others believe that it only affects a small number of children who are already hyperactive or that there is no link at all. More research is being done and evidence collected, but the findings vary and can be misinterpreted.

Reports, research and the media

In 2002, the results from a study on children in the Isle of Wight were reported by the media. They reported that it proved a link between certain additives and poor behaviour. However, soon after this a group that advises the Government said that although the research did suggest that food additives could affect behaviour, it did not *prove* it.

This shows that we need to be careful when listening to reports about scientific studies in the news – some results have been misinterpreted, or reported as being more significant than they actually are.

The results of another, more detailed, study set up by the Food Standards Agency were published in 2007 and clearly showed a link between food additives and poor behaviour. The additives were a mixture of food colourings and sodium benzoate (a preservative). It showed that the effect was greater on younger children – but did not show which specific additives caused the effect.

There have now been many studies on the effects of food additives on behaviour. Some show a link, and some do not. Many food manufacturers are removing artificial additives from some foods due to concerns about their effects – although sometimes they are replaced by natural additives that could have similar effects.

We each have to decide what to do about food additives. Some additives are very important for public health (e.g. preservatives) while others are simply added to make food look better (e.g. colourings). Some have been shown to be safe but others have question marks about them. Food manufacturers will act on research evidence, government laws and public opinion – but the more informed we are, the better decisions we can make when we buy our food.

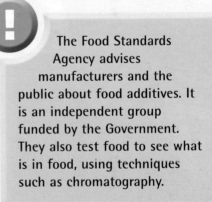

Figure 6.4 *Chromatography is one method used to analyse food additives.*

! The Food Standards Agency advises manufacturers and the public about food additives. It is an independent group funded by the Government. They also test food to see what is in food, using techniques such as chromatography.

Questions

1 What are food additives? *[Total 1]*

2 Why are additives added to food? *[Total 3]*

3 Why do some people worry about food additives? *[Total 2]*

4 Make a table to show advantages and disadvantages of using food additives. *[Total 4]*

5 Why is it important that the Food Standards Agency:
a) tests our food? *[1]*
b) is independent and not funded by food manufacturers? *[1]*
[Total 2]

6 Do you think we should use food additives? Explain your reasoning. *[Total 2]*

Useful elements and compounds

Antoine Lavoisier (1743–1794) carried out a very expensive experiment to prove that diamond was a form of carbon. He burned a diamond to show that it formed carbon dioxide.

There are just over 100 elements. There are millions of compounds, each made by joining elements together in different ways. Many compounds occur naturally but many others are made by chemists. The properties of a compound are very different from those of the elements they are made from. What are some of the common elements that we use everyday? What compounds are they found in? And how do we use these compounds?

Carbon

The element carbon (C) occurs in two main forms – diamond and graphite. Diamonds are beautiful crystals that are very precious – they are the hardest natural substance. Graphite is used in pencils and is a soft, black substance that conducts electricity. Glucose ($C_6H_{12}O_6$), a common sugar, is a naturally occurring compound containing carbon. It is formed in the digestion of carbohydrates and by plants during photosynthesis. Living things use it in respiration. Carbon is also used in some important man-made substances. Polythene ($CH_2CH_2)_n$, is one example – it is used to make **plastic** bags and cling film.

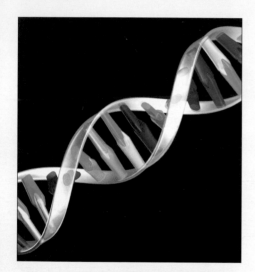

Figure 6.5 *The structure of DNA is very complex.*

Nitrogen

The element nitrogen (N_2) is a colourless, unreactive gas. It makes up 78% of the air. One use of nitrogen is as the gas in food packaging (e.g. crisp packets) because the food will not react with it. DNA is a naturally occurring compound containing nitrogen and other elements such as carbon, hydrogen, oxygen and phosphorus. DNA is found in the nucleus of cells and contains the genetic information that makes up all living creatures. Ammonium nitrate (NH_4NO_3) is a man-made compound used mainly as a fertiliser – millions of tonnes of it are made every year. Without the use of fertilisers it would be difficult to grow enough food to feed everyone in the world. Ammonium nitrate is also used as an explosive.

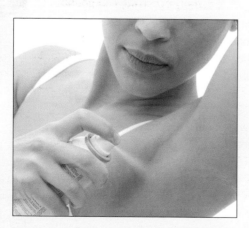

Figure 6.6 *Many antiperspirants contain aluminium chlorohydrate.*

Aluminium

Aluminium (Al) is an important metal. It does not occur naturally but it can be extracted from the ore bauxite (contains aluminium oxide, Al_2O_3). It has many uses including construction (e.g. aeroplanes), power lines, cans and cooking foil. Clay occurs naturally and is mainly made up of minerals made from aluminium, silicon and oxygen (aluminosilicates). Aluminium chlorohydrate [$Al_2Cl(OH)_5$] is a man-made aluminium-containing compound. It is used in antiperspirants and works by blocking sweat pores.

Calcium

Calcium (Ca) is a very reactive metal. It does not occur naturally but it can be extracted from ores such as calcite (contains $CaCO_3$). It is used to extract some other metals and in making alloys. Hydroxylapatite $[Ca_{10}(PO_4)_6(OH)_2]$ is a naturally occurring compound containing calcium – it makes up a large proportion of our bones and teeth. Calcium hydroxide $[Ca(OH)_2]$ is a man-made compound containing calcium and is used as a cheap alkali, in some hair-removal creams and in sewage treatment. Limewater (used to test for carbon dioxide) is a solution of calcium hydroxide in water.

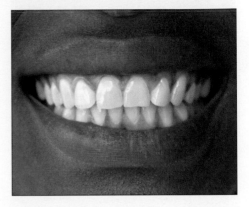

Figure 6.7 *Teeth contain hydroxylapatite.*

Chlorine

Chlorine (Cl_2) is a pale green, toxic gas. It does not occur naturally but can be made by the electrolysis of salt (NaCl) solution. Chlorine is added to water to kill bacteria and it was used as a poison gas in World War I. Salt is a naturally occurring compound that has many uses, including flavouring food, preserving food and melting (or preventing) ice on roads.

Sodium hypochlorite (NaClO) is a man-made compound containing chlorine. It is a bleach – for example, it is used in household bleach. There are several different commercial bleaches, but most are chlorine-containing compounds.

Questions

1 Calcium is a reactive metal that fizzes when added to water. There is some calcium in teeth. Explain why your teeth do not fizz when you drink a glass of water. *[Total 2]*

2 Chlorine is a toxic gas. There is some chlorine in salt. Explain why salt is not toxic. *[Total 2]*

3 Chemistry is all about how to make new substances from raw materials found on Earth. Give three examples of useful substances made from raw materials found on Earth. *[Total 3]*

4 Make a table for the elements potassium, copper and phosphorus to show some of their uses. You should include:

- some uses of the element
- an example of a naturally occurring compound and its uses
- an example of a man-made compound and its uses. *[Total 9]*

5 Antiperspirants contain aluminium compounds. There is some evidence that aluminium compounds are linked to Alzheimer's disease. Find out what Alzheimer's disease is and some arguments/ evidence for/ evidence against the use of aluminium compounds in antiperspirants. Present your findings in a suitable way. *[Total 4]*

2 Elements, compounds and mixtures

Figure 6.8 *Investigating how fast sugar dissolves.*

How fast does sugar dissolve?

There are several **variables** that affect how long it takes a solute to dissolve in a solvent. Kate and Jonathan carried out a series of experiments to investigate how different variables affect the time it takes for sugar to dissolve in water.

In some experiments they changed the temperature of the water; in some the mass of sugar; in some the volume of water. They also tested different types of sugars because they knew from their research that different types of sugar have different size crystals. They stirred the mixture in each experiment in the same way.

Their results are shown in Table 6.2.

Experiment	1	2	3	4	5	6	7	8
Type of sugar	table sugar	table sugar	table sugar	table sugar	table sugar	caster sugar	sugar cubes	brown sugar
Mass of sugar (g)	10	10	10	5	20	10	10	10
Volume of water (cm^3)	200	100	100	100	100	100	100	100
Temperature of water (°C)	21	43	21	21	21	21	21	21
Time to dissolve (s)	26	10	35	18	69	27	90	48

Table 6.2

Questions

1 a) What is the **dependent variable** in each of these experiments? [1]

b) What are the four different **independent variables** in these experiments? [1]

[Total 2]

2 a) What is the effect of temperature on the time it takes sugar to dissolve? [1]

b) Which experiments did you use to work this out? [1]

c) State the variables that must be controlled (kept the same) to investigate the effect of temperature. [1]

[Total 3]

3 a) What is the effect of mass of sugar on the time it takes sugar to dissolve? [1]

b) Which experiments did you use to work this out? [1]

c) State the variables that must be controlled to investigate the effect of the mass of sugar. [1]

[Total 3]

4 a) Which type of sugar dissolves fastest? [1]

b) Which experiments did you use to work this out? [1]

[Total 2]

Solubility curves

Ben and Rebecca carried out an investigation to see how changing the temperature affects the amount of potassium bromide that dissolves in water. They put 10 cm³ of water in a boiling tube, and measured how many spatula loads of potassium bromide dissolves at different temperatures. Their results are shown in **Table 6.3**.

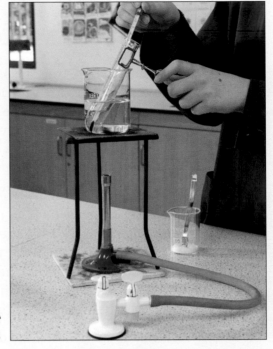

Figure 6.9 *Investigating how temperature affects solubility.*

Table 6.3

Temperature (°C)	21	32	40	48	63	71
Spatula loads of potassium bromide	1	2	3	5	7	8

Questions

1 a) What is the independent variable in this investigation? *[1]*

b) What is the dependent variable in this investigation? *[1]*

c) Give the key **control variables** to make this investigation fair. *[2]*

[Total 4]

2 Plot a graph of the results and draw a line of best fit. The independent variable should be on the *x*-axis. *[Total 4]*

3 a) Ben wrote this conclusion for the experiment:
Increasing the temperature changes the amount of potassium bromide that dissolves.
What key information is missing from this conclusion? *[1]*

b) Write a better conclusion for this experiment. *[1]*

[Total 2]

4 Measuring the mass of potassium bromide in 'spatula loads' is not very precise.

a) Explain why this is not very **precise**. *[1]*

b) Suggest a more precise way of doing this. *[1]*

[Total 2]

Dalton's atomic theory

In about 350 BC, the Greek philosopher Democritus suggested that matter was made up of tiny particles called **atoms** (with open space between them). Democritus was the first person to use the word atom, which comes from the Greek word *atomos* meaning something that cannot be divided. Although the idea of atoms had been around for a long time, not all scientists accepted it. In the early 1800s, John Dalton suggested many new ideas about atoms which became the basis for modern chemistry.

Dalton was born in 1766 near the Lake District. He was very intelligent, and by the age of twelve had taken over as the teacher at his local school. In 1793, when he was 27, he took up a teaching post at New College in Manchester. In 1800, Dalton left the college and joined the Literary and Philosophical Society. Scientific activity in Manchester was centred on this college.

While in Manchester, he developed his theory about atoms. His key ideas were:

Figure 6.10 *John Dalton (1766–1844).*

- everything is made up of tiny particles called atoms.
- atoms cannot be broken up into smaller particles or destroyed.
- in an element, all the atoms are identical and have the same mass.
- the atoms of each element are different to those in all the other elements.
- compounds are made from bigger particles, which are made by atoms joining together (we now call these particles molecules).
- atoms combine in simple whole number ratios when they combine to form compounds.

Dalton made up symbols for the atoms of each element, which are shown in Figure 6.11. He used these to represent the formula of compounds and was the first to see the importance of writing formulas. Some of his formulas are shown in Figure 6.12.

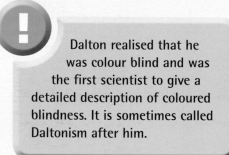

! Dalton realised that he was colour blind and was the first scientist to give a detailed description of coloured blindness. It is sometimes called Daltonism after him.

Not all of Dalton's formulas were correct, however, because he believed that atoms combined in the simplest way possible. For example, he thought that water would have the formula HO because hydrogen and oxygen would combine in the ratio 1:1 (rather than 2:1 (H_2O)). If there was more than one substance made from combinations of the same atoms, then he assumed that in one substance the atoms combined in the ratio 1:1 and in the other 2:1. This can be seen in his formulas for what we now know as carbon monoxide and carbon dioxide.

? **1** What important ideas has John Dalton contributed to science?

[Total 3]

Dalton's atomic theory

Figure 6.11 *Dalton's symbols and atomic weights.*

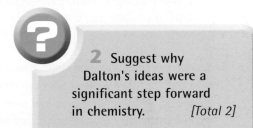

Figure 6.12 *Some of Dalton's formulas.*

Although his ideas were not immediately accepted by all scientists and were not completely correct, they marked a very significant step forward in chemistry.

2 Suggest why Dalton's ideas were a significant step forward in chemistry. *[Total 2]*

Questions

1 a) Who first thought that matter was made of atoms? *[1]*
b) What is the Greek word from which our word *atom* comes? *[1]*
c) What does this Greek word mean? *[1]*
[Total 3]

2 a) Dalton got the formula of some substances wrong. Use his symbols to draw the correct formula of:
i) water (H_2O)
ii) ammonia (NH_3)
iii) methane (CH_4) *[3]*
b) Explain why Dalton got some of his formulas wrong. *[1]*
[Total 4]

3 a) Look carefully at the diagrams. What do you think we call 'azote' today? *[1]*
b) We now know that some of the substances in Dalton's list are compounds, not elements. Name two examples. *[2]*
[Total 3]

End of section questions

1 Saucepans are made out of metal but have a plastic handle.

a) State two properties of metals that make them good for making saucepans. [2]

b) Give the main reason that the handle is made out of plastic, not metal. [1]

[Total 3]

2 a) There are many elements, compounds and mixtures all around us. Decide whether each of the following is an element, compound or mixture. Draw up a table with appropriate headings and add each name to the correct column of your table.

gold   ethanol   silver
oxygen   salt   sea water   [4]

b) Think of one more example each of an element, a compound and a mixture from everyday things around you and add them to your table. [3]

[Total 7]

3 Sophie put some iron and sulphur in a test tube and mixed them together. Iron is a grey metal that is magnetic, and sulphur is a yellow powder. When she heated them, they glowed bright red and formed a grey solid.

a) Sulphur and iron are elements. What is an element? [1]

b) Before she heated the test tube, Sophie could separate the iron from the sulphur with a magnet. After heating the iron and sulphur, she could no longer separate the iron from the sulphur. Explain why she could no longer separate them. [1]

c) The compound produced is called iron sulphide. What is a *compound*? [1]

d) A chemical reaction takes place between the iron and the sulphur. What is a *chemical reaction*? [1]

e) Write a word equation for the reaction between iron and sulphur. [1]

[Total 5]

4 a) Name the elements from which the following compounds are made:

i) potassium bromide
ii) magnesium sulphide
iii) magnesium sulphate. [3]

b) What do you think the following compounds are called?

i) $CuCl_2$
ii) $NaNO_3$ [2]

[Total 5]

5 Which of the diagrams in Figure 1 represents the particles in:

a) an element whose particles are atoms [1]
b) an element whose particles are molecules [1]
c) a compound [1]
d) a mixture of an element and a compound [1]
e) a mixture of two elements [1]
f) a mixture of two compounds? [1]

[Total 6]

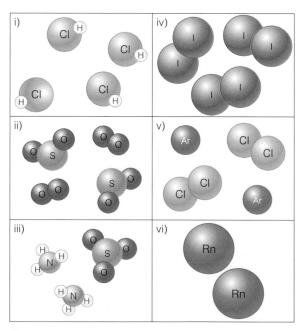

Figure 1

6 Figure 2 shows the particles in a sample of air.
  a) How many different substances are shown in the sample of air? [1]
  b) Is air a mixture or a pure substance? Explain your answer. [2]
  c) Give the formula of each substance in the air. [5]
  d) Decide whether each substance in the air is an element or a compound. [5]
  e) What is the most common substance in air? [1]

[Total 14]

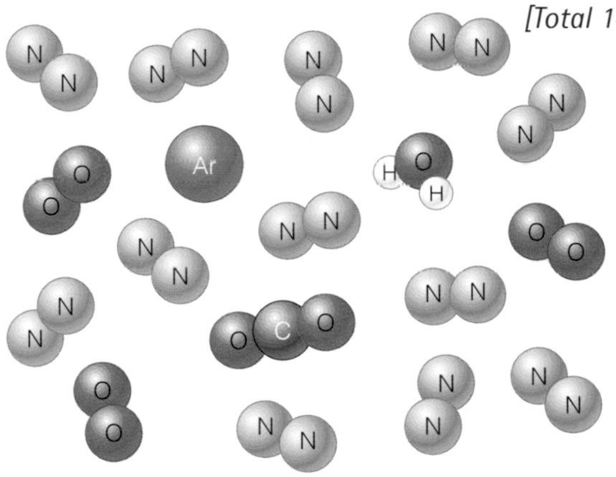

Figure 2

7 a) Use the data in the the table to plot a solubility curve for ammonium chloride. [4]

Temperature (°C)	0	20	40	60	80	100
Solubility (g per 100 g of water)	29	37	46	55	65	77

  b) Describe the relationship between the temperature and the solubility of ammonium chloride. [1]
  c) What mass of ammonium chloride dissolves in 100 g of water at 90 °C? [1]
  d) What is the lowest temperature at which 40 g of ammonium chloride will dissolve in 100 g of water? [1]
  e) If a saturated solution of ammonium chloride in 100 g of water at 70 °C is heated up to 90 °C, how much more ammonium chloride can dissolve? [1]

[Total 8]

8 You are given a mixture of water, toluene, cyclohexane and salt. Salt dissolves in water, but not toluene or cyclohexane. Water is immiscible with toluene and cyclohexane, but toluene and cyclohexane are miscible with each other. Cyclohexane has a lower boiling point than toluene. How could you separate all four substances from each other, so that you end up with all four? (Hint: start by separating the toluene and cyclohexane from the salt and water.)

[Total 4]

9 P Many substances dissolve in water. What factors might affect the amount of a substance that dissolves in water? For example, how would you investigate the effect that temperature has on the amount of potassium bromide that dissolves in water?

10 P Some substances conduct electricity. What factors might affect how well a solution of salt in water conducts electricity? For example, how would you investigate the effect that changing the concentration of the salt solution has on how well it conducts?

11 R There are just over 100 known elements. Make a colourful poster about one element, containing both writing and drawings/pictures. You could write about some or all of the following:
  ○ where we find the element on Earth, or how we make it from other substances
  ○ what the element is like
  ○ what the element is used for.

12 R Some elements are difficult to classify as either a metal or a non-metal, and are sometimes called metalloids. Silicon is a metalloid. Find out about the properties of silicon, which of its properties are typical of metals, which of its properties are typical of non-metals, and find the names of some more elements that are metalloids.

Water and solutions

3.1 Water

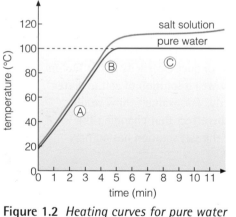

Figure 1.1 *Molecules of water.*

What are the main properties and uses of water? Water is the commonest substance on the surface of the Earth and is essential to all life. We should know about the structure and properties of water, and understand the changes which can occur to water in our environment.

Water molecules

Water is the simplest compound of hydrogen and oxygen. The molecules of water have two hydrogen atoms joined to one oxygen atom – so the formula of water is H_2O.

Heating water

When water is heated, its temperature rises and it eventually **boils**. If we draw a line graph of the temperature changes which occur as water is heated, we will obtain a **heating curve**. Figure 1.2 shows two heating curves, one for pure water and one for a solution of salt in water.

Note that:

- as the water is heated, the temperature rises steadily until it reaches its boiling point.
- if heating is continued after it has started to boil, the temperature remains constant as the energy is used to overcome forces between particles rather than make it hotter.
- the boiling point for pure water is exactly 100 °C.
- when impurities such as salt are added, water's boiling point rises above 100 °C and the temperature does not stay constant during boiling.

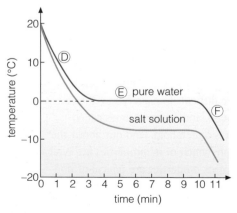

Figure 1.2 *Heating curves for pure water and salt solution.*

Cooling water

If water is cooled, its temperature falls and the water eventually freezes. Figure 1.3 shows two **cooling curves**, one for pure water and one for a solution of salt in water.

Note that:

- the freezing point for pure water is exactly 0 °C.
- impurities, such as salt, lower water's freezing point below zero and the temperature does not stay constant during freezing.
- if cooling continues after freezing the temperature of ice can drop further.

Figure 1.3 *Cooling curves for pure water and salt solution.*

This explains why salt is put on our roads in winter. The salt lowers the freezing point of water and ice does not form so easily.

Testing for water

There are two simple chemical tests which can be used to show the presence of water.

- Crystals of anhydrous copper sulphate change colour from white to blue.
- Cobalt chloride paper changes colour from blue to pink.

However, these tests only show that water is present. To prove that a liquid is pure water you would need to check that its boiling point was exactly 100 °C or its freezing point was exactly 0 °C.

The water cycle

It is thought that the amount of water on Earth has been about the same for millions of years. However, the water is constantly changing from one state to another. It goes from the seas into the atmosphere and back to the seas again. These natural changes are known as the **water cycle**. As shown in Figure 1.4, the water cycle never stops. The water you drink today is not new, but has been recycled over millions of years. It is even possible that someone else will have drunk it, thousands of years ago.

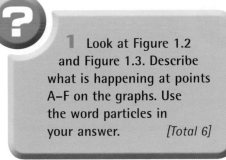

?

1 Look at Figure 1.2 and Figure 1.3. Describe what is happening at points A–F on the graphs. Use the word particles in your answer. [Total 6]

!

Life on Earth depends on a unique property of water. Most solids sink if placed in their liquid form. However, ice is different: it floats. If ice sank, then our seas and lakes would freeze from the bottom up and life could not survive.

?

2 Give three examples of changes of state that occur in the natural water cycle. [Total 4]

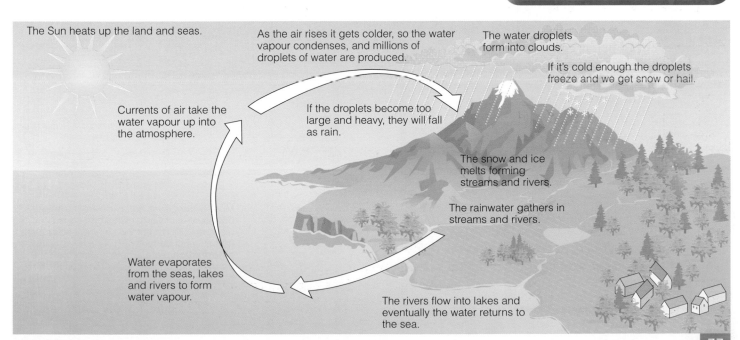

The Sun heats up the land and seas.

As the air rises it gets colder, so the water vapour condenses, and millions of droplets of water are produced.

The water droplets form into clouds.

If it's cold enough the droplets freeze and we get snow or hail.

Currents of air take the water vapour up into the atmosphere.

If the droplets become too large and heavy, they will fall as rain.

The snow and ice melts forming streams and rivers.

The rainwater gathers in streams and rivers.

Water evaporates from the seas, lakes and rivers to form water vapour.

The rivers flow into lakes and eventually the water returns to the sea.

Figure 1.4 *The water cycle.*

If the Earth was completely flat, the water on the planet would form a layer 2.5 km deep over the whole surface.

Our water supply

We all need water for drinking, washing and cooking and so a clean, reliable supply of water is important to our modern lifestyle. Our water mainly comes from lakes and rivers so it has to be treated to make it fit to drink. An outline of a typical water treatment plant is shown in Figure 1.5.

Chemists are involved in many of the stages of water treatment. Their main job is to analyse the water to check that it is safe to drink.

Roughly two-thirds of the Earth's surface is covered in seas. In fact the area of the Pacific Ocean is larger than the total land area of the Earth!

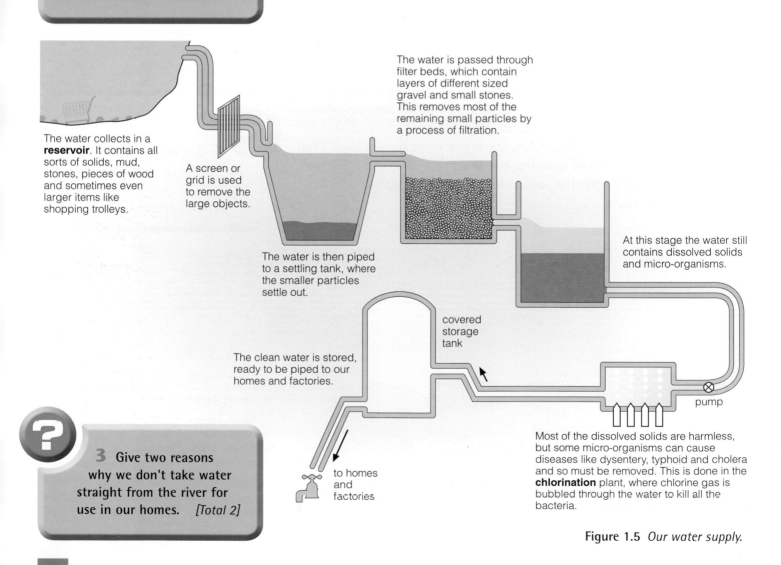

The water collects in a **reservoir**. It contains all sorts of solids, mud, stones, pieces of wood and sometimes even larger items like shopping trolleys.

A screen or grid is used to remove the large objects.

The water is then piped to a settling tank, where the smaller particles settle out.

The water is passed through filter beds, which contain layers of different sized gravel and small stones. This removes most of the remaining small particles by a process of filtration.

At this stage the water still contains dissolved solids and micro-organisms.

covered storage tank

The clean water is stored, ready to be piped to our homes and factories.

to homes and factories

pump

Most of the dissolved solids are harmless, but some micro-organisms can cause diseases like dysentery, typhoid and cholera and so must be removed. This is done in the **chlorination** plant, where chlorine gas is bubbled through the water to kill all the bacteria.

Figure 1.5 *Our water supply.*

3 Give two reasons why we don't take water straight from the river for use in our homes. *[Total 2]*

Problems of pollution

Modern society has created a better standard of living, but it has also created several **pollution** problems. Some of the main sources of water pollution are shown in Figure 1.6.

Water pollution has become a major concern for everyone. Soluble pollutants are particularly dangerous because they can get into the water supply. Sometimes toxic chemicals get into our food chain via the water, and these can cause serious health problems.

One of the largest uses of clean water is for flushing toilets. Every year each one of us flushes about 15 000 litres of water down the toilet.

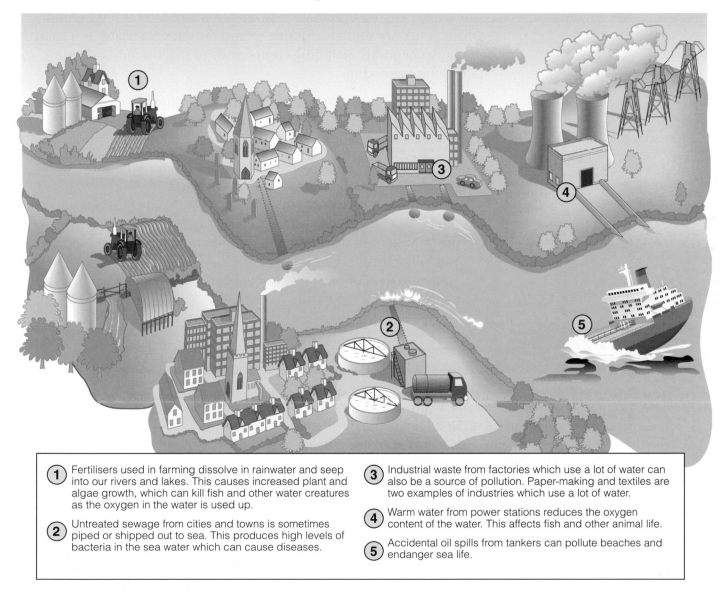

(1) Fertilisers used in farming dissolve in rainwater and seep into our rivers and lakes. This causes increased plant and algae growth, which can kill fish and other water creatures as the oxygen in the water is used up.

(2) Untreated sewage from cities and towns is sometimes piped or shipped out to sea. This produces high levels of bacteria in the sea water which can cause diseases.

(3) Industrial waste from factories which use a lot of water can also be a source of pollution. Paper-making and textiles are two examples of industries which use a lot of water.

(4) Warm water from power stations reduces the oxygen content of the water. This affects fish and other animal life.

(5) Accidental oil spills from tankers can pollute beaches and endanger sea life.

Figure 1.6 *Water pollution.*

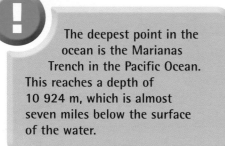

4 Suggest how a river in a city and a river in the countryside would contain different pollutants. *[Total 3]*

5 How could you show that lake water was not pure? *[Total 2]*

The deepest point in the ocean is the Marianas Trench in the Pacific Ocean. This reaches a depth of 10 924 m, which is almost seven miles below the surface of the water.

In recent years most countries have passed laws to control the discharge of industrial and domestic waste. The cleanliness of our rivers, lakes and seas has improved greatly over the last 50 years. However, we must be careful to continue to watch our water sources, as they are essential to all life on this planet.

Resources from the sea

The salt water of the oceans and seas covers most of the Earth's surface. When you evaporate sea water, a white solid is left behind, which is mainly sodium chloride (common salt). Sea water is a source of many chemicals including compounds of magnesium, calcium, potassium and iodine.

If you heat sea water, tap water and distilled water in separate evaporating basins and boil off the water, you can see the difference in terms of dissolved solids.

- The distilled water is pure and leaves no residue when it is evaporated as it contains no dissolved solids.
- The tap water contains a small amount of dissolved solids which can be seen at the bottom of the evaporating basin. This is because the treatment of our water supply only removes undissolved solids and kills germs.
- The sea water contains lots of dissolved solids as can be seen from the 'salt' left in the basin.

Summary

- Water is a compound of hydrogen and oxygen (formula H_2O).
- For pure water, the boiling point is 100 °C, and the melting/freezing point is 0 °C.
- Impurities in water raise the boiling point and lower the freezing point.
- The water cycle describes the changes of state which occur to our natural sources of water.
- The water from our reservoirs is treated by filtration and chlorination before it is supplied to our homes.
- Water pollution from farms, factories, sewage and industrial accidents affects all life forms.
- Sea water is an important source of salt and many other minerals.

Questions

1 Copy and complete the following sentences. Water is a compound of _____ and _____. The formula of water is _____. We can test for water by using cobalt chloride paper which changes from _____ to _____. Water boils at _____ °C and melts at _____ °C. Impurities _____ the boiling point of water. *[Total 4]*

2 Write one sentence for each of the following phrases to explain what each means:
(a) water cycle *[1]*
(b) cloud formation. *[1]*
[Total 2]

3 Look at the drawing of the natural water cycle shown in Figure 1.7
(a) Write down the numbers 1 to 8 and add the correct label from the following list:
rain   river   sea   mountain
snowclouds   sun   lake *[4]*
(b) Write a sentence to describe where each of the following changes occur:
(i) condensation (ii) freezing (iii) evaporation
(iv) melting. *[4]*
[Total 8]

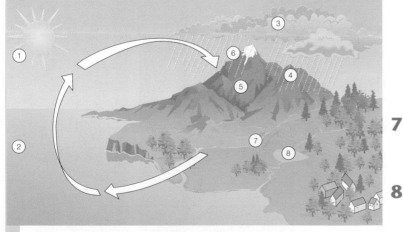

Figure 1.7 *The water cycle.*

4 a) In the water supply (Figure 1.5), where is water stored before purification? *[1]*
b) How are particles of mud and grit removed from dirty water? *[1]*
c) What is put into water to kill any bacteria? *[1]*
[Total 3]

5 To show that tap water contains dissolved solids, some water can be heated in an evaporating basin. Draw an outline diagram of this experiment clearly labelling the following:
evaporating basin   tripod stand
Bunsen burner   tap water *[Total 2]*

6 The table shows how we use water in our homes.

Use of water in our home	Volume used per person per day (l)
Washing ourselves	50
Cooking and drinking	15
Flushing toilets	40
Washing clothes	20
Washing dishes	25
Gardening etc.	10

a) Draw a bar chart to show the use of water in our homes. *[4]*
b) What is the biggest use of water in our homes? *[1]*
c) What is the total volume of water used by each person per day? *[1]*
d) What percentage of the total volume is used for flushing toilets? *[1]*
[Total 7]

7 Write a paragraph about water pollution, describing four sources of water pollution and explaining how they can be a threat to life. *[Total 4]*

8 Explain why sea water can be regarded as an important raw material for the chemical industry. *[Total 2]*

3.2 Acids, alkalis and neutralisation

What are acids and alkalis? How do we tell them apart? What are they used for? Acids and alkalis are very common substances which are found in the home, in industry and in our bodies. Chemists need to be able to recognize the differences between acids and alkalis and be aware of their typical chemical reactions.

Figure 2.1 *Testing with litmus.*

Types of solution

All solutions in water are either **acidic**, **alkaline** or **neutral**. We can tell them apart by using special **indicators**, which change colour depending on the type of solution. Often the indicator is one colour in an acid and a different colour in an alkali.

Litmus is a well known indicator, which is red in acidic solutions and blue in alkaline solutions.

Strong acids and alkalis are **corrosive** liquids that have to be handled carefully. Some acids and alkalis are dangerous, but some weaker acids are not. Many solutions are neither acidic nor alkaline, these solutions are said to be **neutral**.

Some examples of common acids, alkalis and neutral solutions which can be found in and around the house are shown in Figure 2.2.

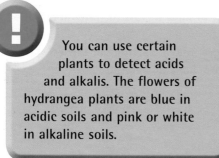

You can use certain plants to detect acids and alkalis. The flowers of hydrangea plants are blue in acidic soils and pink or white in alkaline soils.

1 What is an indicator? [Total 1]
2 What does corrosive mean? [Total 1]

ACIDIC SOLUTIONS

NEUTRAL SOLUTIONS

ALKALINE SOLUTIONS

Figure 2.2 *Types of solution.*

The pH scale

The **pH scale** measures how acidic or alkaline a solution is. The scale runs from below 0 to 14 and above. Neutral solutions have a pH of 7. Acids have a pH less than 7 and alkalis have a pH greater than 7. The pH scale and colours of **universal indicator** are shown in Figure 2.3.

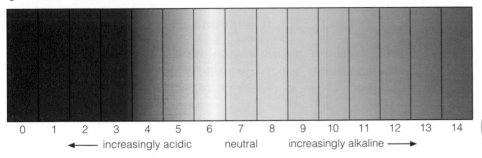

0 1 2 3 4 5 6 7 8 9 10 11 12 13 14

◄—— increasingly acidic   neutral   increasingly alkaline ——►

Figure 2.3 *The pH scale and colours of universal indicator.*

Universal indicator is a mixture of indicators that has a range of colours depending on the pH of the solution. This makes it a very useful indicator and it can be found in most chemistry laboratories as a liquid or soaked into paper.

Acids and alkalis in the laboratory

Many different acids and alkalis are used in the laboratory. Here are some examples of common laboratory acids and alkalis:

acids:
- hydrochloric acid
- sulphuric acid
- nitric acid

alkalis:
- sodium hydroxide
- potassium hydroxide
- ammonia

Many of the acids and alkalis used in the laboratory can be dangerous and bottles of these substances will show the 'corrosive' hazard warning sign.

! A Danish chemist called Sorenson invented the pH scale. Sorenson worked for the Carlsberg brewery. The brewing of beers and lagers requires the pH of solutions to be carefully controlled.

?
3 What colour would universal indicator turn in the following solutions:
a) bleach b) vinegar
c) vodka   d) baking powder?
[Total 4]
4 Why would it be difficult to test the pH of orange juice with universal indicator?
[Total 1]

! The word acid means sour tasting. Many of our favourite drinks contain acids. Tea, coffee, fruit juices like orange and lemon, and fizzy drinks like cola all contain acids. We seem to like the tangy sour taste.

Figure 2.4 *Take care with acids.*

5 Describe what happens to the pH of an acid as it is neutralised.
[Total ?]

In 1949 John Haig murdered a woman in London. He thought that he had destroyed the body in a bath of sulphuric acid. However, 'The Acid Bath Murderer' had made a vital mistake: sulphuric acid will not destroy plastics. His victim was identified by her false teeth and he was found guilty and sentenced to death by hanging.

6 What colour changes will occur when an acid containing universal indicator is neutralised by an alkali?
[Total 2]

Remember the poem

'Here lie the bones of Samuel Jones
He'll never breathe no more
What he thought was H_2O . . .
. . . was H_2SO_4'

(Note: H_2O is water and H_2SO_4 is sulphuric acid).

Always be careful when handling any solutions in the laboratory. Wear eye protection at all times, wash any spills with lots of water and report all accidents to your teacher.

Neutralisation

When an acid is added to an alkali, or an alkali is added to an acid, they cancel each other out. If the correct amounts are added, a neutral solution can be formed. This special kind of chemical reaction is called a **neutralisation** reaction. It is a common reaction in the chemistry laboratory and occurs in many situations in real life.

We can follow a neutralisation reaction by using an indicator. In the example below, sodium hydroxide is being added to hydrochloric acid. Universal indicator is used to follow the reaction.

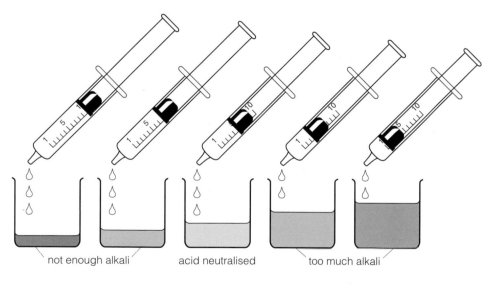

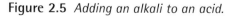
not enough alkali   acid neutralised   too much alkali

Figure 2.5 *Adding an alkali to an acid.*

As the alkali is added the solution becomes less acidic and the pH rises towards 7 (neutral). We have to be careful to add the exact amount of alkali needed to neutralise the acid. If we add too much alkali the solution will become alkaline. If we add too little alkali the solution will still be acidic.

The same reaction occurs if the acid is added to the alkali. Once again care has to be take to add the correct amount of acid to neutralise the alkali. As the acid is added the solution becomes less alkaline and the pH falls towards 7 (neutral).

Neutralisation in the laboratory

The amount of acid or alkali required for neutralisation will depend on the nature and concentration of each solution. To follow a neutralisation reaction, chemists use special apparatus to measure the volumes of liquids accurately. The technique is called **titration**, and it is used in all chemistry laboratories to investigate the concentration and nature of acidic and alkaline solutions.

Figure 2.6 *Titration of acid and alkali.*

Neutralisation in real life

Acids and alkalis commonly occur in nature and the home. Here are some examples of neutralisation in real life situations.

- Too much acid in the stomach causes indigestion. The medicines to cure indigestion will contain alkalis, like magnesium hydroxide, to neutralise the excess stomach acid.
- Some plants do not grow well in acidic soils. To reduce the acidity, farmers and gardeners spread an alkali called **lime** on the soil to neutralise the acid. This helps the plants grow stronger.
- An alkali like baking soda (sodium bicarbonate) is used to neutralise a bee sting, which is acidic.
- An acid, like vinegar, is used to neutralise a wasp sting, which is alkaline.

Figure 2.7 *Curing an acid soil with lime.*

Figure 2.8 *A wasp sting is alkaline.*

Summary

- Acids and alkalis are types of solution which are found in the laboratory and the home.
- Indicators are substances which change colour in acids and alkalis.
- The pH scale measures acid and alkaline properties: below 7 is acidic, 7 is neutral and above 7 is alkaline.
- Universal indicator has a range of colours depending on the pH of the solution.
- When acids and alkalis are added together they cancel out – this is called neutralisation.
- An exact volume of acid and alkali is required for neutralisation.
- Treating indigestion, bee stings, wasp stings and acidic soil are examples of neutralisation reactions.

Questions

1 Copy and complete the following sentences.
Acids have a pH that is _____ than 7 and turn universal indicator _____ or _____. Alkalis have a pH that is _____ than 7 and turn universal indicator _____ or _____.   *[Total 3]*

2 Write one sentence for each of the following words to explain what each means:
a) neutralisation   *[1]*
b) acid   *[1]*
c) indicator   *[1]*
d) pH scale.   *[1]*
    [Total 4]

3 Look at the table
In each case name the solution(s) which
(a) would turn universal indicator blue   *[1]*
(b) are neither acidic nor alkaline   *[1]*
(c) is most acidic   *[1]*
(d) would turn universal indicator orange or red.   *[2]*
    [Total 5]

Solution	pH
A	1
B	3
C	5
D	7
E	10

4 Touching nettles can irritate the skin and cause blisters. This is due to methanoic acid in the sting of the nettles. Rubbing with the leaf of a dock plant can reduce the irritation, because certain alkaline chemicals in the dock leaves counteract the methanoic acid.
Explain the chemistry involved in treating a nettle sting with dock leaves. You should include all the following words in your answer:
    alkali   neutralise   acid   *[Total 3]*

5 Rita and Sahid carried out a neutralisation. In their experiment they found that 20 cm³ of sodium hydroxide solution was exactly neutralised by 10 cm³ of hydrochloric acid solution.
(a) Describe the experiment Rita and Sahid would carry out to find the volumes of acid and alkali needed for neutralisation.   *[3]*
(b) Explain how they would know when neutralisation had occurred.   *[1]*
(c) Describe any safety precautions they should have taken when carrying out this experiment.   *[2]*
(d) What volume of the hydrochloric acid would be needed to neutralise 50 cm³ of the same sodium hydroxide solution?   *[1]*
    [Total 7]

3.3 Reactions of acids

What are the main products formed when acids react? As seen in subsection 3.2, neutralisation reactions occur all around us. Chemists should be able to identify the products formed in the reactions of acids and write chemical equations to represent the changes which occur.

Products of neutralisation

When an acid is added to an alkali, a neutralisation reaction occurs. An indicator, which changes colour at the neutral point, can be used to tell us when the reaction is complete. Chemists have carried out many neutralisation experiments. In each case, they find that when an acid reacts with an alkali, a **salt** and water are formed. We can write a general word equation for this reaction:

acid + alkali → salt + water

In chemistry the term 'salt' is used to describe a group of compounds formed from acids. It does not just refer to common salt which you use on food.

The neutralisation of hydrochloric acid and sodium hydroxide is shown in Figure 3.1. Just enough acid is added to exactly neutralise the alkali. The resulting solution is poured into an evaporating basin and heated. The salt which is formed is dissolved in the water and cannot be seen. However, when the water is evaporated crystals of the salt are left in the basin. In this case, the salt is called sodium chloride. The common name for sodium chloride is table salt, but there are many other types of salt. You can write a word equation for this reaction, because you know the reactants and products.

?

1 What happens during a neutralisation reaction?   [Total 1]

2 Usually when an acid is added to an alkali the salt formed cannot be seen. Where is the salt?   [Total 1]

3 How could you find out how much acid was needed to neutralise an alkali?   [Total 2]

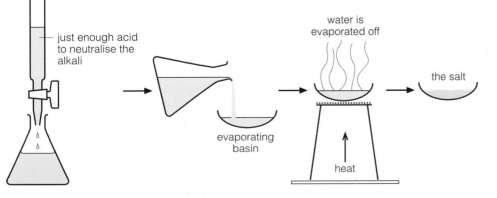

Figure 3.1 *Products of neutralisation.*

> **!** A container of common salt or table salt is not pure sodium chloride. Traces of another edible salt, called magnesium carbonate, are added to help it flow.

> **?** **4** Write a word equation for the reaction between nitric acid and sodium hydroxide. *[Total 2]*

hydrochloric acid + sodium hydroxide → sodium chloride + water
(reactants)   (products)

All reactions between acids and alkalis are similar. The type of salt that is formed depends on the acid and alkali used. Here are some examples of other neutralisation reactions:

hydrochloric acid + calcium hydroxide → calcium chloride + water

sulphuric acid + potassium hydroxide → potassium sulphate + water

nitric acid + lithium hydroxide → lithium nitrate + water

Note that different acids produce different types of salt:

- hydrochloric acid produces chloride salts
- sulphuric acid produces sulphate salts
- nitric acid produces nitrate salts
- phosphoric acid produces phosphate salts.

Acids can also react with metals, metal oxides and metal carbonates to produce salts. These reactions are similar but not exactly the same.

Reaction of acids and metal oxides

Experiments show us that all metal oxides react with dilute acids. When an acid reacts with a metal oxide, a salt and water are always formed. We can also write a general word equation for this reaction:

acid + metal oxide → salt + water

The reaction between sulphuric acid and copper oxide is shown in Figure 3.2. Heat is used to speed up the reaction. The black copper oxide reacts and a blue solution of the salt is formed. The word equation for this reaction is:

sulphuric acid + copper oxide → copper sulphate + water

The salt produced is called copper sulphate. As this salt is blue and soluble, a blue solution is formed.

Figure 3.2 *Copper oxide reacting with sulphuric acid.*

Reaction of acids and metal carbonates

Metal carbonates are compounds that contain carbon and oxygen as well as a metal. It can be shown by experiment that all metal carbonates react with dilute acids. When an acid reacts with a metal carbonate a salt, water and carbon dioxide are produced. The general word equation for this reaction is:

acid + metal carbonate → salt + water + carbon dioxide

The reaction between nitric acid and calcium carbonate is shown in Figure 3.3. During the reaction, the metal carbonate reacts and bubbles of gas are produced.
The word equation for this reaction is:

nitric acid + calcium carbonate → calcium nitrate + water + carbon dioxide

The salt produced is called calcium nitrate. As this salt is soluble, it forms in solution. As it is white, it forms a colourless solution and cannot be seen.

The gas is bubbled through **limewater**, which turns cloudy showing that the gas is carbon dioxide. (The test for carbon dioxide is that it turns limewater cloudy.)

Sherbet sweets contain a mixture of citric acid, sodium hydrogencarbonate and icing sugar. When eaten, the acid dissolves and reacts with the sodium hydrogencarbonate. The sherbet 'fizzes' on the tongue as carbon dioxide gas is produced by the neutralisation reaction.

5 Write a word equation for each of the following reactions:
a) lead oxide and nitric acid [2]
b) sodium carbonate and sulphuric acid. [2]
[Total 4]

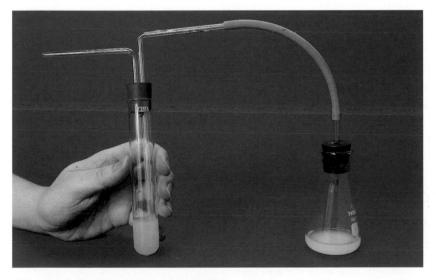

Figure 3.3 *Calcium carbonate reacting with nitric acid.*

Bases and neutralisation

Metal hydroxides, metal oxides and metal carbonates are all examples of **bases**. A base is a substance that reacts with an acid to produce a salt and water. Some examples of common bases are shown in Table 3.1. Metal oxides are also called basic oxides because they neutralise acids.

Table 3.1

Some common bases		
Metal hydroxides	**Metal oxides**	**Metal carbonates**
sodium hydroxide	copper oxide	calcium carbonate
lithium hydroxide	calcium oxide	zinc carbonate
potassium hydroxide	lead oxide	nickel carbonate

Alkalis are bases that can dissolve in water. Many of the soluble bases are metal hydroxides. Some examples of common alkalis are:

- sodium hydroxide
- potassium hydroxide
- lithium hydroxide
- ammonia.

Bases can be described as the opposite of acids. They are sometimes called neutralisers or **antacids** as they cancel out or neutralise acids.

> Neutralisation occurs when an acid reacts with a base to produce a salt and water.

6 Explain what a base is. *[Total 1]*

Alkalis can often feel slippery, like bicarbonate of soda and soap which are used for cleaning. Sodium hydroxide solutions also feel slippery, but be careful because it is very corrosive. Its old name was caustic soda.

7 What is the difference between an alkali and a base? *[Total 1]*

Reactions of acids and metals

Experiments show that many metals also react with dilute acids. When an acid reacts with a metal, a salt and hydrogen are formed. The general word equation for this reaction is:

$$\text{acid} + \text{metal} \rightarrow \text{salt} + \text{hydrogen}$$

The test for hydrogen is that it pops or explodes if a lighted splint is brought near to it.

The reaction between hydrochloric acid and zinc metal is shown in Figure 3.4. During the reaction, the metal reacts and bubbles of gas are produced.

The word equation for this reaction is:

hydrochloric acid + zinc → zinc chloride + hydrogen

The salt produced is called zinc chloride. As this salt is soluble, it forms in solution. As it is white, it forms a colourless solution and cannot be seen.

The gas is collected over water and a lighted taper is brought close to the mouth of the test tube. The gas explodes with a 'pop' showing that the gas is hydrogen.

The reactions of metals and acids are dealt with in more detail in subsections 5.1 and 5.2.

Acid rain

Soluble **non-metal** oxides are called acidic oxides because they form acids when they dissolve in water. As rainwater contains dissolved carbon dioxide from the atmosphere, this explains why it is naturally acidic. However, in some areas other non-metal oxides like sulphur dioxide and nitrogen dioxide are present in the air. These oxides are mainly produced by the burning of fuels and they dissolve in the rainwater making it even more acidic. Some of the effects of acid rain are caused by the reactions of acids described in this section.

○ Acid rain reacts with metal oxides and so washes these essential minerals out of the soil. This affects plant growth and life in rivers and lakes. Many lakes in Scandinavia, and some lochs in Scotland, now contain hardly any fish due to the effects of acid rain.
○ Acid rain damages buildings made of limestone and marble. These rocks are mostly calcium carbonate and acids react with all metal carbonates.
○ Acid rain damages iron and steel objects like railings and car bodies, because acids react with most metals.

Due to government regulations and the work of scientists, acid rain is becoming less of a problem in Britain. This improvement has been brought about by:

○ burning less fossil fuels.
○ removing sulphur from fossil fuels before they are burned
○ removing sulphur dioxide from flue gases.

Figure 3.4 *The reaction between zinc and hydrochloric acid.*

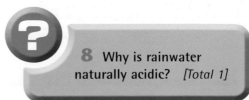

Figure 3.5 *Effects of acid rain.*

?

8 Why is rainwater naturally acidic? *[Total 1]*

More about salts

Salts are an important group of chemicals that have a variety of properties and uses. Sodium chloride, common salt, is just one natural example of this group. Some other examples of salts that can be found in nature are, potassium chloride – used as a healthier substitute to common salt – and potassium nitrate which is used as a fertiliser and in gunpowder.

Many other salts can be manufactured in industry by neutralisation reactions. The type of salt formed depends on the acid and base used. Most soluble salts can be prepared by neutralising an acid with excess insoluble base. The excess base is then removed by **filtration** and the solid salt obtained by **evaporation** of the water in the solution. Some examples of manufactured salts are:

- copper sulphate, which is used as a weed killer and insecticide, and is made from sulphuric acid and copper oxide.
- calcium phosphate, which is used in fertilisers and baking powder, and is made from phosphoric acid and calcium carbonate.
- magnesium sulphate, which is used to make Epsom salts and in the preparation of fabrics, and is made from sulphuric acid and magnesium carbonate.

Summary

- A base is a substance that reacts with an acid to produce a salt and water.
- Bases are the opposite of acids and are sometimes called antacids or neutralisers.
- Metal oxides, metal hydroxides and metal carbonates are all examples of bases.
- An alkali is a base that can dissolve in water.
- Neutralisation occurs when an acid reacts with a base to form a salt and water.
- Acid + alkali → salt + water.
- Acid + metal oxide → salt + water.
- Acid + metal carbonate → salt + water + carbon dioxide.
- Some metals also react with acids producing a salt.
- Acid + metal → salt + hydrogen.
- Acid rain is rainwater which is more acidic than normal.

Questions

1 Copy and complete the following sentences.
When an _____ reacts with a base we say
a_____ reaction has occurred. Neutralisation
reactions always produce a_____
and _____. *[Total 2]*

2 The letters of the names of three acids have been
jumbled up. Rearrange the letters to make the names
of three common acids:
a) crushlipu acid *[1]*
b) drycholorich acid *[1]*
c) cintri acid. *[1]*
[Total 3]

3 The reactions of acids can produce two different
gases. Name the two gases which can be produced
and describe a test for each of them. *[Total 6]*

4 Write a sentence which links each of the following
pairs of words:
a) acid and metal oxide *[2]*
b) acid and metal carbonate. *[2]*
[Total 4]

5 Copy and complete the following neutralisation
equations:
a) sulphuric acid + magnesium →
_____ + _____ *[2]*
b) _____ + potassium hydroxide →
potassium nitrate + _____ *[2]*
c) copper carbonate + hydrochloric acid →
_____ + _____ + _____ *[3]*
d) _____ + _____ → zinc
phosphate + water *[2]*
[Total 9]

6 Which acid and base would you use to make the
following salts:
a) cobalt chloride *[2]*
b) iron sulphate *[2]*
c) zinc nitrate? *[2]*
[Total 6]

7 Write a single sentence containing all of the
following words:
salt   alkali   products   acid   *[Total 4]*

8 a) Why is our rainwater getting less acidic? *[1]*
b) What kind of chemical could be used to remove
the acidic sulphur dioxide from flue gases? *[1]*
c) Will our rainwater ever be neutral?
Explain your answer. *[1]*
[Total 3]

9 Read the following passage and answer the questions
which follow.
When excess powdered zinc carbonate is added to
some dilute hydrochloric acid, a chemical reaction
occurs. During the reaction, some of the powder
appears to dissolve and a gas is given off. When the
reaction is finished, the excess zinc carbonate can be
removed by filtration and the salt formed can be
obtained by evaporation of the water.
a) What is the name of the gas given off during the
reaction? *[1]*
b) How do we know when the reaction is finished?
[1]
c) What is the name of the salt formed during the
reaction? *[1]*
d) What two chemical terms could be used to
describe the reaction which occurs when zinc
carbonate is added to hydrochloric acid? *[2]*
e) Draw a labelled diagram of the filtration process
used to remove the excess zinc carbonate. Include
labels for the filter funnel, filter paper and name
the residue and filtrate. *[2]*
[Total 7]

10 The labels from bottles of hydrochloric acid, sodium
hydroxide and potassium carbonate solutions have
fallen off. Using only three test tubes and three
pieces of magnesium metal, describe how you
could find out what was in each bottle. Include any
safety precautions you need to take in your answer.
[Total ?]

3 Water and solutions

Figure 4.1 *The scientific method.*

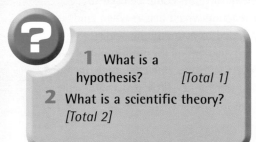

1 What is a hypothesis? [Total 1]

2 What is a scientific theory? [Total 2]

The scientific method

How scientists work

To really understand chemistry, we need to understand the way scientists think and work. That is, we need to understand the 'scientific method'.

The scientific method starts with a question – Why? How? What? Generally it involves something we have seen, and it is usually something that can be measured. For example, 'How does the mass of salt dissolved in water affect its boiling point?'

Using books, scientific papers and the Internet, modern scientists will then research what is already known about the question. Then they would form a hypothesis – an educated guess at an answer to the question. For example, a **hypothesis** for the question above might be 'the greater the mass of salt dissolved, the higher the boiling point.'

A series of experiments will be planned and carried out, making careful measurements and observations. The experiments would be repeated to make sure that the results were as reliable as possible. All the results would be recorded accurately.

The results from the experiments will then be analysed and a conclusion formed. The conclusion should answer the original question and allow you to check the hypothesis, to see if it was correct. After the tests have been repeated by different scientists, a **law** or **theory** might be made to describe what happens and to explain the facts.

Finally the results and conclusions from the experiments will be made available to other scientists. This could involve presentations at conferences, articles in a magazine or an Internet site. Whatever method of communication is used, it has to be clear and accurate. Other scientists have to be able to repeat the experiments and check the results so that they can comment on them and review them thoroughly.

Joseph Black and the discovery of 'fixed air'

In 1755 the Scottish chemist Joseph Black (1728–1799) presented a lecture to the Philosophical Society of Edinburgh on his experiments concerning 'magnesia alba' and the gas called 'fixed air'.

His main findings were:
- heating magnesia alba produced fixed air and a solid called magnesia usta
- when magnesia usta was left open to the air, it slowly turned back into magnesia alba
- fixed air was also produced during the manufacture of alcohol, the burning of charcoal, respiration in animals and when sulphuric acid was added to magnesia alba.

Black's main conclusions were that:
- the difference between magnesia alba and magnesia usta was the gas called fixed air
- gases could combine with solids
- air was not an element but a mixture of gases, including small amounts of fixed air.

Black published a paper in 1756 on this subject and it immediately made a contribution to chemistry. Not only did it improve the understanding of gases, it also emphasised the importance of making careful measurements during experiments. This greatly influenced the work of other chemists, like Priestley and Lavoisier.

Figure 4.2 *Joseph Black (1728–1799).*

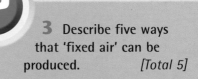

! The modern names are:
- magnesia alba is magnesium carbonate
- magnesia usta is magnesium oxide
- fixed air is carbon dioxide.

? **3** Describe five ways that 'fixed air' can be produced.   *[Total 5]*

Figure 4.3 *Eighteenth century chemist working with gases.*

Questions

1 What is the difference between a hypothesis and a conclusion?   *[Total 4]*

2 Joseph Black became famous for his investigation into fixed air.
a) How did Black communicate his ideas to others? *[1]*
b) If Black was alive today, how else might he have communicated his findings?   *[2]*
c) What would other scientists do with his results? *[2]*
   [Total 5]

3 a) Name two scientists influenced by Black. *[1]*
b) Explain his most important contribution to chemistry.   *[1]*
   [Total 3]

4 Using the correct chemical names, write word equations to represent the following reactions:
a) heating magnesia alba   *[2]*
b) forming magnesia alba by leaving magnesia usta in air.   *[2]*
   [Total 4]

5 Using a labelled diagram, describe how you would collect a sample of fixed air.   *[Total 5]*

6 Which stages in the scientific method are illustrated by each of the drawings in Figure 4.1   *[Total 5]*

3 Water and solutions

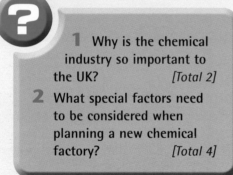

Figure 4.4 *The chemical industry can cause pollution when uncontrolled.*

?

1 Why is the chemical industry so important to the UK? [Total 2]

2 What special factors need to be considered when planning a new chemical factory? [Total 4]

The chemical industry

Planning for the chemical industry

The chemical industry and all its products have helped to improve our standard of living. The industry is also a major contributor to our economy. The UK chemical industry is the fifth largest in the world – it employs over half a million people and is our largest export earner.

All industries must make a profit. Therefore, when planning a new industry many factors need to be considered – availability of materials, transport routes, distance to markets, the workforce and so on. When planning a new chemical industry, there are some other special factors that need to be considered – such as health and safety, the control of hazardous substances and the effects on the local environment.

The sulphuric acid industry

Sulphuric acid is one example of an important chemical – the amount of sulphuric acid used in a country was, at one time, taken as a measure of its wealth.

In the UK, most sulphuric acid is made by the **Contact Process**, using sulphur, air and water as the raw materials. The main stages in the process are outlined in Figure 4.6.

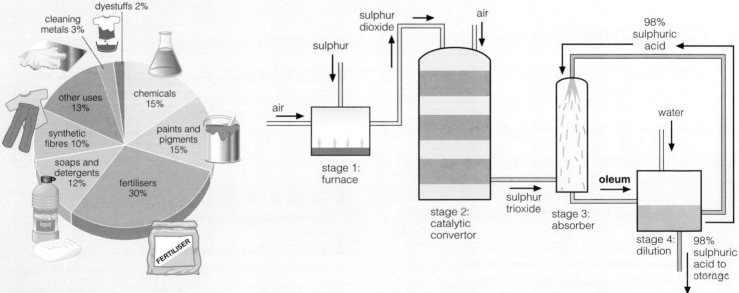

Figure 4.5 *The uses of sulphuric acid.*

Figure 4.6 *The manufacture of sulphuric acid by the Contact Process.*

The handling and use of all chemicals is controlled by government health and safety regulations. Concentrated sulphuric acid is toxic and corrosive, so workers handling the acid need to wear acid-resistant gloves and eye protection. Under certain conditions the acid can produce the toxic gas sulphur dioxide, so good ventilation is needed to prevent the build-up of dangerous fumes.

 3 What industry uses the most sulphuric acid?
[Total 1]

Figure 4.7 *Great care is needed when handling sulphuric acid.*

Figure 4.8 *Sulphur dioxide emissions are monitored carefully.*

4 The COSHH Regulations (2002) describe the controls you need to take when handling hazardous chemicals. Suggest what the letters 'COSHH' might stand for.
[Total 1]

Many chemicals can cause pollution to our environment. In making sulphuric acid, steps have to be taken to make sure there are no acid spills into streams or rivers. In addition, the sulphur dioxide gas made in the first stage of the process must be contained – it is a major contributor to acid rain.

Questions

1 Answer the following questions about the manufacture of sulphuric acid.
   a) What is the name of the process, and what are the three main raw materials needed? [4]
   b) Write word equations for the reactions occurring in stages 1 and 2. [4]
   [Total 8]

2 a) What is the normal concentration of the sulphuric acid manufactured? [2]
   b) Explain the safety precautions you would take if you were using concentrated sulphuric acid. [4]
   [Total 6]

3 Imagine that a sulphuric acid plant is going to be set up in your area.
   a) List five factors that would need to be considered in deciding on the site for the factory. [5]
   b) What benefits could the factory bring to your area? [2]
   c) What problems might the factory cause? [2]
   [Total 9]

4 List five different jobs that could be created by a new chemical factory. [Total 5]

5 Draw a bar chart showing the uses of sulphuric acid – see Figure 4.5. [Total 3]

End of section questions

1 a) Draw a diagram of a molecule of water and give its chemical formula. [2]

b) Imagine that you are a molecule of water in the sea. Describe the changes of state which must occur for you to form part of a cloud, fall as snow on the hills and eventually find your way back to the sea again. [4]

[Total 6]

2 Describe and explain how universal indicator can be used to find out if a solution is acidic, alkaline or neutral. [Total 3]

3 Read the passage below then answer the questions which follow.

The United Kingdom water industry supplies 19 500 million litres of water every day to 58 million people. It has 2200 water treatment plants and 8300 sewage treatment plants. Most of this water comes from its 687 reservoirs and 500 rivers. About one-third comes from underground sources through 1562 boreholes. Only about 3% of the water is used for drinking and cooking. Most of the water is used for flushing toilets and washing.

a) How much water is used each day in the United Kingdom? [1]

b) Calculate the average volume of water used by each person in the country. [1]

c) Calculate how much water is used in the United Kingdom for drinking and cooking. [1]

d) What is the total number of water and sewage treatment plants in the United Kingdom? [1]

e) What is the main use of the water supplied to our homes? [1]

[Total 5]

4 Scientists find answers to questions by doing experiments. Explain how and why scientists communicate what they have found out to other scientists. [Total 4]

5 The diagram below shows a pH scale. The pH of vinegar is shown on the scale. Copy and complete the scale by adding the following solution names at the correct place:

nitric acid   bleach   sugar   sodium hydroxide

[Total 4]

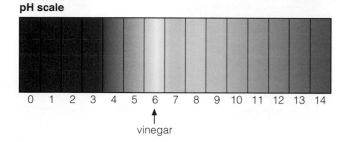

pH scale

6 Common acids, alkalis and neutral solutions are found almost everywhere. Construct a table with appropriate headings to include four examples of each of these types of solution. [Total 7]

7 In each of the following examples state what would happen to the pH of the solution printed in bold.

a) Water is added to **hydrochloric acid**. [1]

b) Hydrochloric acid is added to **bleach**. [1]

c) Sodium hydroxide is added to **salt solution**. [1]

d) Water is added to **salt solution**. [1]

[Total 4]

8 The chemical name for vinegar is ethanoic acid. The equation for the reaction of ethanoic acid with sodium hydroxide is:

ethanoic acid + sodium hydroxide → sodium ethanoate + water

Write out the word equations for ethanoic acid reacting with:

a) magnesium [2]

b) sodium carbonate [2]

c) iron oxide. [2]

[Total 6]

9 There are many examples of neutralisation reaction equations. Copy and complete the following word equations:

a) sulphuric acid + sodium hydroxide →
_____ + _____ [2]

b) _____ + _____
→ magnesium nitrate + hydrogen [2]

c) zinc oxide + _____ →
zinc chloride + _____ [2]

d) phosphoric acid + sodium carbonate →
_____ + _____ +
_____ [3]

[Total 9]

10 Explain the old saying, 'bicarb for bees and vinegar for vasps'. (Hint: it has something to do with neutralisation and there is meant to be a spelling error.) [Total 4]

11 Imagine you have been asked to prepare a dry sample of the soluble salt nickel chloride. You are given powdered nickel carbonate, a suitable acid and normal laboratory apparatus. Describe, with the aid of labelled diagrams and chemical equations where appropriate, each of the stages in the preparation of the salt. The stages are: neutralisation, filtration and evaporation. [Total 6]

12 A group of pupils collected two different samples of rainwater and carried out tests on both samples. Their results are shown in the table below.

Sample	Where collected	Test pH	Evaporation of water
Sample 1	Pure rain water collected as it fell from the sky.	5.6	No solid left behind after evaporation.
Sample 2	Collected after it had passed through some limestone rocks.	6.8	0.2 g of solid left behind after evaporation.

a) What kind of solution is the rainwater? [1]
b) What kind of reaction must occur between the rainwater and the limestone rock? [1]
c) What kind of substance is the solid left behind after evaporation? [1]
d) When hydrochloric acid is added to some limestone rock, calcium chloride and carbon dioxide are formed. Name the chemical which must be in the limestone rock. [1]

[Total 4]

13 Sketch a heating curve and a cooling curve for the substances shown in the table below.

Substance	Melting (freezing) point (°C)	Boiling point (°C)
sodium chloride	801	1423
silicon oxide	1601	2230

14 **P** When a metal carbonate reacts with an acid, carbon dioxide gas is always produced. What factors might affect the volume of gas that is produced? For example how would you investigate the effect of the acid concentration on the volume of carbon dioxide produced?

15 **P** Indigestion tablets neutralise excess stomach acid. How would you investigate which indigestion tablets neutralise most acid, and therefore which are the best value for money?

16 **R** We use a lot of water and this leads to a large volume of waste water which has to be cleaned before it is released into the environment. Find out about what happens to the different types of waste water, and how sewage treatment works.

17 **R** The manufacture and uses of sulphuric acid is dealt with in this subsection. Find out about some of the uses of the other common acids like hydrochloric acid, nitric acid or phosphoric acid.

4.1 The Earth

What is the structure of the Earth, and what is inside it? Nearly all of the substances that we use are from or have been made from materials in the Earth.

The structure of the Earth

The Earth has a diameter of about 12 800 km. It is thought to consist of layers as shown in Figure 1.1. The nearer the centre, the hotter the temperature, going from about –50 °C at the edge of the atmosphere to over 4000 °C at the centre of the Earth.

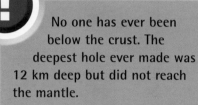

No one has ever been below the crust. The deepest hole ever made was 12 km deep but did not reach the mantle.

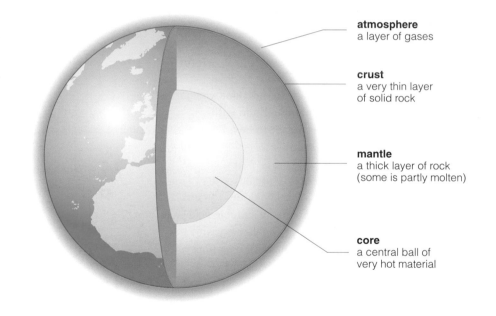

atmosphere
a layer of gases

crust
a very thin layer of solid rock

mantle
a thick layer of rock (some is partly molten)

core
a central ball of very hot material

Figure 1.1 *The structure of the Earth.*

The structure of the Earth has been worked out using information from seismic waves (waves that pass through the Earth from, for example, earthquakes).

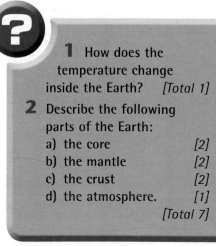

1 How does the temperature change inside the Earth? *[Total 1]*

2 Describe the following parts of the Earth:
a) the core [2]
b) the mantle [2]
c) the crust [2]
d) the atmosphere. [1]
[Total 7]

At the centre of the Earth is the **core**. The outer part is thought to contain molten iron from which the Earth's magnetic field originates. Next is the **mantle** which is mainly solid rock, but near the crust some of the mantle is molten. The outer layer is called the **crust** and is very thin compared with the mantle and core. The crust is not flat, having low parts under the oceans and high parts in mountainous regions. We live on the **continental crust** which is about 35 km thick on average. Under the oceans the crust is known as **oceanic crust** and is only about 6 km thick. There is also the **atmosphere** around the Earth which contains a mixture of gases, including the oxygen that we need to survive.

The lithosphere

The outer part of the Earth (the crust and some of the upper mantle) is called the **lithosphere**. This consists of a series of separate pieces called **tectonic plates**. These huge slabs of rock are moving very slowly, at a speed of only a few centimetres each year.

It is thought that over 200 million years ago all the continents were joined together in one giant land mass, called Pangaea. As a result of the movement of the plates, Pangaea slowly split up moving the continents to their present positions. The plates are still moving slowly. Many features of the crust, such as mountains and volcanoes, occur where the plates meet. For example, the Himalayas have formed by the meeting of the Indo-Australian plate, carrying India, with the Eurasian plate.

> **!** The Atlantic Ocean is widening by a few centimetres each year due to the movement of tectonic plates.

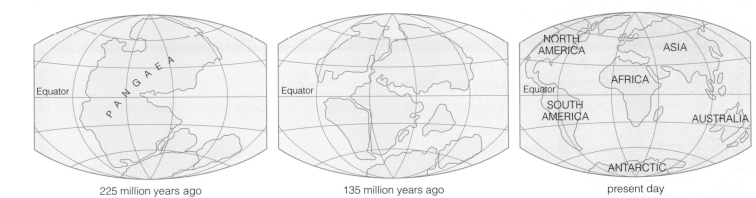

225 million years ago   135 million years ago   present day

Figure 1.2 *The movement of the Earth's continents.*

Minerals

Rocks are made up of minerals. A **mineral** is a chemical element or compound that was formed naturally on or within the Earth. However, coal and other substances that are formed from the remains of living creatures are not classed as minerals.

Minerals are often found in the form of **crystals** (crystals are solids with a regular shape and flat surfaces which reflect light). The crystals of some minerals can be beautiful and quite large, such as some diamonds and rubies. They are also rare which makes them very valuable.

Minerals usually have a different name to their chemical name. For example, the mineral quartz is silicon dioxide (SiO_2) and calcite is calcium carbonate ($CaCO_3$).

Figure 1.3 *A diamond and a ruby.*

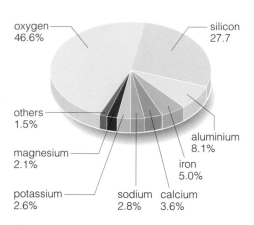

oxygen 46.6%
silicon 27.7
others 1.5%
aluminium 8.1%
magnesium 2.1%
iron 5.0%
potassium 2.6%
sodium 2.8%
calcium 3.6%

Figure 1.4 *The composition of the Earth's crust.*

Some rocks contain only one mineral, such as the rock metaquartzite which only contains the mineral quartz. However, most rocks contain a mixture of minerals, such as granite which contains the minerals feldspar, quartz and mica.

There are over 3000 known minerals, but only a few are commonly found in rocks. All minerals have different physical properties and they can be identified by a series of simple tests. Properties commonly used include colour, how they reflect light, density, crystal shape, hardness and how they break.

Figure 1.4 shows which atoms the minerals in the Earth's crust contain. There is much silicon and oxygen, and they readily combine with each other and other atoms to form silicate minerals. Silicate minerals make up over 98% of all rocks in the crust.

Summary

- The Earth has three main layers: the crust, the mantle and the core.
- The lithosphere (the crust and upper part of the mantle) consists of separate pieces called tectonic plates that are moving slowly.
- Rocks are made up of minerals.
- A mineral is a chemical element or compound that was formed naturally on or within the Earth.

Questions

1 Copy and complete the following sentences.
At the centre of the Earth is the _____.
The next layer is the _____, with the
_____ at the surface. The _____ is
very thin compared with the other layers.   *[Total 2]*

2 a) Draw a diagram to show all the layers of the Earth.   *[4]*
   b) The Earth has a magnetic field. What is thought to be inside the Earth that causes this field, and where is it?   *[2]*
   [Total 6]

3 a) What is the lithosphere?   *[2]*
   b) What is a tectonic plate?   *[1]*
   c) What is happening to tectonic plates that is responsible for features on the Earth such as mountains?   *[1]*
   [Total 4]

4 a) What are rocks made of?   *[1]*
   b) What is a mineral?   *[1]*
   c) Explain why coal is not classed as a mineral.   *[2]*
   d) Explain why most minerals are silicates.   *[2]*
   [Total 6]

4.2 Rocks

How were all the different types of rocks found on the Earth formed? They formed in different ways and have different properties.

The three main groups of rocks

There are many different types of rocks, but they can be classified into three main groups depending on how they are formed. These three groups of rocks are called **igneous**, **sedimentary** and **metamorphic** rocks.

Igneous rocks

The inside of the Earth is very hot and some of the rock is molten. This molten rock is called **magma**. If the magma cools down, the minerals will crystallise forming **igneous rock**.

If magma escapes onto the Earth's surface, for example through a volcano, it is called **lava**. Lava cools and crystallises quickly on the Earth's surface. If it cools and solidifies underground, then it crystallises much more slowly. The more slowly a liquid cools and turns into a solid, the bigger the crystals formed. Igneous rocks formed underground (**intrusive** igneous rocks) have much bigger crystals than those formed on the surface (**extrusive** igneous rocks). The crystals in extrusive igneous rocks are often so small that they can only be seen with a microscope.

Basalt
(an extrusive igneous rock)

Granite
(an intrusive igneous rock)

Figure 2.1 *Igneous rocks.*

> **!**
> The world's deepest mine is in South Africa and is 3.5 km deep. The temperature at the bottom of this mine is over 50 °C.

> **?**
> 1 Describe how igneous rocks are formed. *[Total 2]*
> 2 What is the difference between magma and lava? *[Total 2]*
> 3 a) What is the difference between an extrusive and an intrusive igneous rock? *[2]*
> b) Why do intrusive igneous rocks have bigger crystals than extrusive igneous rocks? *[2]*
> *[Total 4]*

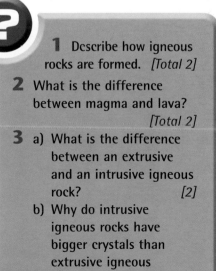

Weathering of rocks

Over time all rocks get broken up into smaller bits or even dissolved by various processes of **weathering**.

4 a) What is
   weathering?   *[1]*
b) **What is the difference
   between physical,
   chemical and biological
   weathering?**   *[3]*
c) **Give one example of
   each type of weathering
   in part b).**   *[3]*
          [Total 7]

Physical weathering

Physical weathering is where forces cause rocks to break up. There are two main methods:

- **By the freezing and thawing of water.**
  Water expands when it freezes. If water gets into a crack in a rock and then freezes, as it expands it will force the crack to open further. As the ice melts, the water can go further into the now bigger crack and if it freezes again, it will force the crack to open even further. This repeated freezing and thawing causes pieces of rock to break off.

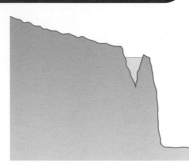

Rainwater collects in a crack.

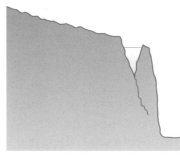

The temperature falls below 0°C. The water freezes and expands, making the crack bigger.

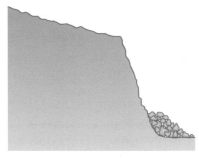

Eventually, after repeated freezing and thawing, rock breaks off.

Figure 2.2 *Freeze-thaw weathering.*

- **By the expansion and contraction of rocks (exfoliation).**
  Rocks expand as they get hotter and contract as they cool down. If rocks repeatedly expand and contract, it can cause them to break up. This is common in desert areas where it is hot during the day and cold at night.

Figure 2.3 *Exfoliation.*

Chemical weathering

Chemical weathering is where the rock undergoes chemical reactions with substances such as water. For example, the mineral calcite (calcium carbonate) in **limestone** reacts with rainwater. Rainwater is slightly acidic due to carbon dioxide from the air dissolving in rain. Other substances from the soil and decaying plant material also dissolve in rainwater once it has fallen and make it more acidic. ('Acid rain' is rain that is more acidic than normal due to air pollution.)

Biological weathering

Biological weathering is where plants and animals cause the rocks to break up. For example, the roots of plants can grow into rocks and break them apart and animals can damage rocks as they burrow into the ground.

Erosion

The broken up pieces of rock are moved by the wind, gravity, the water in rivers, streams and the sea, and by the ice in glaciers. As they move they get worn down and break up more. They also wear away the rocks that they travel over. This is called **erosion**. For example, rocks are smoothed as they move along rivers, forming pebbles.

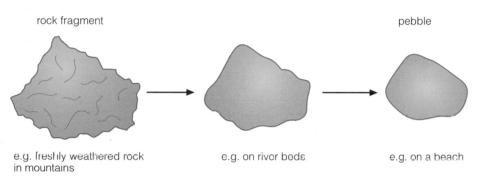

rock fragment   pebble

e.g. freshly weathered rock   e.g. on river beds   e.g. on a beach
in mountains

Figure 2.4 *Rocks are rounded off as they travel.*

5 What is the difference between weathering and erosion? [Total 2]

6 Describe two changes that happen to rocks as they are eroded. [Total 2]

Sedimentary rocks

The rock fragments formed by weathering and erosion that are carried in rivers are called **sediment**. These rock fragments vary in size from lumps of rock to sand and clay. When rivers reach the sea, the water flow slows down and the sediment settles to the bottom (deposition). Over many years, more sediment builds up on top pushing down and squeezing the water out (**compaction**). Minerals from the water cement the sediment together (**cementation**) to make **sedimentary rock**.

Figure 2.5 *Sandstone (formed from sand) and conglomerate (formed mainly from pebbles).*

7 a) What is sediment? [1]
b) Describe how sedimentary rocks are formed. [3]
c) Name three sedimentary rocks. [3]
[Total 7]

Figure 2.6 *Layers are clearly visible in this rock face of sedimentary rock.*

When the sediment settles, it forms layers. These layers can often be seen in the sedimentary rock.

Some sedimentary rocks are made from organisms that were once living. Coal is a sedimentary rock made from the remains of trees and other plants. Most limestones are made from the shells and skeletons of sea creatures. The creatures died and fell into the sediment. Their bodies decayed away, leaving their shells or skeletons which became the limestone.

There are many minerals dissolved in sea water. If the water evaporates, the minerals are left behind and may build up as sedimentary rocks. This happens mainly in places with hot climates. The rocks are formed as the sea water evaporates from lagoons (shallow pools of sea water) or inland seas.

Metamorphic rocks

Rocks are sometimes changed into harder crystalline rocks called **metamorphic rocks** by very high pressures and/or temperatures. The structure of the minerals changes and new crystals are formed. The rocks that become metamorphic rocks do not melt, otherwise they would form magma.

Figure 2.7 shows some metamorphic rocks and the rocks from which they are formed. The sedimentary rock mudstone forms different metamorphic rocks depending on the conditions.

8 a) Describe how metamorphic rocks are formed. [2]
b) Name the metamorphic rock formed from:
 i) limestone
 ii) sandstone
 iii) mudstone. [3]
 [Total 5]

metaquartzite (formed from sandstone)

slate, schist, gneiss (all formed from mudstone)

Marble (formed from limestone)

Figure 2.7 *Metamorphic rocks.*

One way in which the changes can happen is shown in Figure 2.8. If some magma makes its way into an area of sedimentary rock, then the heat can cause the sedimentary rock closest to the magma to turn into metamorphic rock.

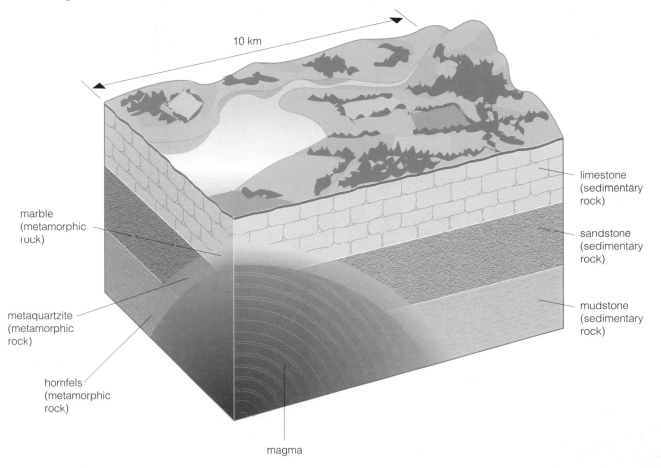

Figure 2.8 *The effect of magma on sedimentary rocks.*

Looking at the three groups of rocks

We can often tell the differences between the three groups of rocks by looking at their texture and the minerals they contain.

- Igneous rocks are hard and have randomly arranged, interlocking crystals of minerals.
- Sedimentary rocks are often softer and are made up of separate grains of minerals cemented together. Broad layers or bands can often be seen.
- Metamorphic rocks are mostly hard and consist of mineral crystals. Unlike igneous rocks, they may be arranged in fine bands or layers.

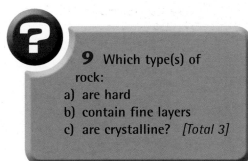

9 Which type(s) of rock:
a) are hard
b) contain fine layers
c) are crystalline? *[Total 3]*

Figure 2.9 shows the textures of some typical igneous, sedimentary and metamorphic rocks, all made up from the minerals quartz, mica and feldspar.

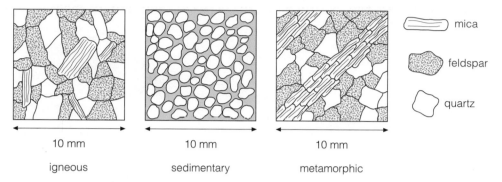

10 mm
igneous

10 mm
sedimentary

10 mm
metamorphic

mica

feldspar

quartz

Figure 2.9 *The texture of a typical rock from each group.*

The rock cycle

The three groups of rock are recycled over millions of years. All rocks are weathered to form sediment. This sediment hardens to form sedimentary rocks. Sedimentary and igneous rocks can be changed into metamorphic rocks. Metamorphic rocks can partly melt and form magma. Magma solidifies to form igneous rocks and so on. These changes are summarised in the **rock cycle**.

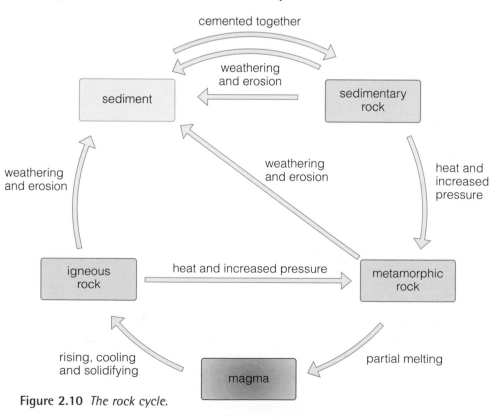

cemented together

weathering and erosion

sediment

sedimentary rock

weathering and erosion

heat and increased pressure

weathering and erosion

weathering and erosion

igneous rock

heat and increased pressure

metamorphic rock

rising, cooling and solidifying

partial melting

magma

Figure 2.10 *The rock cycle.*

Fossils

Fossils are the remains or imprints of plants and animals that lived millions of years ago. Nearly all fossils occur in sedimentary rocks – the remains would be destroyed by the heat and pressure involved in the formation of igneous and metamorphic rocks.

Many of the fossils that have been found were of sea creatures. When a creature died, it fell into the sediment at the bottom of the sea. The soft parts of the creature decayed, but the harder parts, like shells or skeletons, could remain as the sediment hardened to form sedimentary rock. However, these harder parts of creatures often dissolved away, leaving a mould which filled with other substances.
Many creatures are soft bodied – they do not have a shell or skeleton.

? **10** What is a fossil? [Total 1]
11 Most fossils are found in sedimentary rocks. Explain why few fossils are found in metamorphic rocks and igneous rocks. [Total 1]

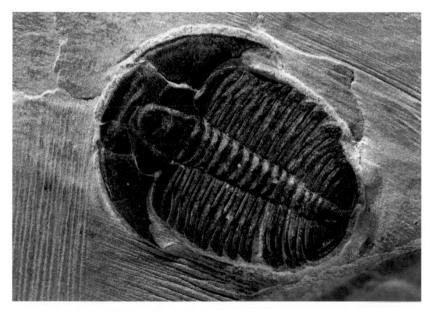

Figure 2.11 *A trilobite fossil.*

? **12** Explain how most fossils were formed. [Total 4]
13 Explain why very few fossils are found of creatures with soft bodies. [Total 2]

Some – such as jellyfish – have been found preserved as fossil imprints but the conditions have to be exactly right for this to happen. Very few fossils of soft-bodied creatures are found.

Fossils can be used to date the rocks in which they are found. A fossil found in a rock will be from a creature that lived at the same time as the sediment deposited. This means that the rock will be the same age as the fossil. However, not all fossils are useful for dating – the only ones that are useful are from species that survived for just a few million years, such as some types of trilobites.

! Fossils have been found on Mount Everest showing that its rock was once under the sea – it has been pushed up as two tectonic plates collide.

Structure and types of soil

Much of our land is covered in **soil** which consists of two main things:

- rock fragments of different sizes – from large rocks to pebbles, sand and clay (from the weathering of rocks)
- **humus** (the decayed remains of plants, in the main, and animals).

Soil also contains air, water and dissolved minerals.

Soils are all different and what a soil is like depends very much on the rocks it was formed from, how much humus it contains and the local climate. The main types of soils are as follows.

- **Clay soils.** The rock particles in clay soils are very small. This leaves only very small gaps between the rock particles, and so clay soils do not drain well. This means that clay soils can easily become water-logged. Air cannot get into the soil, which leads to poor plant growth.
- **Sandy soils.** In sandy soils the rock particles are bigger. This means there are bigger gaps between the particles, allowing the soil to drain well and contain enough air. However, sandy soils can dry out very quickly and do not hold nutrients so well. This leads to poor plant growth.
- **Loam soils.** Loam is soil with a mixture of sand and clay particles. This sort of soil is ideal for plant growth.

Soil is made up of layers. The layer nearest the surface is called topsoil, with subsoil underneath it and then rock fragments. The closer to the surface, the more humus there is in the soil. Plants and animals live in the topsoil, so the topsoil is often covered with dead leaves (leaf litter) and other decaying vegetation. This explains why it contains most humus.

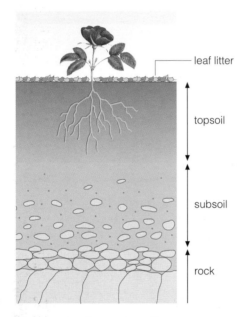

leaf litter

topsoil

subsoil

rock

Figure 2.12 *Layers in soil.*

Summary

- Igneous rocks are made when magma cools down and crystallises. The more slowly it crystallises, the larger the mineral crystals.
- Sedimentary rocks are formed from the hardening of sediment over time.
- Metamorphic rocks are formed by the action of heat and/or increased pressure on other rocks.
- All rocks are eventually weathered, which means they are broken down into smaller pieces.
- Rocks are recycled and changed from one group to another over millions of years.
- Soil consists of small fragments of rock, humus, air, water and dissolved minerals.

Questions

1 Copy and complete the following sentences.
There are three main groups of rocks: _____,
_____ and _____ rocks. All rocks
are made up from _____. *[Total 2]*

2 Draw a table giving some important information
about igneous, sedimentary and metamorphic rocks.
There should be four columns: rock group; what the
rock is formed from; how it is formed; two examples.
  [Total 9]

3 Figure 2.13 shows the texture of two igneous rocks, A
and B. One was formed on the Earth's surface and
one underground.
  a) Which rock was formed on the Earth's surface? *[1]*
  b) Explain why the rocks have a different
     appearance. *[3]*
  c) What is the name for igneous rocks formed on the
     Earth's surface? *[1]*
  d) What is the name for igneous rocks formed below
     the Earth's surface? *[1]*
  e) For each rock sample, give one example of a rock
     that it could be. *[2]*
  [Total 8]

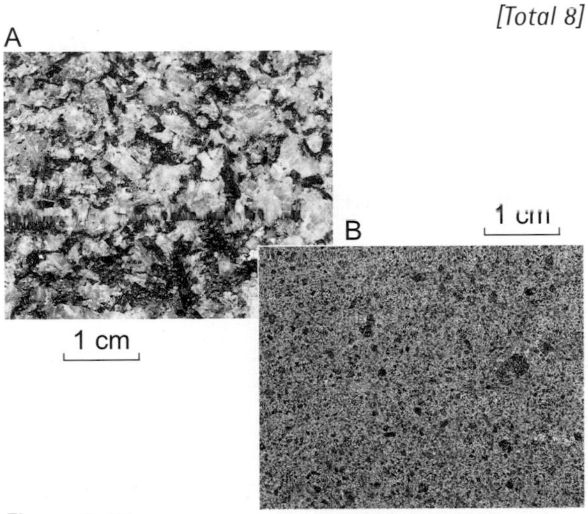

A

B

1 cm

1 cm

Figure 2.13

4 a) What is weathering? *[1]*
  b) Explain clearly the difference between chemical,
     physical and biological weathering. *[3]*
  [Total 4]

5 All rocks are weathered. Explain clearly how each of
the following breaks up rocks:
  a) plant roots *[2]*
  b) freezing water *[3]*
  c) rain water *[2]*
  d) extremes of hot and cold. *[3]*
  [Total 10]

6 a) Two cottages were built out of stone. One was built
     out of granite and the other out of sandstone.
     i)   What rock group does granite belong to?
     ii) What rock group does sandstone belong to?
     iii) Which cottage will stand up to the
          weather best? *[3]*
  b) Slate is often used for roofing tiles.
     i)   What rock group does slate belong to?
     ii) Explain why slate is a good material for
          making roofing tiles. *[4]*
  [Total 7]

7 a) What is soil made up of? *[5]*
  b) What is humus? *[1]*
  c) Explain why sandy soils drain better than clay
     soils. *[2]*
  d) Name the type of soil that is best for growing
     crops. *[1]*
  e) Explain why the type of soil in part d) is the best
     for growing crops. *[2]*
  f) Soils are very different. Give three things that
     affect the type of soil. *[3]*
  [Total 14]

8 a) Explain why some fossils can be used to date
     rocks. *[1]*
  b) Explain the limitations of using fossils to
     date rocks. *[1]*
  [Total 2]

4.3 The air and combustion

What is air and what happens when a substance burns? Although we cannot see it, air is all around us, is vital for life and takes part in many chemical reactions.

The atmosphere and air

The **atmosphere** is the mixture of gases that surrounds the Earth. The atmosphere gets thinner as you go further from the Earth's surface. It is difficult to say exactly where the atmosphere stops.

Air is the mixture of gases in the lower part of the atmosphere. About 99% of the air is made up of just two gases, nitrogen and oxygen, with only small amounts of other gases. The amount of water vapour in the air, although small, changes and so the exact composition of air changes. However, the composition of dry air stays constant and is shown in Table 3.1.

Table 3.1

Gas	% in dry air
nitrogen (N_2)	78
oxygen (O_2)	21
argon (Ar)	0.9
carbon dioxide (CO_2)	0.04
other gases	traces

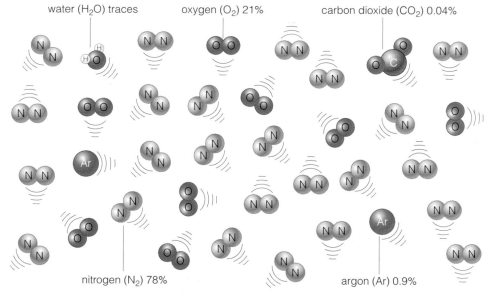

Figure 3.1 *The gases in air.*

There are other substances in the air that pollute it. The main sources of air pollution are the burning of fossil fuels and the release of man-made chemicals into the atmosphere. Air pollution is studied in subsection 4.4.

1 a) What is air? [1]
b) List the four main gases in air in order of decreasing abundance. [1]
c) Name the most abundant element found in air. [1]
d) Name the most abundant compound found in air. [1]
[Total 4]

Finding the amount of oxygen in air

The apparatus shown in Figure 3.2 can be used to find the percentage of oxygen in a sample of air.

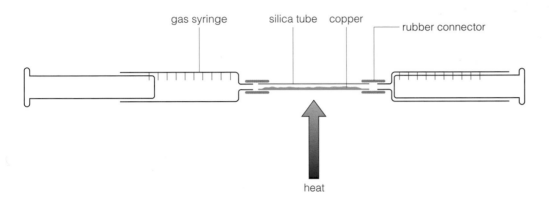

Figure 3.2 *Finding the percentage of oxygen in air.*

Method

The volume of air in the syringes is measured at the start of the experiment. The copper is then heated strongly as the air is passed slowly from one syringe to the other. The process is continued until there is no further change in the volume of gas.

Finally, the apparatus is allowed to cool and the volume of air in the syringes is measured again. The change in volume is due to the loss of oxygen which is removed as it reacts with the copper to form copper oxide.

Results

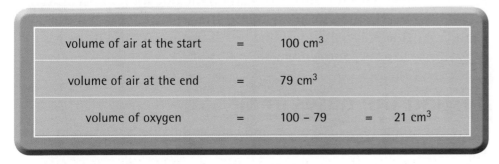

volume of air at the start	=	100 cm^3		
volume of air at the end	=	79 cm^3		
volume of oxygen	=	100 – 79	=	21 cm^3

Conclusion

This sample of air contains 21% oxygen.

Figure 3.3 *The diver obtains oxygen from the oxygen tank and the fish use dissolved oxygen in the water.*

!

Bubbles of nitrogen form in the blood of deep-sea divers as they surface. This is called 'the bends' and it can be fatal. Divers have to spend hours in decompression chambers to allow their bodies to get used to the change in pressure to avoid 'the bends'.

!

Although oxygen gas is colourless, liquid oxygen is pale blue. It is also magnetic and a tube of liquid oxygen can be attracted to a magnet.

Properties and uses of the gases in air

Fractional distillation of liquid air can be used to separate the gases. The air is first cooled and compressed to turn it into a liquid. The gases can be separated because they have different boiling points (see subsection 2.5).

All the gases in air are colourless and have no smell, but they differ in other properties and uses.

Nitrogen, the most abundant gas in air, is insoluble in water and does not react easily with other substances. As nitrogen is so unreactive, the gas is used for packaging foods. However, nitrogen *can* be made to react and is used to make ammonia and nitric acid. Both of these compounds are used to make fertilisers. Plants and animals need nitrogen-containing compounds to make proteins.

Oxygen is soluble in water and reacts with many other substances. The presence of oxygen in air and water is essential to life on Earth. Oxygen is needed for respiration, the process by which living things release energy from sugars. Cylinders of gas that include oxygen are used in hospitals to help patients with breathing difficulties, and by underwater divers. Oxygen is also needed for combustion, and substances burn better if more oxygen is present. Oxygen is used along with the fuel gas acetylene (ethyne) to produce a very high temperature flame in oxyacetylene burners.

Argon is insoluble in water and is extremely unreactive. Ordinary light bulbs are filled with argon so that the filament does not burn out.

Carbon dioxide is soluble in water but is fairly unreactive. There are only small amounts of carbon dioxide in the air, but it is important to all living things. Green plants need carbon dioxide for photosynthesis, the process that produces carbohydrates and replaces oxygen in the air. Carbon dioxide is also used in some fire extinguishers and is the gas in fizzy drinks like beer and lemonade.

Testing the gases in air

There are simple tests for oxygen and carbon dioxide, as shown in Figure 3.4. However, there are no specific tests for nitrogen and argon.

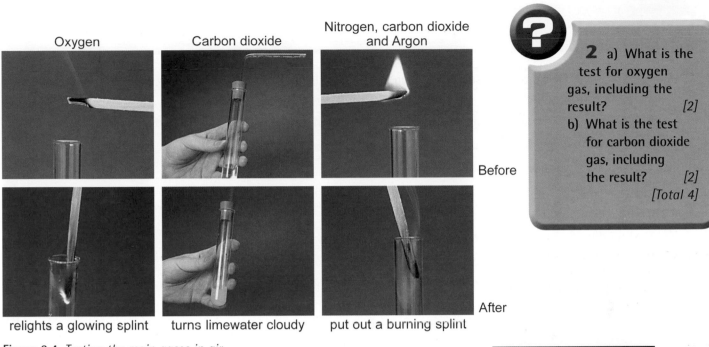

Oxygen | Carbon dioxide | Nitrogen, carbon dioxide and Argon

Before

After

relights a glowing splint | turns limewater cloudy | put out a burning splint

Figure 3.4 *Testing the main gases in air.*

2 a) What is the test for oxygen gas, including the result? *[2]*

b) What is the test for carbon dioxide gas, including the result? *[2]*

[Total 4]

Combustion (burning)

Oxidation is said to take place when a substance reacts with oxygen. Some substances catch fire when they react with oxygen. This is called **burning** or **combustion**. When substances react with oxygen, new substances called oxides are formed.

For example, when magnesium is burned it forms magnesium oxide. The word equation is:

magnesium + oxygen → magnesium oxide

When hydrogen sulphide is burned, it forms water (i.e. hydrogen oxide) and sulphur dioxide. The word equation is

hydrogen sulphide + oxygen →   water   + sulphur dioxide
                                (hydrogen oxide)

The fire triangle

A fire needs three things – a **fuel**, oxygen and heat. This can be shown by the fire triangle. To put a fire out you need to remove one (or more) of these three things. For example, many fire extinguishers, including those containing water and carbon dioxide, work by stopping oxygen getting to the fire and cooling the fire down. If somebody catches fire, you could wrap them up in a fire blanket, or use something like a coat. This stops oxygen getting to the fire.

Figure 3.5 *Magnesium burning.*

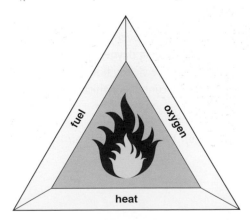

Figure 3.6 *The fire triangle.*

Summary

○ Air is a mixture of nitrogen (78%) and oxygen (21%) with small amounts of argon, carbon dioxide, water and other gases.

○ The gases in air can be separated by fractional distillation of liquid air.

○ Nitrogen and argon are both unreactive.

○ Oxygen is needed for respiration and burning.

○ Oxygen relights a glowing splint.

○ Plants need carbon dioxide for photosynthesis.

○ Carbon dioxide turns limewater cloudy.

○ Oxidation is the reaction of a substance with oxygen.

○ Combustion is a rapid reaction in which a substance combines with oxygen, catches fire and gives out energy.

○ A fuel, oxygen and heat are all needed for combustion.

Questions

1 Copy and complete the following sentences.
Air is a mixture of gases. The four main gases in air, in order of decreasing abundance, are _____, _____, _____ and _____
_____.   [Total 2]

2 Give one use for each of the following gases:
oxygen   nitrogen   carbon dioxide   argon.
[Total 4]

3 Susan has been given three stoppered test tubes containing oxygen, nitrogen and carbon dioxide. Describe clearly how Susan could find out which test tube contained which gas.
[Total 3]

4 a) Which gas in the air is used up when substances burn?   [1]

b) Write word equations to show what happens when the following substances are burned:
i)   iron
ii) carbon
iii) sulphur
iv) octane (formula C_8H_{18})
v)   ammonia (formula NH_3)
vi) ethanol (formula C_2H_6O).   [6]
[Total 7]

5 a) The fire triangle shows the three things that are needed for a fire. What are they?   [3]

b) There are different types of fire extinguisher for different types of fire.
i)   Explain how a water extinguisher puts out a paper fire.
ii) Explain how a carbon dioxide extinguisher puts out an electrical fire.
iii) Why should you not use a water extinguisher on an electrical fire?   [4]
[Total 7]

4.4 Fossil fuels

What are fossil fuels and what is produced when they are burned? Most of the world's energy comes from burning fossil fuels, but their burning does cause some problems.

The formation of fossil fuels

The most common **fossil fuels** are **coal**, **crude oil** and **natural gas**. They were all formed in similar ways over millions of years.

Coal was formed from the remains of trees and other plants that died in swamps. They were buried by more plants and mud that squashed them. Over millions of years, in the absence of any air, the heat and pressure caused chemical changes to take place turning the plant remains into coal. The coal is often deep underground and we have to obtain it by mining.

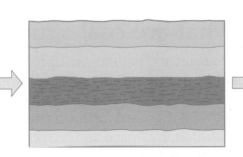
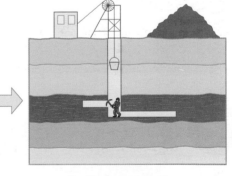

Trees and other plants die and are buried in swamps.

Coal is formed over millions of years as sediment builds up on top.

Coal is dug out of mines.

Figure 4.1 *The formation of coal.*

Oil and natural gas were formed from sea creatures which died and fell into the sand on the sea bed. In time, more and more were buried and squashed by the weight of the sand. Over millions of years, in the absence of any air, the heat and pressure caused chemical changes to take place turning the remains into crude oil and natural gas. They are deep underground and we have to obtain them by drilling.

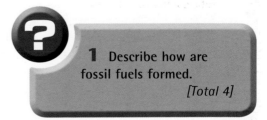

?

1 Describe how are fossil fuels formed.

[Total 4]

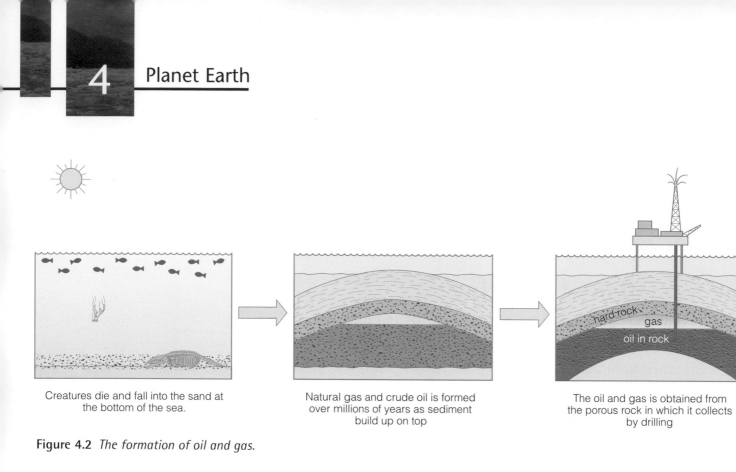

Figure 4.2 *The formation of oil and gas.*

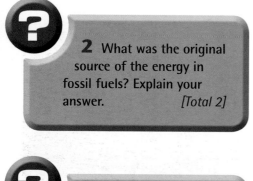

2 What was the original source of the energy in fossil fuels? Explain your answer. [Total 2]

3 What are crude oil and natural gas made up of? [Total 1]

The plants that formed coal and the creatures that formed crude oil and natural gas all obtained their energy from the Sun by photosynthesis. This means that the original source of all the energy in fossil fuels is the Sun.

What are coal, crude oil and natural gas?

Crude oil and natural gas are mainly mixtures of **hydrocarbons**, although they do contain small amounts of other substances. Hydrocarbons are compounds that contain hydrogen and carbon only. They are discussed further in the next subsection. Coal consists mainly of carbon, hydrogen and oxygen, but it also contains small amounts of other substances such as sulphur.

Combustion of fossil fuels

The reason that we burn fossil fuels is to release energy. For example, natural gas is often burned in cookers, central heating boilers and Bunsen burners. Fossil fuels release a great deal of energy when they burn. Burning is a chemical reaction and the experiment in Figure 4.3 shows what is formed when a hydrocarbon is burned.

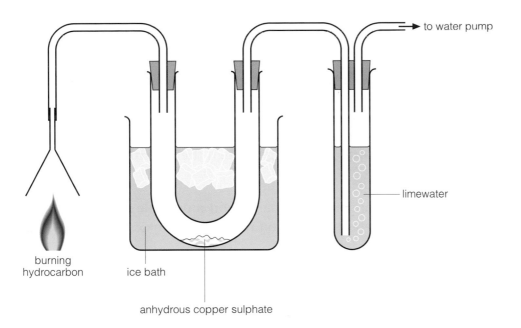

to water pump

limewater

burning
hydrocarbon

ice bath

anhydrous copper sulphate

Figure 4.3 *Testing for the products from the combustion of a hydrocarbon.*

The anhydrous copper sulphate turns from white to blue proving that water is produced. The **limewater** turns cloudy showing that carbon dioxide is produced.

The word equation for the combustion of any hydrocarbon is shown below, though the reason that they are burned is to release energy, not to make carbon dioxide and water!

hydrocarbon + oxygen →   water   + carbon dioxide
(hydrogen oxide)

Incomplete combustion

Sometimes there is not enough oxygen for a substance to burn completely. This is known as **incomplete combustion**. When a hydrocarbon undergoes incomplete combustion, carbon monoxide and/or carbon (soot) is formed rather than carbon dioxide. The word equations are:

hydrocarbon + oxygen → water + carbon monoxide

hydrocarbon + oxygen → water + carbon

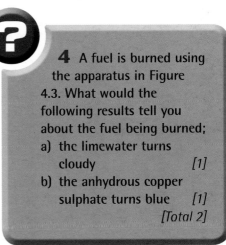

4 A fuel is burned using the apparatus in Figure 4.3. What would the following results tell you about the fuel being burned;
a) the limewater turns cloudy   [1]
b) the anhydrous copper sulphate turns blue   [1]
              [Total 2]

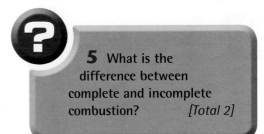

5 What is the difference between complete and incomplete combustion?   [Total 2]

Air pollution from burning fossil fuels

Carbon dioxide

All fossil fuels contain carbon, so when they are burned they produce carbon dioxide. There is a small amount of carbon dioxide in the air (about 0.04%), but so many fossil fuels are being burned that the amount of carbon dioxide in the air is increasing. This is thought to be responsible for **global warming** through the **greenhouse effect**.

Carbon monoxide

When fossil fuels are burned, some carbon monoxide is produced due to incomplete combustion. Carbon monoxide is toxic.

Soot

Incomplete combustion of fossil fuels also forms soot (carbon) particles which are carried in the air and can blacken buildings and damage health.

It can also reduce the amount of sunlight reaching the Earth, causing global dimming.

Figure 4.4 *Houses of Parliament in London before and after the soot was cleaned off.*

Sulphur dioxide

Most fossil fuels contain small amounts of sulphur which produces sulphur dioxide when the fuel is burned. Sulphur dioxide is harmful to the breathing system of humans and other animals. Sulphur dioxide also reacts with air and rainwater to make **acid rain** which damages metal, stone, brick, plants and animals. It can also make lakes too acidic for fish to survive.

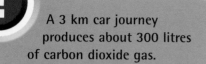

! A 3 km car journey produces about 300 litres of carbon dioxide gas.

! Many people have been killed in their homes by carbon monoxide. Poorly serviced gas boilers and gas fires can give out this toxic gas.

! Rain water is naturally acidic. The pH of rain should be between 5 and 6. This is due to carbon dioxide dissolved in the rain. 'Acid rain' is rain that is more acidic than this.

Nitrogen oxides

When fossil fuels are burned in engines or furnaces, the temperatures reached are so high that oxygen and nitrogen in the air can react together. This forms nitrogen oxides which, like sulphur dioxide, are harmful to the breathing system and cause acid rain.

Reducing pollution

There are several ways to reduce pollution from burning fossil fuels. Some examples are as follows.

- Lean-burn car engines carefully control the amount of air and fuel so there is less incomplete combustion resulting in less carbon monoxide (and less unburned fuel) being given out.
- Catalytic converters in car exhausts reduce the amount of carbon monoxide and nitrogen oxides reaching the atmosphere.
- Power stations can build plants to remove sulphur dioxide from the waste gases (flue-gas desulphurisation plants).

One way to reduce the amount of carbon dioxide being released is to burn fewer fossil fuels. However, as the amount of energy the world needs is increasing, it would need a massive increase in the use of other energy sources like nuclear, wind and solar power to do this.

Renewable and non-renewable fuels

Another problem with burning fossil fuels is that they will eventually run out. Fossil fuels are **non-renewable** (finite) because, once used, we cannot replace them as they took millions of years to form. Oil and natural gas are rapidly running out, and although coal will last for several hundred years it will eventually run out too.

There are some **fuels** that are **renewable**. Examples are alcohol, biodiesel and wood which are made from plants. They are renewable because more plants can be grown to replace those used. They are described as **carbon neutral**. This means that for every molecule of carbon dioxide they produce when they burn, a molecule of carbon dioxide is absorbed by the plants from which they are made when they grew. Therefore, growing and burning such fuels does not increase the amount of carbon dioxide in the air.

There are other renewable energy sources, such as solar, wind and tidal power. These do not cause the same pollution problems as fossil fuels, but there are difficulties obtaining enough energy from them.

?

6 Explain:
   a) why the substances listed below may be formed when fossil fuels are burned. [5]
   b) what environmental problems the substances listed below cause? [5]

- soot
- carbon monoxide
- carbon dioxide
- sulphur dioxide
- nitrogen oxides

[Total 10]

!

On average, each person in the UK uses 1.4 tonnes of oil, 1.2 tonnes of natural gas and 1.0 tonnes of coal per year.

?

7 What is the difference between a renewable and a non-renewable fuel? Give two examples of each. [Total 4]

8 What does it mean if a fuel is carbon neutral? [Total 2]

Summary

- Coal, crude oil and natural gas are fossil fuels.
- The burning of fossil fuels produces pollutants such as carbon dioxide, carbon monoxide, soot, sulphur dioxide and nitrogen oxides.
- The amount of carbon dioxide in the atmosphere is increasing and is thought to be causing global warming.
- Sulphur dioxide and nitrogen oxides cause acid rain.
- Fossil fuels are non-renewable because they cannot be replaced once they have been used.
- Sugar (used to make alcohol) and wood are renewable fuels because more can be grown to replace that which is used.

Questions

1 Copy and complete the following sentences.
Fossil fuels were formed from the remains of _____ and _____. The remains were buried and decayed over _____ of years in the absence of _____ under heat and _____. Three common fossil fuels are _____, _____ and _____.
[Total 4]

2 Jack carried out an experiment (similar to that in Figure 4.3) to see whether carbon dioxide and water were formed when he burned some substances.

For each of the following substances:
a) hydrogen   c) propane (C_3H_8)
b) magnesium   d) glucose ($C_6H_{12}O_6$)

decide whether:
i) the white anhydrous copper sulphate will turn blue (which it does if it comes into contact with water)
ii) the limewater will go cloudy (which it does if carbon dioxide is bubbled through it).   *[Total 4]*

3 Cars are a major source of air pollution. The main problems are carbon dioxide, carbon monoxide, nitrogen oxides and unburned hydrocarbons in the exhaust gases.
a) i) Explain why carbon dioxide is formed in car engines.
   ii) What environmental problem is increasing amounts of carbon dioxide in the air thought to be causing?   *[3]*
b) i) Explain why carbon monoxide is formed in car engines.
   ii) Why is carbon monoxide in the air a problem?   *[2]*
c) i) Explain how nitrogen oxides are formed in car engines.
   ii) What problems do these nitrogen oxides cause?   *[3]*
d) What do cars with petrol engines have in their exhaust system to reduce the amount of carbon monoxide, unburned hydrocarbons and nitrogen oxides in their exhaust gases?   *[1]*
[Total 9]

4.5 Chemicals from oil

What is crude oil and how can we obtain useful products from it? Crude oil is one of our most precious resources. Not only does it provide us with many different **fuels**, but many useful substances such as **plastics**, medicines and detergents are made from it.

What is crude oil?

Crude oil is a runny, dark brown liquid. It is a mixture of many different chemicals, but most of them are hydrocarbons. **Hydrocarbons** are compounds made out of carbon and hydrogen only, but their molecules can have very different sizes. The number of carbon atoms in each hydrocarbon molecule varies from 1 to over 100. Figure 5.1 shows two hydrocarbon molecules.

C_4H_{10} $C_{20}H_{42}$

Figure 5.1 *Two hydrocarbon molecules.*

Oil refining

Crude oil is of little use in its natural form, but the substances in it are very useful once they are separated from each other. The separation process takes place in an oil refinery and is called fractional distillation.

Figure 5.2 *An oil refinery – fractional distillation is carried out in the tall towers.*

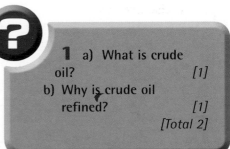

?

1 a) What is crude oil? [1]

b) Why is crude oil refined? [1]

[Total 2]

Fractional distillation takes place in tall towers called fractionating towers. It separates the hydrocarbons because they have different boiling points. The boiling points of the hydrocarbons depend on the size of their molecules. The larger the molecules, the higher the boiling point because more energy is needed to separate the molecules.

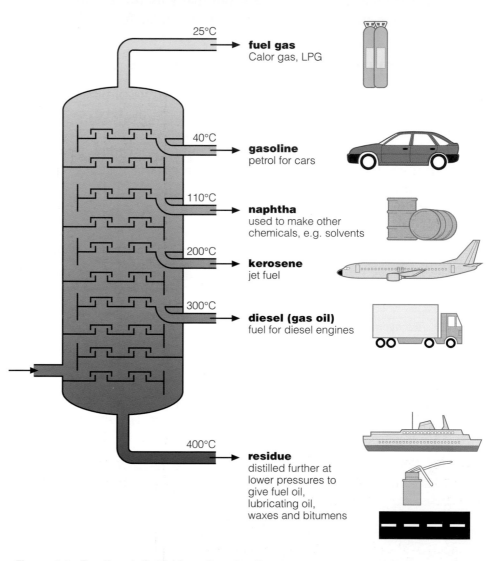

Figure 5.3 *Fractional distillation of crude oil.*

- The crude oil is heated so that most of it turns into gas. It is then put into a fractionating tower which is hotter at the bottom than it is at the top.

As the hot gases rise up the tower, they cool down and turn back into liquids (condense). The different substances in the crude oil have different boiling points and so condense at different temperatures. Those with high boiling points turn back into liquids near the bottom of the tower. Those with lower boiling points do not become liquids until they are near the top of the tower.

The liquids are trapped on trays as they condense. These trays are designed to allow the gases to rise up, but not to let the liquids fall back down the tower.

The process separates the crude oil into **fractions**. Each fraction is still a mixture of hydrocarbons, but all the hydrocarbons in a fraction have molecules of a similar size. The fractions have different uses because the hydrocarbons in the different fractions have different properties. For example, the fractions nearer the top are more flammable (catch fire more easily).

Figure 5.3 shows a fractionating tower along with some uses of the fractions. The hydrocarbons with higher boiling points collect in the residue at the bottom. They are taken off and distilled further at low pressure to separate them into more fractions.

Cracking

The gasoline fraction is in greater demand than the other fractions because it is used for petrol in cars. To meet this demand, another process called **cracking** is carried out at the oil refinery. In this process, fractions containing big hydrocarbon molecules are broken down into smaller ones by heating, often in the presence of a catalyst (a catalyst is a substance that speeds up a reaction but does not get used up itself). In addition to producing more gasoline, other molecules are produced that are very useful for making many other substances, such as plastics.

Making useful substances

Many of the fractions from crude oil are used as fuels, such as petrol and diesel in cars and lorries, kerosene in aircraft and fuel oil on ships. However, some of the other chemicals are put to other important uses. The naphtha fraction and some of the chemicals produced in cracking are used to make substances such as plastics, artificial fibres (e.g. polyesters), detergents, paints, solvents, explosives and many medicines.

2 Outline how fractional distillation separates the substances in crude oil. [Total 4]

3 What is a fraction? [Total 1]

4 a) Which fraction is used for fuel in most cars? [1]
b) Which fraction is used for jet fuel? [1]
[Total 2]

5 Why are fractions containing bigger hydrocarbon molecules cracked? [Total 2]

Petrol sold in the summer is different to petrol sold in the winter.
Winter petrol contains more hydrocarbons with lower boiling points. This allows the petrol to vaporise more easily to start the engine on cold days.

Figure 5.4 *Some useful products made from chemicals in crude oil.*

The petrochemical industry

The **petrochemical industry** drills for crude oil and separates out the different chemicals to be used as fuels or made into other substances. This is a major employer in the UK and very important to the economy.

What will happen when oil runs out?

We are rapidly using up our supplies of oil. As it starts to run out, its price will rise and people will be forced to use cheaper alternatives. This will probably happen in your lifetime. There are alternatives however, and we can make many of the same chemicals from coal. We have sufficient coal to last for hundreds of years.

Summary

- Crude oil is a mixture of many different hydrocarbons.
- Hydrocarbons are compounds that contain carbon and hydrogen only.
- Crude oil is not very useful unless the hydrocarbons are separated into fractions by fractional distillation.
- Each fraction contains a mixture of hydrocarbons with similar boiling points and similar sized molecules.
- The hydrocarbons in crude oil are used as fuels or to make useful substances like plastics, solvents, medicines and clothing fibres.

Questions

1 Copy and complete the following sentences.
Crude oil is a _____ fuel. It is a mixture of
many different compounds called _____.
These compounds are separated at an oil
_____ by _____ _____.
[Total 2]

2 Crude oil is a mixture of many hydrocarbons.
a) What is the main use of the hydrocarbons in
crude oil? *[1]*
b) What is a hydrocarbon? *[2]*
c) What is the formula of the hydrocarbon shown in
the diagram? *[1]*

d) Give five other types of chemical that are made
from hydrocarbons in crude oil. *[5]*
[Total 9]

3 The hydrocarbons in crude oil are separated into
fractions by fractional distillation.
a) Give one use for each of the following fractions:
i) diesel
ii) gasoline
iii) kerosene. *[3]*
b) What property of the hydrocarbons in crude oil
allows them to be separated by fractional
distillation? *[1]*
c) Briefly explain how the fractional distillation of
crude oil works. *[3]*
d) Which of the fractions listed in part a) contains
the largest molecules? *[1]*
e) Which of the fractions listed in part a) contains
the hydrocarbons with the lowest boiling points?
[1]
[Total 9]

4 Many of the larger hydrocarbon molecules from
crude oil are cracked.
a) What is cracking? *[1]*
b) Why is cracking necessary? *[1]*
c) How are the molecules cracked? *[2]*
d) What are the main uses of the products of
cracking? *[2]*
[Total 6]

5 Crude oil is running out.
a) What will happen to the price of oil as reserves
get low? *[1]*
b) What might be used to produce the chemicals
that we get from crude oil at the moment? *[1]*
[Total 2]

6 Use the data in the table to draw a pie chart of
energy sources in the UK. *[Total 2]*

Source	Percentage (%)
coal	16
oil	35
natural gas	37
nuclear fuel	11
others	1

7 Explain why the petrochemical industry is
important to the UK. *[Total 4]*

8 Oil is running out. What will happen as oil supplies run
out? List as many consequences as you can. *[Total 6]*

Uses of rocks as building materials

Rocks are very useful building materials – some examples are given in Table 6.1. Some building materials – such as concrete and brick – are man-made, although some of these are made using rocks found naturally.

Rock	Type of rock	Uses in building	Useful properties	Problems with its use
limestone	sedimentary	as building stone	easily cut into shape	reacts slowly with rainwater
sandstone	sedimentary	as building stone	easily cut into shape	poor resistance to weathering
granite	igneous	as building stone (very good for decorative parts of buildings), as attractive when polished gravestones	very hard, good resistance to weathering,	difficult to cut to shape
marble	metamorphic	as building stone (very good for decorative parts of buildings)	very hard, good resistance to weathering, attractive when polished	difficult to cut to shape and expensive
slate	metamorphic	as roofing tiles	hard, strong, good resistance to weathering, splits into thin, flat sheets	

Table 6.1 *The main rock groups.*

?

1 Why is granite a good rock for making stone steps? [Total 1]

2 Why is slate a good rock for making roofing tiles? [Total 1]

3 Why is sandstone a poor rock for making a statue? [Total 1]

Figure 6.1 *Peak District cottage made of limestone.*

Figure 6.2 *Polished granite is very decorative.*

Uses of rocks as building materials

Very large quantities of rock are used as building materials. These rocks are taken from **quarries** – these are massive areas, often in the countryside, where rock is taken from the ground.

It costs a lot of money to move heavy, bulky rocks around the country. This means that builders often use local rocks in their construction. For example, many homes in the Peak District are built using **limestone** because there is a lot of limestone in the area.

Quarries bring both benefits and problems – so there are many factors to consider before a quarry is started. Some of these are shown in Table 6.2.

Figure 6.3 *A quarry.*

Benefits	Problems
• creates jobs for local people • brings more money to the area	• creates a large hole in the landscape • very noisy • could reduce tourism • more traffic, especially lorries, on local roads • dust and dirt in the air

Table 6.2 *Good or not so good?*

Continuing to quarry rocks in the way we do now will destroy the landscape – and some rocks would end up in short supply. It is not **sustainable** to keep quarrying rocks in the quantities that we do now. Ways must be found to reduce the amount of rock that we quarry – **recycling** some building materials is one example of how this could be done.

Questions

1 Why do builders often use local rocks in building? [Total 1]

2 In what ways might a quarry bring money to the area near it? [Total 2]

3 Imagine that a company wanted to build a quarry near where you live. Present arguments for and against the building of the quarry. Be specific to the area where you live. [Total 6]

4 Explain why quarrying as we do today is not sustainable. [Total 2]

The Indian Ocean tsunami warning system

Many people have been killed in earthquakes and volcanic eruptions. It is difficult to predict when these may happen, even though developments in science and technology are being used to help. It is important to have systems to detect these events and to inform people who may be affected.

On 26th December in 2004, a massive earthquake struck under the Indian Ocean. The earthquake happened about 100 miles to the west of Sumatra, the biggest island in Indonesia. It happened at a depth of nearly 20 miles under the seabed. The earthquake caused the sea floor to rise several metres and produced a **tsunami** (tidal wave). The tsunami was not very tall in deep water, but in shallow water near coastlines it reached up to 10 metres high.

! The deadliest earthquake was in China in 1556 – it killed 830 000 people.

! The size of earthquakes is measured on the Richter scale – the earthquake that caused the Asian tsunami was measured at 9.0. For every one unit higher an earthquake is on the Richter Scale, it is ten times more powerful. In 2008, there was a small earthquake in the UK that measured 5.2.

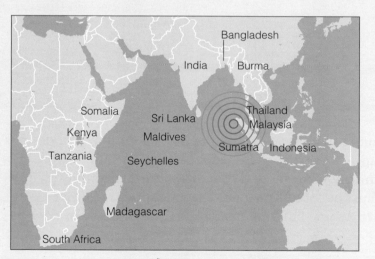

Figure 6.4 *The regions affected by the tsunami.*

Indonesia was affected very badly, along with Sri Lanka, India and Thailand. The waves travelled a long way, with the furthest reported death being 5000 miles away in South Africa. It is estimated that about 250 000 people were killed by the tsunami – many more were injured and up to 5 million people lost their homes.

Following this disaster, it was agreed at a United Nations conference to set up a tsunami early-warning system for the Indian Ocean. There is already one in place for the Pacific Ocean. By June 2006, the detection system was in place. It includes **seismic wave** detectors that detect earthquakes almost as soon as they happen – seismic waves are those that travel through the Earth. There are also undersea detectors looking for signs of a

? **1** Explain what a tsunami is and how it is produced. [Total 3]
2 Why is it important to be able to either predict or detect as soon as possible natural events such as earthquakes, volcanic eruptions and tsunamis. [Total 2]

The Indian Ocean tsunami warning system

tsunami by measuring changes in the pressure of water above a set of detectors. Information from these is processed by powerful computers and is sent by satellite to tsunami-monitoring stations around the region.

It takes time for a tsunami to travel so, unless the earthquake is near a coastline, there is a chance of warning people to evacuate to safety. Detecting a tsunami is not the only part of an early-warning system. The biggest problem is having a system for communicating information to all the people. In many of the areas where the 2004 tsunami hit, many people do not have a television, radio or telephone and they live in remote places – one possible solution is to use sirens. It is believed that most of the people killed in the 2004 tsunami would have been saved if such a system had been in place.

Figure 6.5 *Destruction caused by the tsunami.*

Two years later, almost 25 000 people were evacuated to safety in Java after the Pacific Ocean early-warning system detected a tsunami, but more than 600 people were still killed. This confirms that however well we use advances in science and technology for detection, we must also work to ensure that systems are in place to get the message to as many people as possible.

The Indian and Pacific Ocean systems are to be part of an international early-warning programme for many types of natural disasters – earthquakes, volcanic eruptions, tsunamis, floods and hurricanes. This requires many countries working together and scientists working with many other people, including governments and relief organisations, in order to produce a system that will save lives.

Figure 6.6 *Many people live in remote areas.*

Questions

1 These questions are about the 2004 tsunami in the Indian Ocean.

  a) The map shows that Malaysia was close to the centre of the earthquake. Why do you think that there were far fewer deaths in Malaysia than in other countries in the area? [1]

  b) Why would a tsunami early-warning system have saved many lives in Sri Lanka and India? [1]

  c) Why would a tsunami early-warning system not have saved so many lives in Indonesia? [1]

  [Total 3]

2 a) Describe how the Indian Ocean tsunami early-warning system detects a tsunami. [3]

  b) What is the most difficult element of a system for preventing deaths when there is a natural disaster? [1]

  [Total 4]

3 a) Describe how advances in science and technology are being used to save lives through early-warning systems for natural disasters. [2]

  b) Explain why it is important for scientists to work with others and to communicate clearly with many different people in the development of international early-warning systems. [1]

  [Total 3]

Global warming

Most people have heard about **global warming**. In simple terms, the theory is that the Earth is getting warmer due to the increasing amount of carbon dioxide in the atmosphere. However, there is still a great deal of debate among scientists about this theory.

Carbon dioxide – a greenhouse gas

There is no doubt that the amount of carbon dioxide in the atmosphere is increasing. Table 6.3 shows how it has changed in recent years at Mauna Loa in Hawaii. It is shown in parts per million (ppm). 316 ppm equals 0.0316% of air. There is similar data from other parts of the world that supports this.

The increase is thought to be due to the increased burning of fossil fuels and destruction of much of the world's rainforests (trees remove carbon dioxide from the air for photosynthesis).

But why is an increase in carbon dioxide in the atmosphere a problem? Carbon dioxide traps heat on the Earth, rather like glass in a greenhouse. Heat from the Sun can pass through the glass in a greenhouse, but the glass stops heat escaping. This makes it warmer inside the greenhouse than outside. Carbon dioxide in the atmosphere behaves like the glass in a greenhouse. It allows heat from the Sun to reach the Earth, but stops some of the Earth's heat escaping.

Is global warming happening?

Many people believe that the increasing levels of carbon dioxide and its role in the greenhouse effect are causing the temperature of the Earth to rise. However, there are many variables other than the amounts of greenhouse gases in the atmosphere that affect the Earth's temperature. Scientists are not certain how these will change or what their combined effect will be. The majority of scientists believe that the overall effect for the Earth will be that it becomes warmer.

There is evidence that the Earth is already getting warmer. The average temperature of the Earth rose by over 0.5°C in the last century, however some believe this could be due to natural variations in temperature. There are many different predictions about how much the temperature may rise, but even a small rise of a degree or two could have serious consequences.

Table 6.3

Year	CO_2 (ppm)
1960	317
1965	320
1970	326
1975	331
1980	339
1985	346
1990	354
1995	361
2000	369
2005	380

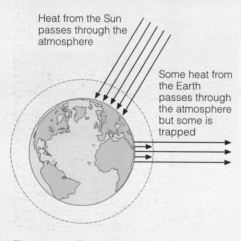

Heat from the Sun passes through the atmosphere

Some heat from the Earth passes through the atmosphere but some is trapped

Figure 6.7 *The atmosphere acting like a greenhouse.*

The further away from the Sun a planet is, the colder it is, except for Venus. Venus is hotter than Mercury even though it is further from the Sun. This is thought to be due to the greenhouse effect on Venus. The atmosphere on Venus is 96% carbon dioxide.

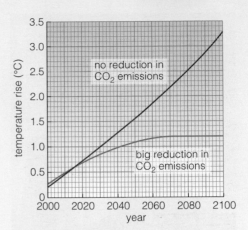

The effects of global warming

It is difficult to predict exactly what will happen if global warming is happening. A number of important effects have been suggested:

- A rise in sea levels due to the water in the oceans expanding and part of the ice caps melting. This would lead to parts of some low lying countries, such as Bangladesh, disappearing under the sea.
- A change in climate making some parts of the world hotter and some parts wetter.
- Land currently used for farming becoming desert in some parts of the world.
- Some species of plants and animals becoming extinct or migrating to different parts of the world.

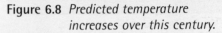

Figure 6.8 *Predicted temperature increases over this century.*

Theories and predictions

Scientists often make predictions based on a theory. If experimental evidence agrees with their theory, then other scientists may accept the theory. We are still waiting for conclusive evidence that the Earth is really getting warmer and whether this is due to the increase in carbon dioxide levels. We cannot be certain which scientists have the best theory about the effect of increasing carbon dioxide levels on the climate and by how much the temperature will rise. As with all science, some theories will be shown to be better than others as the evidence becomes stronger.

However, can we take the risk of waiting to see if these scientists are right before taking action?

?

1 What is thought to have caused the increase in the amount of carbon dioxide in the atmosphere? [2]

2 Why is it important that data about increasing levels of carbon dioxide are taken from several different places around the world? [1]

Questions

1 a) Use the data in Table 6.3 to plot a graph, showing the line of best fit, to show how the average carbon dioxide level has changed from 1960 to the present day. Plot the year across the x-axis from 1960 to now. You should plot the carbon dioxide level up the y- axis from 300 ppm to 400 ppm. [4]
   b) Describe what the graph tells you. [1]
   c) Explain why this has happened. [2]
   [Total 7]

the last century? [1]
   b) Besides increasing carbon dioxide levels, what other explanation is there for the Earth possibly getting warmer? [1]
   c) By how much could the temperature rise in the next century if the scientists who predict global warming are correct? [1]
   d) How will we be able to tell if the scientists who predict global warming are correct? [2]
   [Total 5]

2 Many scientists think that increasing levels of carbon dioxide will result in global warming.
   a) By how much did the average temperature rise during

3 What do you think we should do to prevent global warming? [3]

Fuels: reducing the problems

Problems of using fossil fuels

Burning fossil fuels has become essential for modern life – however, it is not without its problems. Firstly, they are non-renewable and will run out sometime. Crude oil, from which petrol and diesel are separated, will run out during your lifetime if we continue to burn it at the current rate. It is not **sustainable** to keep burning fossil fuels. Secondly, burning fossil fuels produces substances that harm our planet. Table 6.4 summarises these substances and suggests some ways in which their problems can be reduced.

In each case, one possible answer is to burn fewer fossil fuels. One way of achieving this is to become more energy-efficient. Much energy is wasted at the moment and if we reduce this amount then fewer fossil fuels would have to be burned.

Figure 6.9 *Huge quantities of fossil fuels are burned for providing warmth, generating electricity and powering cars.*

Substance	Main problem caused	Ways to reduce the problem
carbon dioxide (CO_2)	global warming	• burn fewer fossil fuels
carbon monoxide (CO)	toxic gas	• burn fewer fossil fuels • ensure that there is a good supply of oxygen when the fuel is burned • use catalytic converters in car exhausts
carbon/ soot (C)	blackens buildings	• burn fewer fossil fuels • ensure that there is a good supply of oxygen when the fuel is burned
sulphur dioxide (SO_2)	causes acid rain	• burn fewer fossil fuels • remove sulphur from fuel before burning • flue-gas desulphurising systems in power stations remove sulphur dioxide before the waste gases are released
nitrogen oxides (NO, NO_2)	causes acid rain	• burn fewer fossil fuels • use catalytic converters in car exhausts

Table 6.4 *The products of burning fossil fuels.*

Alternative fuels

We must also look for alternative fuels and energy sources that do not cause these problems. There are several alternative energy sources – including wind, nuclear, solar and hydroelectric power. There are also several possible alternative fuels such as **biofuels**. Biofuels are fuels made from plants and are **carbon neutral**. Some alternative fuels are listed in Table 6.5, along with benefits and drawbacks of each one.

There are many countries around the world that are committed to cutting carbon dioxide emissions and using alternative energy sources and fuels. As technology improves, these alternatives, along with those still to be developed, will become cheaper and replace the use of fossil fuels.

A person's 'carbon footprint' is the amount of carbon dioxide produced by all their activities – heating their home, getting from one place to another, buying a loaf of bread, using a plastic bag etc.

Fuel		Benefits	Drawbacks
biofuels	bioethanol	• renewable (made from sugar) • carbon neutral	if large quantities of this fuel are used, massive amounts of farm land are needed to grow enough sugar crops to make it
	biodiesel	• renewable (made from vegetable oils, e.g. rapeseed oil) • carbon neutral	if large quantities of this fuel are used, massive amounts of farm land are needed to grow enough vegetable oil crops to make it
hydrogen		• the only waste product is water	it is used in fuel cells, which are expensive to produce at present

Table 6.5 *Alternative fuels.*

Questions

1 a) Why is the continued burning of fossil fuels damaging to the environment? [2]

b) Why is the continued burning of fossil fuels not sustainable? [1]

[Total 3]

2 What three things could be done to reduce the amount of fossil fuels that are burned? [Total 3]

3 a) What are biofuels? [1]

b) Give two advantages of biofuels. [2]

c) Give one disadvantage of biofuels. [1]

[Total 4]

4 a) List the things that you believe governments should do to reduce the amount of fossil fuels burned. [3]

b) List all the things that you can do personally to reduce the amount of fossil fuels burned. [3]

[Total 6]

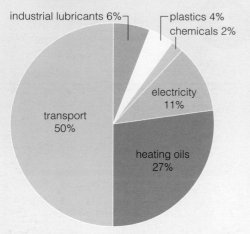

Figure 6.11 *The uses of crude oil.*

Uses of crude oil

Crude oil is one of the most important and valuable natural resources on the planet. It is separated at oil refineries into more useful substances (fractions) such as liquefied petroleum gases (LPG), petrol, diesel, kerosene and fuel oil. At present, almost 90% of crude oil is burned for transportation, heating or generating electricity.

Crude oil is likely to run out in your lifetime, yet it has so many other uses that are very important to modern life. Examples of other substances made from crude oil include plastics (e.g. polythene), clothing fabrics (e.g. polyesters), medicines (e.g. aspirin), paints, detergents, solvents and explosives. Some of the fractions are used as lubricants (e.g. engine oil).

Polymer/ plastic	Common name	Properties	Uses	Examples
poly(ethene)	polythene	flexible	bags, cling film	
poly(propene)	polypropene	flexible	crisp packets, carpets	
poly(chloroethene)	PVC	tough	window frames, gutters, pipes, electrical cable coatings	
poly(tetrafluoroethene)	Teflon/ PTFE	tough, slippery	frying pan coatings, stain proof carpets	
poly(methyl 2-methylpropenoate)	Perspex	tough, hard, clear	shatter-proof windows	

Table 6.6 *Common plastics and their uses.*

By the time crude oil runs out, alternative ways of making these substances will be needed. There are ways of doing this – for example from coal – but it is not as easy.

The main type of product made from crude oil is plastics. **Plastics** are used to make so many things that we use in modern life – Table 6.6 gives some examples of plastics and their uses.

Disposal of plastics

We produce more than 5 million tonnes of plastic each year in the UK. One big problem with the use of plastics is their disposal – there are three common ways of disposing of rubbish: bury it in landfill, burn it in an incinerator or recycle it.

Over 70% of the rubbish in the UK is buried in the ground at landfill sites. This is very easy to do, but a lot of land is being used up and it is not sustainable to keep on doing this. Also, most plastics are not biodegradable, which means they do not decay away over time. This means the plastics will still be buried in the ground thousands of years from now. Some new plastics are being made that are **biodegradable**.

Another common disposal method is to burn waste plastics in an incinerator. This avoids the problems of landfill and modern incinerators are cleaner producing less waste gases. However, they do still produce some carbon dioxide which is a greenhouse gas.

The third way is to recycle plastics. This can be done by melting down waste plastic and re-moulding into new products. However, there are many different types of plastics and they have to be separated before they are melted down – this takes time and is therefore expensive. The cost could be reduced by getting the public to separate plastics when they recycle them. This could be done using the small number stamped on most plastics showing which type they are.

1 What is the main use of the chemicals in crude oil? [Total 1]

2 What other substances are made from the chemicals in crude oil? [Total 4]

3 Why are shatterproof windows made from Perspex? [Total 2]

4 Which property of Teflon makes if suitable for the coating inside frying pans? [Total 1]

Figure 6.12 *The symbol for poly(propene).*

Questions

1 Most of the chemicals from crude oil are burned. Do you think this is a good use of them? Explain your answer. [Total 2]

2 Plastics are very useful materials that have improved modern life – what is the problem with using so much plastic? [Total 1]

3 Make a table to show the three ways in which plastics are disposed of. Your table should describe what each method does, and give some advantages and disadvantages. [Total 9]

4 Some new plastics are being made that are biodegradable. Explain what this means and why it is useful. [Total 2]

End of section questions

1 a) Briefly explain how you could distinguish:
   i) an igneous rock from a metamorphic rock
   ii) an igneous rock from a sedimentary rock
   iii) a sedimentary rock from a metamorphic rock. *[3]*
   b) Figure 1 shows four rocks. Decide whether each one is an igneous, sedimentary or metamorphic rock. *[4]*
   [Total 7]

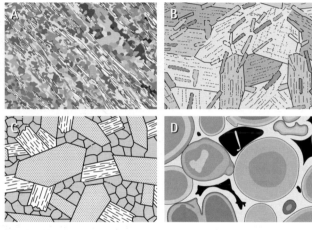

Figure 1

2 Look at Figure 2 and put the events that formed it into the correct order.
   A mudstone formed
   B sandstone folded
   C sandstone weathered and eroded
   D volcano formed
   E sandstone formed   *[Total 4]*

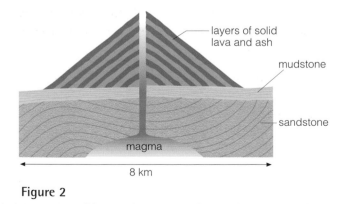

Figure 2

3 Study Figure 3 which shows a rock face and then answer the questions in as much detail as you can.

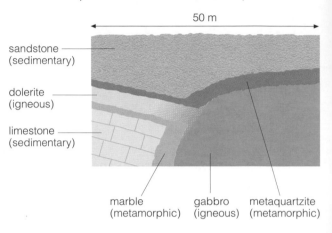

Figure 3

a) Name the three main groups of rock. *[3]*
b) Gabbro and dolerite are igneous rocks. Explain how they were formed. *[2]*
c) i) How will the appearance of the dolerite and gabbro differ?
   ii) Explain why their appearance is different. *[4]*
d) Limestone and sandstone are sedimentary rocks. Explain how they were formed. *[2]*
e) Marble and metaquartzite are metamorphic rocks. Explain how they were formed. *[2]*
f) Name one more example each of an igneous, sedimentary and metamorphic rock. *[3]*
   [Total 16]

4 a) Describe how coal was formed. *[4]*
   b) Explain why coal is classed as sedimentary rock. *[2]*
   [Total 6]

5 Write word equations to show what happens when the following substances are burned in air:
   a) calcium *[1]*
   b) phosphine (PH_3) *[1]*
   c) butane (C_4H_{10}). *[1]*
   [Total 3]

6 The pie chart in Figure 4 shows the gases in dry air.

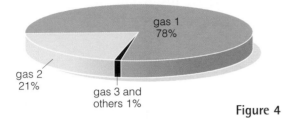

gas 1
78%

gas 2
21%

gas 3 and
others 1%

Figure 4

a) Give the name and formula of gases 1, 2 and 3. *[6]*
b) One of the other gases in the air is only present in trace quantities, but is thought to be causing the greenhouse effect. Give the name and formula of this gas. *[2]*

[Total 8]

7 a) Natural gas (methane, CH_4) is burned in a Bunsen burner. When you heat glassware you should have the air hole open. This lets more air mix with the methane.
 i) What colour is the flame when the air hole is open?
 ii) Write a word equation for the burning of methane with the air hole open. *[2]*
b) You should not heat glassware with the air hole closed because the glass blackens.
 i) What colour is the flame when the air hole is closed?
 ii) Explain why the glassware blackens.
 iii) Write a word equation for the burning of methane with the air hole closed. *[4]*

[Total 6]

8 a) Is crude oil a pure substance? Explain your answer. *[2]*
b) The fractions separated from crude oil are mainly used as fuels. Name the fraction used as fuel for each of the following:
 i) aeroplanes
 ii) lorries
 iii) cars. *[3]*

[Total 5]

9 Kerosene is one of the fractions produced in the fractional distillation of crude oil.
a) Describe how crude oil was formed. *[4]*
b) What does crude oil consist of? *[1]*
c) What is a hydrocarbon? *[2]*
d) Explain how the kerosene fraction is separated from crude oil. *[3]*
e) Write a word equation to show what happens when kerosene is burned. *[1]*

[Total 11]

10 P Magma is molten rock. What factors might affect how well magma flows. For example, how would you investigate the effect of changing the temperature of magma on how well it flows? You cannot use real magma, but syrup is a good liquid to use in its place.

11 P If a glass jar is placed over a candle, the candle burns for a short time and then goes out. What factors might affect how long a candle burns inside a glass jar. For example, how would you investigate the effect of changing the size of the jar on how long the candle burns?

12 R The Earth has a crust, mantle and core. We have never dug down below the crust, so how do we know? Find out how scientists have investigated the structure of the Earth.

13 R Find out about six renewable energy sources. Find out how they work and their main advantages and disadvantages.

14 R Power stations that burn fossil fuels have taken steps to reduce sulphur dioxide pollution. Find out about the methods that they use to do this.

5.1 Properties and uses of metals

What makes metals so valuable and useful? Thousands of years ago humans used metals like copper and iron to make weapons and tools. These metals are still in use today and are just as important as they were to early humans.

Physical properties of metals

Metals are among our most important resources. Most of the elements in the Periodic Table are metals and they have a wide variety of uses. The five most-used metals, in decreasing order of use, are iron, aluminium, copper, zinc and manganese. However, lead, magnesium, chromium, nickel and many others are just as important to our everyday lives.

The general **physical properties** of metals are:

- hard and strong
- solids (only mercury is a liquid at room temperature)
- shiny (when polished)
- good **conductors of heat**
- good **conductors of electricity**
- dense (have a high **density**)
- **malleable** and **ductile**.

These properties make metals suitable for a large number of uses. However, some metals are better than others in a particular situation.

- Copper, silver and gold are good conductors of electricity and are ductile, which means they can be drawn out into wires. This is why copper is used in electrical cables and circuits, and gold and silver are sometimes used for electrical contacts.
- Iron and steel are both hard and strong. Therefore, they are used to construct bridges, buildings and motor cars. Iron is by far the most useful metal and makes up over 90% of all metal production. The main disadvantage of using iron is that it tends to rust.
- Aluminium is a good conductor of heat and is malleable. It is used to make saucepans and thin cooking foil. It is also used to make aeroplanes, because it is a low density metal.
- Gold and silver are malleable, ductile, shiny and unreactive. They are used to make intricate jewellery which keeps its good looks and does not tarnish.

(The properties of substances are described in detail in subsection 2.1.)

1 Describe the differences in properties between a wooden spoon and a spoon made of silver.
[Total 4]

Pure gold is not hard enough to be used in jewellery, so an alloy of gold and copper is generally used. The purity of the gold is measured in carats. 24 carat represents pure gold. Jewellery is usually made from 18 carat gold, which is 75% gold and 25% copper.

Figure 1.1 *Uses of metals.*

Alloys

Mixing a metal with one or more other elements can change its properties. A mixture of a metal with other elements is called an **alloy**. The properties of a metal are often improved by mixing, and alloys have many important uses. The properties of some alloys are given in Table 1.1.

2 What are alloys and why are they important?

[Total 2]

Table 1.1

Alloy	Mixture of metals	Improved properties	Uses
steel	iron and carbon plus other metals	stronger than pure iron	girders for buildings, car bodies
solder	tin and lead	lower melting point than pure metals	connecting electrical circuits
duralumin	aluminium and copper	lighter than copper, stronger than aluminium	aeroplane bodies, alloy wheels

Chemical properties of metals

Metals are found on the left-hand side of the Periodic Table. We usually recognise metals by their physical properties. However, most metals have similar **chemical properties** as well. The most important chemical reactions of metals are with oxygen, water and acids, which are common substances found in nature. Although the chemical properties of metals are similar, they do not all react in exactly the same way.

Metals and oxygen

Many substances on the Earth's surface, including metals, will react with the oxygen in the air. The shiny surface of most metals becomes dull in time. This is caused by a slow chemical reaction between the metal surface and oxygen. The reaction forms just one product, a surface coating of the metal oxide. A general word equation can be written for the reaction of metals and oxygen:

metal + oxygen → metal oxide

For example, the dull appearance of the metal lead is due to a coating of lead oxide. The word equation is:

lead + oxygen → lead oxide

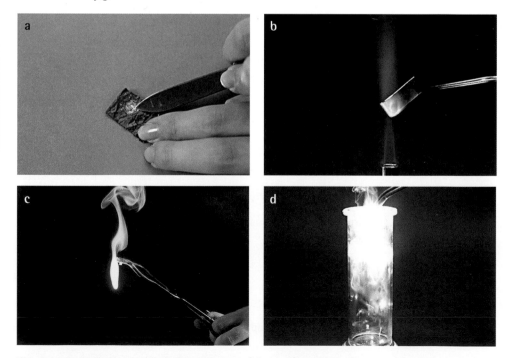

Figure 1.2 *Metals reacting with oxygen: a) lead; b) copper; c) magnesium in air; d) magnesium in oxygen.*

3 What is the difference between a chemical property and a physical property? *[Total 2]*

The bright light of shooting stars and the sparks in sparklers are both produced by the reaction of iron with oxygen. Fine iron powder is used to make sparklers, and shooting stars are tiny meteorites, which are lumps of iron from space.

4 Write a word equation for the reaction which occurs when aluminium is burned in oxygen. *[Total 3]*

If the surface is scratched then the shiny lead metal can be seen underneath.

Heating can speed up the reaction with oxygen. If a piece of copper is heated, it quickly becomes coated in black copper oxide. The word equation is:

copper + oxygen → copper oxide

Some metals will burn in air. For example, magnesium burns brightly and is used in flash bulbs and distress flares. This reaction is even faster if the burning metal is placed in a gas jar of pure oxygen. The word equation is:

magnesium + oxygen → magnesium oxide

Only a few metals, like gold and platinum, are unaffected by heating in air. These very unreactive metals do not form compounds easily with any other element. Gold and platinum are ideal for making into jewellery because they don't react with oxygen and so stay shiny.

Metals and water

Most materials on the Earth's surface will at some time come into contact with water. Metals react with water in different ways. A few metals, like potassium, sodium and calcium, are so reactive that they will react quickly with cold water. The reactions can be quite violent and always make two products, a metal hydroxide and hydrogen gas. The general word equation is:

metal + water → metal hydroxide + hydrogen

The reaction of sodium with water produces enough heat energy to melt the metal. Round globules of liquid sodium move about the surface of the water, propelled by the hydrogen gas that is formed during the reaction. The word equation is:

sodium + water → sodium hydroxide + hydrogen

> **!** If mercury is absorbed into the body it can cause brain damage. The phrase 'mad as a hatter' originated from the health problems caused by the use of mercury in the manufacture of top hats.

> **!** Potassium, sodium and lithium are the only metals that are less dense than water and so are the only metals that float on water. However, it would not be a good idea to make a ship out of them!

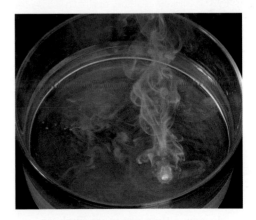

Figure 1.3 *Potassium reacting with cold water.*

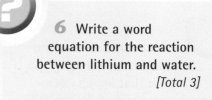

5 Why is the reaction between potassium and water carried out in a glass trough? [Total 2]

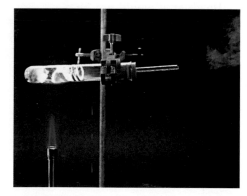

6 Write a word equation for the reaction between lithium and water. [Total 3]

Figure 1.4 *Magnesium reacting with steam.*

Accidents at nuclear power stations are very rare. However, if explosions do occur they are more likely to be caused by hydrogen, produced when steam accidentally reacts with metals, than by a nuclear reaction.

The reaction of potassium and water is even more violent. In this case, the heat given out ignites the hydrogen gas, and the metal appears to burn. Lilac flames shoot out, as the metal travels across the surface of the water. The word equation is:

potassium + water → potassium hydroxide + hydrogen

The same type of reaction occurs with calcium, but it is less violent.

Metals like potassium and sodium are so reactive that they are stored under oil. This prevents them coming in contact with water and oxygen, and so they keep longer.

Heating the water, to produce steam, can speed up the reaction with metals. Some metals that don't appear to react with cold water react violently with steam. When metals react with steam a slightly different reaction takes place, producing a metal oxide and hydrogen gas. The general word equation is:

metal + steam (water) → metal oxide + hydrogen

If a cleaned piece of magnesium ribbon is placed in water, it reacts slowly. After a while, bubbles of hydrogen gas can be seen forming on the magnesium. However a violent reaction takes place between magnesium ribbon and steam. The word equation is:

magnesium + steam → magnesium oxide + hydrogen

Aluminium, zinc and iron also react with steam, but not as quickly as magnesium.

Lead, copper, mercury, silver, gold and platinum do not react with water or steam. For this reason copper is a good choice of metal for hot water pipes, because it does not react with boiling water and is cheaper than the other metals that do not react.

Metals and acids

Acids are found in many places in our environment and are in everyday use in industry and the home. Most metals react with dilute acids. The reaction forms two products, a salt and hydrogen. A general word equation can be written for the reaction of metals with acids:

acid + metal → salt + hydrogen

For example, when magnesium metal is added to sulphuric acid, the metal reacts and bubbles of hydrogen gas are produced. A salt called magnesium sulphate is also formed, which is dissolved in the water. The presence of hydrogen can be confirmed because it 'pops' if a lighted splint is brought near. The word equation is:

magnesium + sulphuric acid → magnesium sulphate + hydrogen

Other metals like zinc, iron, nickel, tin and lead all react with dilute acids. Some react faster than others, but they all produce a salt and hydrogen gas.

Zinc reacts fairly slowly with dilute sulphuric acid, producing bubbles of hydrogen gas. As the zinc slowly disappears, a solution of zinc sulphate is formed. The word equation is:

zinc + sulphuric acid → zinc sulphate + hydrogen

Iron reacts very slowly with dilute sulphuric acid, producing some bubbles of hydrogen gas. Iron sulphate is formed in solution, but even a small piece of iron would take a long time to react completely. The word equation is:

iron + sulphuric acid → iron sulphate + hydrogen

The formation of salts is dealt with in detail in subsection 3.3.

A few metals like copper, mercury, silver, gold and platinum do not react with most dilute acids.

Potassium and sodium, which react quickly with cold water, are too dangerous to react with dilute acids. This is because their reactions would be so fast that they could cause explosions.

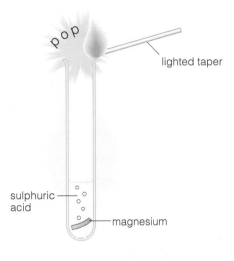

Figure 1.5 *Reaction of magnesium and sulphuric acid.*

7 Write a word equation for the reaction between lead and nitric acid. *[Total 3]*

Liquid sodium and potassium, two of the most reactive metals, are used as a coolant in some nuclear reactors.

Summary

- The main physical properties of metals are that they are strong, hard, shiny, good conductors of heat and electricity, malleable and ductile, and have high densities.
- Alloys are metals mixed with one or more other elements, to improve their properties.
- Many metals react with oxygen, water and acids.
- Metal + oxygen → metal oxide.
- Metal + water → metal hydroxide + hydrogen.
- Metal + steam → metal oxide + hydrogen.
- Metal + acid → salt + hydrogen.

Questions

1 Copy and complete the following sentences.
An alloy is a _____ mixed with other _____. Metals are generally strong, hard and good conductors of _____ and _____. Most _____ react with _____ to produce metal oxides.

[Total 3]

2 Explain the following by referring to the properties of the metals.
a) Hot water pipes are made out of copper. *[1]*
b) Steel is used to make kitchen sinks and car bodies. *[1]*
c) Aluminium is used to make aircraft bodies. *[1]*
d) Electrical cables are made of copper. *[1]*

[Total 4]

3 Copy and complete the following word equations for the reactions of metals:
a) calcium + water → _____ + _____ *[2]*
b) sodium + oxygen → _____ *[1]*

c) aluminium + steam → _____ + _____ *[2]*
d) nickel + sulphuric acid → _____ + _____ *[2]*

[Total 7]

4 Describe two ways in which you could speed up the reaction of a metal with air. *[Total 2]*

5 Briefly explain each of the following.
a) The metal potassium is stored under oil. *[2]*
b) If a piece of sodium metal is cut with a knife, the shiny metal at the cut soon goes dull. *[2]*

[Total 4]

6 Write word equations to fit the following descriptions of the reactions of metals.
a) Cleaned aluminium foil reacts with nitric acid producing a gas. *[2]*
b) Small pieces of barium metal react quickly with cold water. *[2]*
c) When nickel is heated in air its surface changes colour. *[2]*

[Total 6]

5.2 The reactivity series

How do metals differ in their reactivity? Not all metals react with oxygen, water and acids and some metals react faster than others under the same conditions. These differences in the way metals react can be used to develop a reactivity series of metals. This reactivity series can be extremely useful to chemists.

The reactivity series

The reactions of metals with oxygen, water and acids show a pattern in the reactivity of the metals. Observing how quickly different metals react can be used to place them in an order of reactivity. The list of metals in order of how quickly they react is called the **reactivity series**.

Figure 2.1 shows the reactions of five different metals with dilute sulphuric acid. The metals used are calcium, magnesium, zinc, iron and lead. To make the test fair, the same volume and concentration of acid is used in each test tube, and all the metals are the same form and size. The order of reactivity can be found by observing the rate at which bubbles of hydrogen gas are produced.

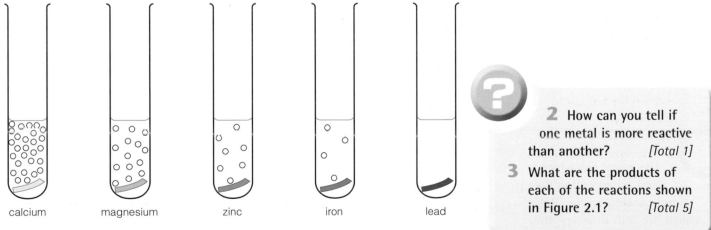

calcium   magnesium   zinc   iron   lead

Figure 2.1 *Which metal reacts fastest?*

This experiment allows us to form a reactivity series for these metals.

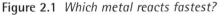

calcium	most reactive (fastest formation of gas)
magnesium	
zinc	
iron	
lead	least reactive (no visible reaction)

?

1 Write general word equations for three different reactions of metals. *[Total 3]*

?

2 How can you tell if one metal is more reactive than another? *[Total 1]*

3 What are the products of each of the reactions shown in Figure 2.1? *[Total 5]*

Further experiments, using a range of metals, can be used to construct a larger reactivity series. Table 2.1 lists the metals in order of reactivity, and includes a summary of their main reactions.

Table 2.1

Reactivity series	Reaction with water	Reaction with dilute acids	Reaction with oxygen
↑ potassium sodium calcium	react quickly with cold water		
R E A C T I V I T Y magnesium aluminium zinc iron nickel tin	react quickly with steam but react slowly with cold water	react with dilute acids	react with oxygen
lead copper mercury silver gold platinum	do not react with cold water or steam	do not react with dilute acids	do not react with oxygen

Displacement reactions of metals

The reactivity series can be used to make predictions about other reactions of metals. For example, a chemical reaction occurs when an iron nail is placed in a solution of copper sulphate. The main evidence that a chemical change has taken place is that the nail becomes coated with copper metal.

!

The metal foil which is used for wrapping sweets and cooking is sometimes called 'tin foil'. However, this foil is actually made of aluminium, which is a much cheaper metal.

This is called a **displacement reaction**. The copper is displaced (pushed out) from the copper sulphate solution, and the iron replaces it. Copper metal and iron sulphate are produced. The equation for this reaction is:

iron + copper sulphate → copper + iron sulphate

Similar reactions can occur using other metals and salt solutions, depending on the position of the metals in The reactivity series. Displacement reactions only occur when the metal being added is more reactive than the metal in the salt solution.

Consider the following series of displacement experiments. Small metal pieces were placed in a dimple tray and solutions of the salts were added. The metals and solutions were then observed to see if a reaction would occur.

The results of the experiments are shown in Table 2.2. A ✓ shows where displacement occurred and a ✗ indicates where there was no reaction.

Figure 2.2 *Iron displaces copper from solution.*

Table 2.2 *Displacement reactions.*

Metal	Salt solution				
	magnesium nitrate	iron nitrate	lead nitrate	copper nitrate	silver nitrate
magnesium	✗	✓	✓	✓	✓
iron	✗	✗	✓	✓	✓
lead	✗	✗	✗	✓	✓
copper	✗	✗	✗	✗	✓
silver	✗	✗	✗	✗	✗

?

4 Name three metals which react only very slowly with cold water but would react with iron chloride solution. [Total 3]

5 Write a word equation for the reaction between tin metal and lead nitrate solution. [Total 3]

Silver coins, like the 5, 10, 20 and 50 pence pieces, contain no silver. They are actually made from an alloy of copper and nickel. The alloy is silver in colour, but it is harder wearing and cheaper than silver.

The experiments clearly show a pattern that can be used to confirm the order of metals in the reactivity series. A reaction only occurs when the metal being added is higher in the reactivity series than the metal in the salt.

For example, magnesium can displace iron from iron nitrate solution because magnesium is more reactive than iron. The word equation is:

magnesium + iron nitrate → iron + magnesium nitrate

However, iron cannot displacc magnesium from magnesium nitrate solution because iron is a less reactive metal.

Displacement of metal oxides

Not all displacement reactions involve solutions of metal salts. Metals can also be displaced from solid metal oxides.

If a mixture of powdered zinc and copper oxide is heated, a violent reaction occurs. The zinc displaces the copper producing zinc oxide and copper metal. The equation for this reaction is:

zinc + copper oxide → copper + zinc oxide

This reaction occurs because zinc is more reactive than copper. However, copper cannot displace zinc from zinc oxide because copper is less reactive than zinc.

Figure 2.3 *Using the Thermit reaction to join rails together.*

A well known example of this type of displacement involves the reaction between powdered aluminium and iron oxide. Once started this reaction is very fast and gives out lots of heat which keeps the iron molten. Molten iron and aluminium oxide are formed. The equation for this reaction is:

aluminium + iron oxide → iron + aluminium oxide

This is called the **Thermit reaction**, and it is used in industry to produce small quantities of molten iron at high temperatures. Figure 2.3 shows the reaction being used to weld (join) two railway lines together. The heat produced by the reaction is so great that it melts the ends of the rails and forms a strong joint.

The decomposition of metal carbonates

Heating can be used to break down compounds. For example, when green copper carbonate powder is heated, it breaks down to form black copper oxide and carbon dioxide gas. The equation for this reaction is:

copper carbonate → copper oxide + carbon dioxide

Certain metals give distinctive colours to a flame. For example, potassium gives a lilac flame, while copper is green and strontium is red. The presence of compounds of these metals give fireworks their bright colours.

This is a **decomposition reaction** because the copper carbonate is broken down. Most metal carbonates break down when heated to produce similar products. A general equation can be written for the decomposition:

$$\text{metal carbonate} \xrightarrow{\text{heat energy}} \text{metal oxide} + \text{carbon dioxide}$$

The experiment shown in Figure 2.5 can be used to compare the stability of different metal carbonates.

The **limewater** turns cloudy when carbon dioxide gas is released. How easily a carbonate decomposes can be measured by how quickly the limewater turns cloudy. If a series of metal carbonates is tested, they can be placed in order of their stability.

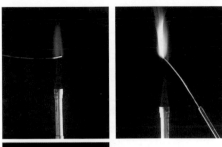

Figure 2.4 *Flame tests: potassium (lilac), copper (green) and strontium (red).*

Most stable
does not
decompose ⟶ sodium carbonate
calcium carbonate
magnesium carbonate
zinc carbonate
Least stable
decomposes
easily ⟶ lead carbonate
copper carbonate

increasing ease of decomposition

decreasing stability of carbonate

The results of these experiments show that there is a link between the reactivity series and the stability of the carbonates. The most reactive metals form the most stable carbonates. Indeed the most reactive metal carbonates do not break down at all, at the temperature produced by a Bunsen burner.

This is a general rule for all metal compounds. The more reactive the metal, the harder it is to break down its compounds. The less reactive the metal, the more easily its compounds decompose.

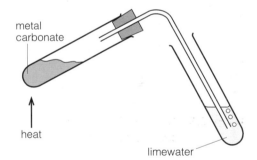

metal carbonate

heat

limewater

Figure 2.5 *Decomposing metal carbonates.*

Using the reactivity series

It is sometimes difficult to compare the reactivity of metals by using their reactions with oxygen, water and acids. Using displacement reactions is the easiest way to produce the reactivity series. The reactivity series is particularly useful to chemists because it can be used to make predictions about how metals will react in different situations.

Remembering the reactivity series

You can use a phrase to help you to remember the reactivity series. Here is one example, where all the capital letters stand for the first letter of the metals in the order of the reactivity series.

Police **S**ergeant **C**harlie **MAZINTL** **C**aught **M**e **S**tealing **G**old **P**late.

Copper was the most used metal in ancient Egypt and it has been estimated that the Egyptians used about 6 tonnes of copper each year. Today, iron is our favourite metal and we use about 600 million tonnes of the metal every year.

6 Titanium metal can be produced by heating titanium chloride with magnesium.
a) What is this type of reaction called? [1]
b) What does this tell you about titanium's place in the reactivity series compared to magnesium? [1]
c) What could you do to find out its exact position in the reactivity series? [2]

[Total 4]

potassium
sodium
calcium
magnesium
aluminium
zinc
iron
nickel
tin
lead
copper
mercury
silver
gold
platinum

In general:

- the reactions of the metals gets stronger and faster as we go up The reactivity series.
- metals higher up the series can displace metals lower down from their compounds.
- compounds of metals higher up the series are more stable than compounds of metals lower down.

Summary

- The reactions of metals with oxygen, water and acids can be used to produce a reactivity series.
- The reactivity series can be used to make predictions about other reactions of metals.
- A more reactive metal can displace a less reactive metal from its compounds.
- Decomposition reactions involve breaking down compounds.
- Most metal carbonates decompose on heating to form a metal oxide and carbon dioxide.
- The more reactive a metal, the more stable its compounds.

Questions

1 Copy and complete the following sentences.
Nickel is between _____ and _____
in the middle of the reactivity series.
A _____ reactive metal can displace a
_____ reactive metal from its
_____. The most stable metal compounds are
formed from the _____ reactive metals.

[Total 3]

2 Write one sentence for each of the following phrases
to explain what each means:
a) reactivity series   *[2]*
b) decomposition reaction.   *[2]*

[Total 4]

3 Rearrange the following list of metals in order of
the reactivity series. Start the list with the most
reactive metal.

iron   magnesium   mercury   zinc   aluminium
sodium   silver   calcium   *[Total 2]*

4 Copy and complete the following reaction equations.
Write 'no reaction' if nothing happens.
a) iron + lead oxide →   *[1]*
b) zinc + nickel sulphate →   *[1]*
c) mercury + lead chloride →   *[1]*
d) magnesium + copper nitrate →   *[1]*

[Total 4]

5 The Thermit reaction is used in the construction of
railway tracks. The reactants in this reaction are
aluminium powder and iron oxide.
a) What does the Thermit reaction produce?   *[2]*
b) Write a word equation for this reaction.   *[1]*
c) What is the chemical name for this type
   of reaction?   *[1]*
d) What would happen if powdered tin was used
   in place of the aluminium? Briefly explain
   your answer.   *[2]*

[Total 6]

6 Imagine that a new metal called dorobium was
discovered, and that the metal was found to lie
between potassium and sodium in the reactivity
series.
a) How should dorobium be stored?   *[1]*
b) Describe the reaction of dorobium with cold
   water and name the products formed.   *[3]*

[Total 4]

7 If a piece of heated magnesium is put into a gas jar
of chlorine, it burns brightly. However, a piece of
heated nickel just changes colour in chlorine gas.
Predict what would happen if heated pieces of the
following metals were placed in gas jars of chlorine:
a) sodium   *[1]*
b) tin   *[1]*
c) platinum.   *[1]*

[Total 3]

8 You are given some pieces of an unknown metal X
and the following apparatus and chemicals:
droppers   dimple tray   solutions of:
iron nitrate, zinc nitrate, nickel nitrate and tin nitrate.
The metal X is thought to be iron, zinc, nickel or tin.
Describe how you could use the given apparatus and
chemicals to discover the identity of metal X. *[Total 3]*

9 Look at the phrase at the bottom of page 151. Make
up your own phrase to help you remember the
reactivity series.   *[Total 2]*

5.3 Finding and extracting metals

Where do all the different metals come from? Rocks that contain metals are among our most valuable natural resources. Finding these special rocks and extracting metals has been an important part of chemistry for many years.

Metals and metal ores

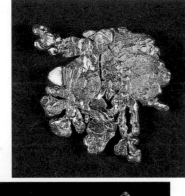

Figure 3.1 *Native gold and silver.*

Small pieces of gold can be found naturally uncombined (as the element) in the ground. For this reason gold has been known and used for thousands of years. Metals that are found free or uncombined in nature are called **native** metals. They are found as elements because they are very unreactive. Platinum and silver are two other metals that can be found in a native state.

Most metals are found in compounds and are not native. This is because they are more reactive and so react with substances around them. For example, most metals react with oxygen and sulphur, forming metal oxides and sulphides.

Rocks from which metals can be extracted are called **ores**. These rocks are not usually pure substances, but are a mixture of compounds. The most common ores usually contain an oxide, sulphide or carbonate of the metal and these compounds have to be broken down to extract the metal.

In 1578 a British ship, on an expedition to Baffin Island, brought back over 1000 tonnes of a shiny yellow mineral that looked like gold. Unfortunately it was not – it was fool's gold which is actually an ore of iron. The ore is called iron pyrites and it is mainly made up of iron sulphide.

Galena

Bauxite

Malachite

Haematite

Cinnabar

Figure 3.2 *Common metal ores.*

Some common examples of ores are:

- haematite, an ore of iron, is mainly iron oxide
- bauxite, an ore of aluminium, is mainly aluminium oxide
- galena, an ore of lead, is mainly lead sulphide
- cinnabar, an ore of mercury, is mainly mercury sulphide
- malachite, an ore of copper, is mainly copper carbonate
- limestone, an ore of calcium, is mainly calcium carbonate.

There are two basic steps involved in obtaining a metal from its ore:

- mining and collecting the ore
- **decomposition** of the compounds in the ore to release the metal.

Extracting metals from ores

The extraction of a metal from its ore involves a chemical reaction to release the metal from its compounds. The more reactive metals form the most stable compounds which are hardest to break down. This explains why the least reactive metals were the first metals to be extracted in large quantities. For example, copper can be extracted from its ore malachite by heating in a charcoal fire. After gold and silver, copper was one of the first metals to be used. Other methods had to be found to decompose the ores of more reactive metals.

The extraction of a metal from its ore is an example of a decomposition reaction. However, it can also be described as a **reduction** reaction, because the ore is **reduced** (broken down) to release the metal. During reduction, the elements combined with the metal are removed and the metal is left free. Many ores are oxides so this means removing oxygen to release the metal.

There are three main methods, that can be used to reduce metal ores and extract metals:

- heat alone
- heat with carbon
- electrolysis.

The industrial process chosen to extract a particular metal has to be the most economic. Therefore, the method used will be the one which works, and is least expensive.

Micro-organisms extract 10% of all the copper produced in the USA. Bacteria like *Thiobacillus ferro-oxidans* obtain the energy they need for life by reducing the copper ore, chalcopyryte, to copper. Extracting copper by this method is much cleaner and cheaper than using other industrial methods.

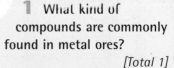

1 What kind of compounds are commonly found in metal ores?
[Total 1]
2 Which factors help in deciding how metals are extracted from their ores?
[Total 2]

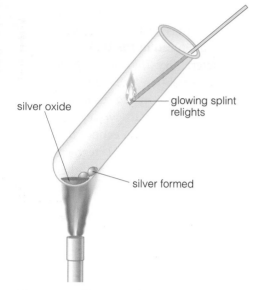

silver oxide

glowing splint relights

silver formed

Figure 3.3 *Decomposing silver oxide.*

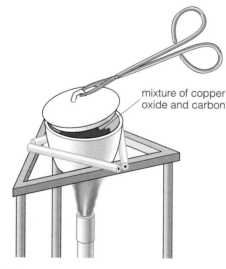

mixture of copper oxide and carbon

Figure 3.4 *Extraction of copper by heating with carbon.*

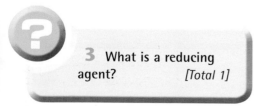

3 What is a reducing agent? [Total 1]

Extraction by heat alone

Heat alone can reduce some of the least stable metal ores to release the metal. Only the least reactive metals can be extracted using this method. For example silver is often found in an ore which contains silver oxide. If it is heated it is reduced, and silver metal and oxygen gas are formed. The reduction of silver oxide is shown in Figure 3.3.

Beads of silver metal can be seen at the bottom of the test tube and the formation of oxygen can be shown as it relights a glowing splint. The word equation is:

heat energy

silver oxide → silver + oxygen

Mercury and silver are usually extracted by **thermal decomposition**. These are two of the less reactive metals, which are found near the bottom of the reactivity series. However, many metal oxides cannot be decomposed by heat alone, and other methods have to be used to extract the metal.

Extraction by heating with carbon

Many ores are metal oxides, and most others can be converted to their oxides by roasting in air. Heating a metal oxide with carbon is another method that can be used to extract metals.

For example, if copper oxide is heated with carbon powder, the oxide is reduced, forming copper metal and carbon dioxide gas. The word equation is:

heat energy

copper oxide + carbon → copper + carbon dioxide

The carbon acts as a **reducing agent**, taking the oxygen away from the metal. The carbon and oxygen combine to form carbon dioxide, and the metal is left free. This is a reduction reaction, because the metal oxide is reduced to release the metal.

Zinc, iron, nickel, tin, lead and copper are usually extracted by heating with carbon. These are metals of moderate reactivity, which are found in the middle of the reactivity series. The reaction is similar to the displacement of a metal from one of its compounds, which was dealt with in the last subsection. Carbon is more reactive than these metals and so can displace them from their oxides.

Extraction by electrolysis

Passing electricity through a molten ore will split up the compound, and so extract the metal. This process is called **electrolysis**. The electrical energy decomposes the compounds and reduces the ore.

For example, aluminium is extracted by the electrolysis of molten bauxite, which consists mainly of aluminium oxide. During electrolysis, the ore is reduced, aluminium forms at the negative electrode and oxygen is produced at the positive electrode.

Copper was probably discovered by chance when people were making coloured vases. 5000 years ago potters used glazes containing coloured copper compounds. These could have been accidentally reduced to copper by the carbon in the fires.

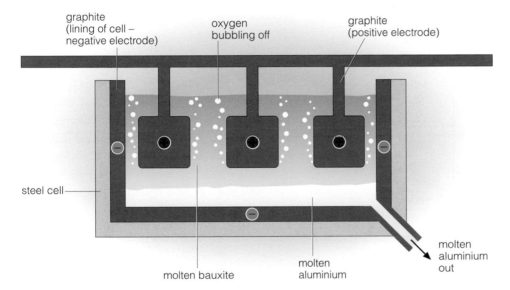

Figure 3.5 *Extraction of aluminium by electrolysis.*

The reduction reaction involves breaking up the aluminium oxide:

$$\text{aluminium oxide} \xrightarrow{\text{electrical energy}} \text{aluminium} + \text{oxygen}$$

Remember, the metal is always formed at the negative electrode during electrolysis. As electrolysis requires large quantities of electricity, it is a very expensive process. Therefore, it is only used when no other method will work. Potassium, sodium, calcium, magnesium and aluminium are all usually extracted by electrolysis. These represent the most reactive metals, which are found at the top of the reactivity series.

Electrolysis is the only way of reducing these ores because they contain the most stable compounds.

For other metals, thermal decomposition or heating with carbon is used because it is cheaper. A summary of methods of extraction is given in Table 5.1.

 4 Why aren't all metals extracted by electrolysis?
[Total 2]

Table 5.1 *Methods of extraction.*

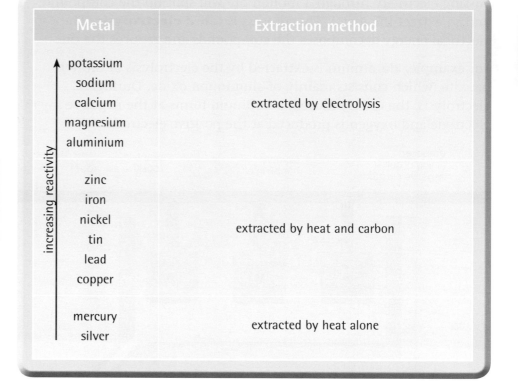

Metal	Extraction method
potassium sodium calcium magnesium aluminium	extracted by electrolysis
zinc iron nickel tin lead copper	extracted by heat and carbon
mercury silver	extracted by heat alone

increasing reactivity

5 Magnesium can displace iron from iron oxide. Suggest why this is not done on an industrial scale to produce iron.

[Total 3]

Summary

- Only the least reactive metals like gold, silver and platinum are found in a native state (as elements).
- Rocks from which metals can be extracted are called ores.
- Decomposition reactions involve breaking down compounds.
- Metals are extracted from compounds in their ores by a reduction reaction.
- The less reactive metals are extracted by heat alone.
- The metals of moderate reactivity are extracted by heating with carbon.
- The most reactive metals can only be extracted by electrolysis.

Questions

1 Copy and complete the following sentences.
The metals silver, _____ and _____
are found uncombined in nature. Most metals are
found combined with other _____ in rocks
called _____. Bauxite, galena and
_____ are examples of metal _____.
[Total 3]

2 Write one sentence for each of the following phrases
to explain what each means:
a) reduction reaction *[2]*
b) native metal. *[2]*
[Total 4]

3 a) What is an ore? *[1]*
b) Give an example of a word equation for a
decomposition reaction which forms a metal oxide
and carbon dioxide. *[2]*
c) Which common method of extracting metals is
most expensive? *[1]*
[Total 4]

4 Copy and complete the table below to show the
method used to extract each of the metals from their
oxides. *[Total 3]*

Table 5.2

Metal oxide	Main method used to extract metal
nickel oxide	
calcium oxide	
mercury oxide	
iron oxide	
magnesium oxide	
lead oxide	

5 Write a word equation for each of the following
chemical reactions:
a) reducing zinc oxide with carbon *[2]*
b) breaking down mercury oxide with heat alone. *[2]*
[Total 4]

6 Explain why, in Britain, the **Bronze Age** started about
1500 BC but the **Iron Age** did not start until 500 BC
(**bronze** is an alloy of copper and tin). *[Total 2]*

7 Suggest why aluminium, the most abundant metal,
was worth more than gold in 1820. *[Total 2]*

8 Read this passage carefully before answering the
questions which follow.
Metals are used everywhere and they are one of our
most precious resources. Most metals are extracted
from ores, but supplies of metal ores are running out.
Calculations show that at the present rate of use,
we have about enough reserves of aluminium for 250
years, copper for 30 years, lead for 20 years and
nickel for 50 years. We must stop wasting our
precious reserves of metals. Much of what we throw
away could be reused. Recycling metals would save
our resources for future use. In addition, large
quantities of energy are needed to extract metals
from their ores, so recycling would also reduce the
amount of energy we use to produce the metals.
a) Which metal has the largest reserves? *[1]*
b) What does recycling mean? *[1]*
c) Describe two advantages of recycling metals. *[2]*
d) Draw a bar chart showing the number of years
left for each of the metals mentioned in the
passage. Remember to give names and units
where appropriate. *[4]*
[Total 8]

9 Imagine your friend has missed the lesson on
extracting metals. Draw up a poster, using labelled
diagrams, equations and tables, to summarise
'Finding and extracting metals'. *[Total 8]*

5.4 Corrosion and rusting

What causes corrosion and rusting and how can we prevent it happening? We see corroded and rusted metal everyday: old cars, railings, bridges and ships all tend to rust. It is a major problem for industrial nations. We must first understand the causes of corrosion and rusting before we can discover ways of preventing it.

Corrosion

Most metals form a dull surface coating when exposed to air. The coating is produced as the metal reacts and forms a compound. For example, magnesium reacts with the oxygen in air to form a coating of magnesium oxide. The word equation is:

magnesium + oxygen → magnesium oxide

This chemical reaction is called **corrosion**.

Similar corrosion reactions occur with other metals like aluminium, zinc and lead. The word equation for aluminium is:

aluminium + oxygen → aluminium oxide

In these examples, the oxide layer formed prevents oxygen getting at the metal underneath. This means that the metal is protected from further corrosion. Scratching the coating removes the oxide layer to reveal the shiny metal.

Corrosion is generally a slow reaction, but the more reactive metals tend to corrode faster. Some metals, like gold and platinum, do not corrode at all.

Rusting

Rusting is the special name given to the corrosion of iron and steel. Iron is relatively abundant and cheap and when made into steel can be made to have a variety of useful properties. Therefore, iron and steel are the most widely used metals in the world and rusting is a common problem.

> The chemical reaction which forms compounds on the surface of a metal is called corrosion.

> **1** Write a word equation for the corrosion of lead in air. *[Total 3]*
> **2** a) Name two metals which will corrode very quickly. *[1]*
> b) Name two metals which won't corrode. *[1]*
> *[Total 2]*

> Great improvements have been made in protecting cars against rust, but unfortunately it still occurs. The most likely places to find rust problems in a car are at the edges of doors, under sills and wings.

Iron and steel usually rust when exposed to air and water. We can show what happens during rusting by setting up a series of experiments.

Investigation into the rusting of iron nails

It is important that we understand the processes involved in rusting, so that we are able to take steps to prevent it. The experiment described here was designed to investigate rusting.

- Five identical iron nails were placed in test tubes as shown in Figure 4.2.
- The test tubes were left for a few days and then examined for the presence of rust.
- The results of the investigation were recorded below each test tube.

Figure 4.1 *Rusting.*

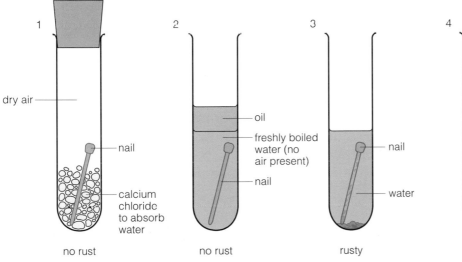

Figure 4.2 *Investigating rusting.*

What causes rusting?

There are two main conclusions from these experiments.

- Both air and water need to be present for iron to rust.
- The presence of salt or acid speeds up the rusting of iron.

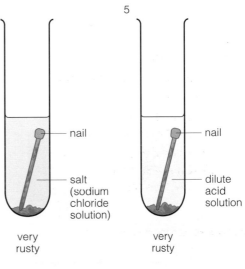

Stainless steel contains iron, nickel and chromium. This alloy does not rust because it forms a surface layer of chromium oxide. This very thin oxide layer is strong and keeps out air and water. (The oxide layer is less than 0.000 000 01 m thick.)

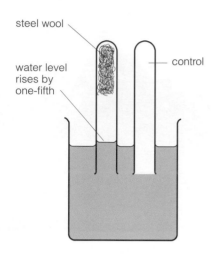

steel wool

control

water level rises by one-fifth

Figure 4.3 *The rusting of iron.*

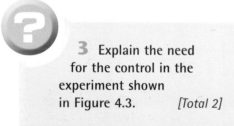

?

3 Explain the need for the control in the experiment shown in Figure 4.3. [Total 2]

Figure 4.4 *A sunken ship*

We can show that iron combines with the oxygen in air during rusting by setting up the simple experiment shown in Figure 4.3.

After a few days, the steel wool has rusted, and the water in the test tube rises about one-fifth of the way up the tube This means that roughly one-fifth of the air has been used. Since about one-fifth (20%) of the air is oxygen, it is reasonable to assume that the iron has combined with the oxygen during rusting.

Rust is actually **hydrated** iron oxide, formed from the reaction of iron with oxygen and water. The word equation is:

iron + oxygen + water → hydrated iron oxide (rust)

These conclusions can be used to explain how rusting occurs in different situations.

- Tanks left in the desert since the end of the Second World War show hardly any signs of rust, because the desert atmosphere contains little or no water.
- Ships that have sunk in deep areas of the oceans hardly rust at all, because there is very little air dissolved in the water of the deepest parts of the ocean.
- Iron and steel structures built in or near to the sea rust very quickly. This is due to the salt dissolved in the sea water, which speeds up rusting.
- Cars and other iron objects corrode more in areas where you get acid rain.

Problems of rusting

The brown flakes of rust, which form during the corrosion of iron and steel, are brittle and weak. This causes them to crumble and break away, exposing the iron underneath. The iron rusts further until it has all corroded away.

The corrosion of iron and steel is a major problem. Rust can destroy any object made of iron, and rusted machinery, cars, bridges, etc., will have to be replaced. This costs the country millions of pounds each year in replacement parts and lost production.

Preventing rusting

Since rusting costs so much money, steps have to be taken to prevent it happening. There are two main ways of protecting iron and steel from corrosion. The first method uses a **physical barrier** to keep out air and water. The second method, called **sacrificial protection**, involves attaching a more reactive metal to the iron. Each of the methods has advantages and disadvantages which makes it useful in different circumstances.

Protection by a physical barrier

For iron or steel to rust, oxygen and water must be present. The simplest way of stopping rusting is to prevent oxygen and water getting at the metal. This can be done is several ways.

- Paint is cheap and easily applied. Painting is used to protect many everyday steel objects like cars, bikes, bridges, etc.
- Oil and grease are good flexible coatings, which are suitable for preventing the corrosion of tools and machinery.
- Plastic coatings are more expensive, but they are strong and long lasting. Wire netting is often coated with plastic to stop it corroding.
- **Tin plating** is used to make the sheet metal for 'tin' cans. These are suitable for food containers, because the tin coating is strong, non-poisonous and prevents corrosion.
- **Electroplating** uses electricity to put a thin coating of an expensive metal onto iron. Metals like chromium and nickel can be used for electroplating. These metals form a hard, shiny, protective coating. Cutlery and taps are frequently electroplated.

The main disadvantage of using any physical barrier to prevent rusting is that the coating has to be maintained. If the coating becomes scratched or broken then air and water will get in to the iron, and it will rust.

?

4 List seven different substances used as a physical barrier to prevent rusting. *[Total 5]*

5 Describe a situation where a physical barrier may not work well. *[Total 2]*

Figure 4.5 *Using a physical barrier.*

> Tin cans are actually 99% steel with a thin coating of tin to prevent corrosion. Baked beans in tomato sauce were especially created for keeping in tin cans.

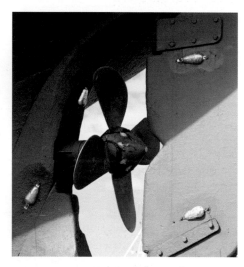

Figure 4.6 *Sacrificial protection on a ship's hull using zinc blocks.*

> Car bodies are attached to the negative terminal of the battery to help reduce corrosion. It doesn't work very well with cars, because the circuit is broken when the engine is switched off. However, attaching to the negative terminal of a power supply can protect some metal structures, such as oil rigs.

Sacrificial protection

Railway lines cannot be painted, or covered in any other material, because the coating would soon wear off. A different method of protection has to be used where coating the metal is difficult or impossible. It was discovered that iron and steel could also be protected from rusting by attaching them to a more reactive metal like magnesium or zinc. To prevent railway lines rusting, bags of magnesium are attached at regular intervals. This unusual method of preventing rusting is called sacrificial protection. Some other examples are described below. In each case, the more reactive metal corrodes protecting the iron from rusting. This is why it is called sacrificial protection. The more reactive metal is sacrificed to save the iron. Examples are:

- blocks of magnesium metal attached to oil rigs in the North Sea
- blocks of zinc bolted to the hulls of iron ships
- bags of scrap magnesium metal attached to underground oil and gas pipes.

The main disadvantage of sacrificial protection is that the more reactive metals used to protect the iron will be used up in time. Therefore the protecting metals have to be replaced regularly, or there will be none left to protect the iron, which will then start to rust.

Galvanising

Steel and iron can be protected from rusting by coating with zinc. This is called **galvanising** and the coating is usually applied by dipping the metal in molten zinc. Some examples of where galvanising is used are:

- girders for bridges and buildings
- some car body panels
- motorway crash barriers
- buckets and roofing nails.

Galvanising is a special form of protection because it involves both a physical barrier and sacrificial protection. The zinc coating keeps out air and water, and if the coating becomes scratched or broken the iron will still be protected because the zinc is a more reactive metal. Therefore, the zinc also sacrificially protects the iron.

Summary

- Corrosion is the formation of compounds on the surface of a metal.
- Rusting is the corrosion of iron and steel.
- Rusting is very costly because the metal is destroyed.
- Both oxygen and water are needed for iron to rust.
- The presence of salt or acid speeds up rusting.
- A physical barrier like paint, oil, grease, plastic coating and metals like tin and chromium can prevent rusting.
- Rusting can also be prevented by sacrificial protection, where a more reactive metal is attached to the iron and corrodes instead of the iron.
- Galvanising is the protection of iron and steel by coating with zinc.

Questions

1 Copy and complete the following sentences.
Corrosion is the formation of a metal _____
on the _____ of a metal. Rusting is the
corrosion of _____ and _____.
[Total 2]

2 Write one sentence for each of the following phrases
to explain what each means:
a) physical barrier [1]
b) sacrificial protection. [1]
[Total 2]

3 The rusting of car bodies is a major problem.
a) Name the two substances which cause iron
to rust. [2]
b) Write a word equation to represent the rusting
of iron. [2]
c) What effect does salt used on roads in winter
have on rusting in cars. [1]
d) Give two ways in which manufacturers protect
cars against rusting. [2]
[Total 7]

4 Sacrificial protection is used to stop railway lines
rusting.
a) Briefly explain why railway lines cannot
be painted. [1]
b) Describe how railway lines are protected. [2]
c) Why do old railway tracks, which are no longer
used, start to rust? [1]
[Total 4]

5 Galvanising is widely used to protect steel.
a) Briefly describe how steel is galvanised. [1]
b) Explain how galvanising can be described as a
'double' protection. [2]
c) Give two examples of where galvanising
is used. [2]
[Total 5]

6 Describe one advantage and one disadvantage of
each of the following forms of rust prevention.
a) Sacrificial protection by attaching to a block
of zinc. [2]
b) Physical protection by using paint. [2]
[Total 4]

5 Metals

Discovering new materials

What are **nanoparticles** and **smart materials**? What are they used for?

Atoms, molecules and nanotechnology

Atoms and molecules are far too small to see, even with the most powerful microscope. They are so tiny that they are measured in **nanometres** (nm), 1×10^{-9} metres.

Nanotechnology

Nanotechnology is the science of building and controlling particles whose sizes range from 10 to 100 nanometres. The idea of building molecules, atom by atom, seems incredible but nanotechnology has enormous potential.

Some useful nanoparticles have already been developed. ICI have produced nanoparticles of titanium dioxide that absorb harmful UV rays. They are used in high-factor sunscreens that appear invisible on the skin and in sun-protective clothing.
Nanocomposite plastics have also been produced – these are stronger and stiffer than ordinary plastics and are used in the car industry, dentistry and medicine.

Some scientists even believe that self-replicating molecules could be built and be programmed to do certain jobs. These **nanobots** could be used to build tiny machines on the molecular scale. However, some people are concerned about possible problems caused by using nanotechnology. For example, some are worried that self-replicating materials could get out of control. Like all advances in science, we must consider the advantages, but still be aware of possible dangers. To weigh up these choices we all need some scientific understanding and we all need to be involved.

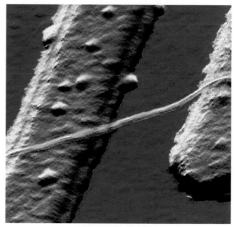
Figure 5.2 *Carbon nanotubes could be used to make smaller and faster computers on the molecular scale.*

One nanometre is one billionth of a metre. A human hair is about 80 000 nm thick. The largest atoms are just over 0.5 nm across.

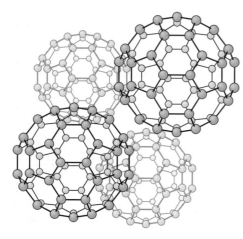
Figure 5.1 *Molecules of **fullerene** have a diameter of approximately 1 nm. Fullerene is an unusual form of carbon, made up of molecules containing 60 carbon atoms (C_{60}).*

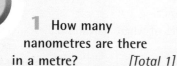

1 How many nanometres are there in a metre? [Total 1]

2 A virus measures 100 nanometres across. What is that in metres? [Total 1]

3 What is special about nanotechnology? [Total 1]

Billions of pounds are being spent on research and development (R&D) into nanotechnology. However, many scientists believe that the creation of useful nanoparticles, that can control their own actions, is a long way off – and may never happen.

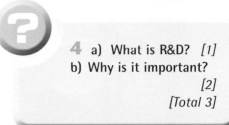

4 a) What is R&D? *[1]*
b) Why is it important?
[2]
[Total 3]

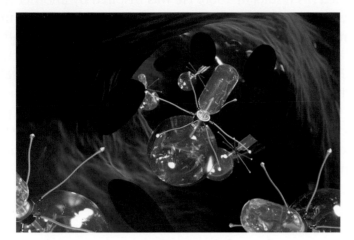

Figure 5.3 *Sometime in the future, doctors might use millions of nanobots to clean up your arteries.*

Smart materials

Another range of new substances that have great potential are 'smart materials'. These substances respond to changes around them in a consistent way. New smart materials can expand or contract through small changes in temperature, pH or electric current. Some scientists think that these could be used as artificial muscles, but much more research is needed.

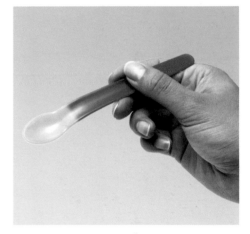

Figure 5.4 *This 'smart spoon' changes colour if the food is too hot.*

Questions

1 What are nanometres, nanoparticles and nanobots? *[Total 3]*

2 This question is about the uses of nanoparticles.
a) List two examples in practice today. *[2]*
b) List three examples of possible uses in the future. *[3]*
[Total 5]

3 What problem could arise from using self-replicating nanoparticles? *[Total 2]*

4 Suggest a possible use for a 'smart fabric' that changes colour with changes in:
a) light *[1]*
b) moisture. *[1]*
[Total 2]

5 Why do we all need some understanding of science? *[Total 2]*

6 Design a poster for a lecture on nanotechnology. Your poster should have an interesting title, and drawings to illustrate the new technology. *[Total 10]*

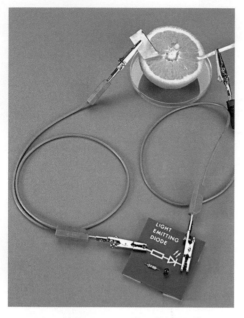

Figure 5.5 *The orange can light the LED.*

Table 5.1

Metals connected in cell	Voltage (V)
magnesium and silver	3.1
magnesium and copper	2.7
magnesium and zinc	1.6
copper and zinc	1.1
silver and copper	0.4

Cells and batteries

An Italian professor, Alessandro Volta, made the first **battery** in 1799 and published his results in 1800. He was inspired by another Italian scientist, called Luigi Galvani, who carried out some strange animal experiments. In 1780, Galvani had noted that if he hung freshly killed frogs over an iron railing using copper hooks, the frogs instantly started to twitch. He thought that the movement was caused by natural electricity in the frogs. This gave Volta the idea to investigate metals and electricity. His experiments showed that it was the metals that produced the electricity and the frog just acted as a solution to complete the circuit. The electrical energy was produced by a chemical reaction between the two metals and the solution.

Electrical cells

Further experiments showed that putting any two metals in a solution of a salt or acid could produce electricity. The arrangement was called a **cell**. Some examples of simple two metal cells are shown in Table 5.1.

- Placing magnesium and copper strips in salt solution makes a simple cell. The voltmeter shows that a voltage of 2.7 V is produced.
- Using the acid in an orange and strips of copper and zinc produces enough electricity to run a digital clock.
- Common metal objects can be used to produce electricity. A gold ring and iron nail dipped in sulphuric acid make a cell, which can light a light-emitting diode (LED).

Every cell has to have two electrodes (often two metals) and a solution of a salt or an acid.

Note that cells are sometimes called batteries, although strictly a battery is two or more cells joined together.

Cell voltage

It can be shown that the **voltage** produced in a cell depends on the metals used. The voltage produced by different cells is shown in Table 5.1.

The largest voltage is produced when a very reactive metal is connected to a very unreactive metal. That is, the voltage is greatest when the metals are furthest apart in the reactivity series.

The development of modern batteries

The first battery consisted of a series of zinc and copper discs, which were separated by cardboard soaked in salt solution. It was called a voltaic pile and it could produce a small, steady electric current. However, it could not produce currents over long periods.

The cells used today have been developed from the voltaic pile.

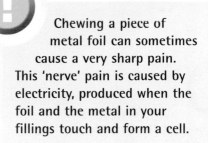

Chewing a piece of metal foil can sometimes cause a very sharp pain. This 'nerve' pain is caused by electricity, produced when the foil and the metal in your fillings touch and form a cell.

- 1868 – The Leclanché cell used carbon electrodes to connect a mixture of manganese dioxide and carbon to a solution of ammonium chloride. It could produce a higher current for a longer time, but it was heavy and the solutions could be spilled.
- 1880 – The zinc–carbon cell was similar to the Leclanché cell. It had a zinc case as one electrode, and a mixture of manganese dioxide and carbon as the other. In-between was cardboard soaked in ammonium chloride solution. The ordinary cell used today is the same zinc–carbon cell. It is cheap and reliable but is only useful for low power appliances.
- 1950 – Alkaline cells are similar to zinc–carbon cells but use potassium hydroxide, an alkaline solution, instead of ammonium chloride. They are more expensive but can produce higher currents and run for longer periods.
- 1970 – Lithium cells were developed to produce a steady current for many years. They are used in heart pacemakers. These are expensive cells which use lithium as one of the electrodes.

Figure 5.6 *The voltaic pile was the first battery.*

Questions

1 List all the chemicals that are needed to make an ordinary zinc carbon cell. *[Total 3]*

2 A voltage is produced when any pair of metals is placed in a solution of salt. Consider the following pairs of metals:

copper/iron   copper/zinc   zinc/silver
silver/iron   copper/silver

a) Which pair of metals would produce the largest voltage, and which would produce the lowest voltage? *[2]*

b) Draw a labelled diagram for one of the above cells showing how it is set up and how the voltage is measured. *[4]*

c) What would be the voltage of the cell formed between zinc and silver. (Hint: look at the voltages of the cells in Table 5.1. *[1]*
[Total 7]

3 a) Who invented the first battery? *[1]*

b) When was the first battery invented? *[1]*

c) What substances were used to make this battery? *[2]*

d) What experiments gave the inventor the idea of how to investigate metals and electricity? *[1]*
[Total 5]

5 | Metals

The price of gold

Golden dreams

Given as a token of love and fought over in wars, gold has fascinated us for thousands of years. It was one of the first metals used by early man and it is still useful today. Gold is used in medicine, dentistry and electronics – but 80% of it is used in jewellery-making.

Gold is valuable because it is rare and has special properties. For example, gold is shiny when polished, easy to bend and shape, is an excellent conductor of electricity and is very unreactive, so it keeps its good looks. But what is the price that we pay for using it – and is the price worth paying?

Gold mining is important for many developing countries, such as Ghana and Uzbekistan. It provides work and training for the people, and brings in foreign investment that helps the economy. It also introduces and enables the development of new technologies – and so helps to improve the general scientific understanding of the population. Developing gold mining also brings about improvements to services like water and electricity, and to road, rail and other transport systems.

Figure 5.7 *New technology, like the use of computers to monitor and control mining operations, can be useful in other areas.*

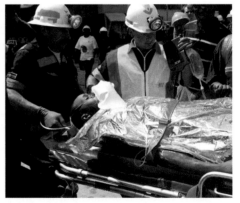

Figure 5.8 *According to international labour organisations, mining is responsible for 5% of the world's workplace deaths every year.*

Unfortunately there are also disadvantages for these countries as a result of gold mining. All mining is dangerous and, although big disasters grab the headlines, everyday accidents make mines particularly dangerous places. Gold mining also produces vast amounts of waste rock. About 20 tonnes of rock and earth are excavated to mine

1 Why was gold one of the first metals that man used? *[Total 1]*

2 Why is gold used to make jewellery? *[Total 3]*

Although most gold is produced in developing countries, over 85% of it is sold and used in the most well-off nations.

3 What fraction of the gold produced is not used to make jewellery? *[Total 1]*

4 Why would gold mining improve transport links in a country? *[Total 2]*

the gold needed to make one wedding ring. This waste rock is not only unsightly; it is also dangerous to humans and to the environment because it contains many poisonous chemicals.

Gold is often extracted from the crushed ore using a chemical called potassium cyanide – this is extremely poisonous. Leaks of potassium cyanide have resulted in loss of life and great damage to the environment.

Most gold mining operations use up vast amounts of water. One mine in America uses over 500 million litres of water a day; more than is needed by a city of over 2 million people. This is a great waste of a precious natural resource.

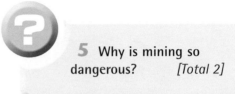

? **5** Why is mining so dangerous?   *[Total 2]*

Figure 5.9 *Pollution from gold mining.*

Figure 5.10 *A waste of water.*

Questions

1 What new technologies would be introduced by gold mining?   *[Total 2]*

2 What compound is commonly used to extract gold, and what problem does this cause?   *[Total 2]*

3 Why do you think gold mining produces so much waste?   *[Total 2]*

4 Make a table, like the one here, and list the benefits and problems of gold mining in a developing country.

Benefits of gold mining	Problems of gold mining

[Total 7]

5 Some people say we should stop buying 'new' gold jewellery because this would stop the exploitation of developing countries.
Do you agree or is there a better solution? Write down some of the main points that support your view.   *[Total 6]*

Scrap yard challenge

Scrap yards look dirty and disorganised. Can we really make money from scrap metal? What are the benefits of collecting and reusing metals?

Any old iron?

Metal recycling is an important industry in the UK – it involves large businesses and local authorities. It is generally a **labour intensive** process employing manual labour as well as highly trained scientists. Up to 60% of our reclaimed metal is exported and the rest is used to save our own natural resources.

Iron and steel

Over 10 million tonnes of iron and steel are produced in the UK every year. The main source of 'new' iron is the ore **haematite**, which is mainly iron oxide. Using **coke** (from coal) and **limestone**, the iron is extracted in a **blast furnace**. The process uses enormous amounts of energy and water.

Figure 5.11 *In the UK, over 13 million tonnes of scrap metals are recycled every year.*

?

1 What mass of recycled metal is exported? [Total 1]

!

Each household uses about 600 steel cans every year.

?

2 Name three natural resources saved by recycling scrap iron and steel. [Total 3]

3 What compound is in the main ore of iron? [Total 1]

4 What is 'cast iron' and why is it not very useful? [Total 2]

Figure 5.12 *Extracting iron is dirty, dangerous work that causes pollution to the air, land and water.*

The **cast iron** produced in the blast furnace is **brittle**, because of high levels of carbon and other impurities. To make it more useful, the iron is converted into steel – this is an alloy of iron that contains less carbon. Mixing different metals with the iron produces different types of steel. Some of the main uses for steel are for buildings, bridges, ships, railways, cars and domestic appliances.

Advantages of recycling iron

About 42% of our iron and steel is made from **recycled** metal. The advantages of this are:

- saving natural resources
- using less energy
- reducing air and water pollution
- producing less carbon dioxide (a **greenhouse gas**)
- using up less water.

The main disadvantage of using scrap steel is that it contains different amounts of different metals. This can be a problem because the properties of a sample of steel depend on the amounts of different metals mixed together.

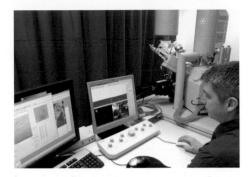

Figure 5.13 *Chemists analyse steel to see if it contains the correct amounts of different metals.*

Recycling iron and steel is important – but the benefits of recycling **non-ferrous** metals (metals other than iron) can be even greater. Extracting recycled aluminium uses just 5% of the energy that is needed to produce the same amount of new metal by electrolysis. The world's copper, lead and zinc resources are all running out and recycling them is essential if we are to preserve our stocks for the future.

Metal	% taken from recycled metal sources
aluminium	39
copper	32
lead	74
iron and steel	42
zinc	20

Table 5.2 *Iron and steel are not the only metals that are recycled.*

! One recycled aluminium can saves enough energy to run a television for three hours.

? **5** Why does recycling aluminium save so much energy? *[Total 2]*

Questions

1 a) What problems are associated with extracting iron from its ore? *[3]*
 b) What is the difference between iron and steel? *[1]*
 [Total 4]

2 a) Name five metals that are recycled. *[1]*
 b) Which common metal is made from mostly recycled metal? *[1]*
 c) List the main benefits gained by recycling metals. *[3]*
 [Total 5]

3 Use the information in Table 5.2 to draw a bar chart to show the percentage of each metal produced from recycled metal. *[Total 3]*

4 Imagine that you have been put in charge of recycling aluminium cans in your school. List five things you would do to encourage others to collect as many cans as possible. *[Total 5]*

End of section questions

1 The following lists of words and definitions have been mixed up. Copy out the list and rearrange the definitions so that they are opposite the correct word.

Word	Definition
alloy	iron being covered in zinc
native metal	rock from which a metal can be extracted
galvanising	metal with other elements added
ore	metal found as an element in nature

[Total 4]

2 Copy the following passage and complete it by choosing the correct words in the brackets.

Iron is the (most/least) important metal to man. Its main ore, haematite, is mainly iron (chloride/oxide). It is extracted from its ore by heating (alone/with carbon). The corrosion of iron is called (rusting/reducing) and needs the presence of (either/both) water (and/or) air. (Underline each of your chosen words.)   *[Total 3]*

3 Explain each of the following facts.
   a) Electrical wires are usually made of copper, although silver is a better conductor of electricity.   *[1]*
   b) Calcium is never used to make kitchen sinks.   *[1]*
   c) In industry, iron is never extracted by electrolysis.   *[1]*
   d) A lifeboat sometimes has a block of zinc attached to its hull.   *[1]*

   [Total 4]

4 In each case name two metals which:
   a) can react with dilute acids, but have a very slow reaction with cold water.   *[1]*
   b) are extracted from their ores by electrolysis.   *[1]*
   c) do not corrode easily under any conditions.   *[1]*
   d) are more reactive than tin but less reactive than zinc.   *[1]*

   [Total 4]

5 Copy and complete the following equations involving metals and their reactions:
   a) potassium + water →   *[2]*
   b) sodium + hydrochloric acid →   *[2]*
   c) lithium + oxygen →   *[2]*

   [Total 6]

6 Give one advantage and one disadvantage for the following uses of metals:
   a) iron used for fences.   *[2]*
   b) gold used for coins.   *[2]*
   c) aluminium used for warships.   *[2]*

   [Total 6]

7 Explain the meaning of sacrificial protection, and give two examples of where it might be used.

   [Total 4]

8 Iron can be protected from rusting by a physical barrier.
   a) How does a physical barrier stop iron rusting?   *[1]*
   b) Name four different ways of protecting iron using a physical barrier.   *[4]*

   [Total 5]

9 Explain why zinc is such a good coating to use to protect iron from rusting.

   [Total 4]

10 Look at Figure 1. Each test tube contains an identical iron nail.
   a) In which test tube will the iron nail rust most quickly?   *[1]*
   b) In which test tube will the iron nail rust most slowly?   *[1]*
   c) Briefly explain your answers to parts a) and b).   *[2]*

   [Total 4]

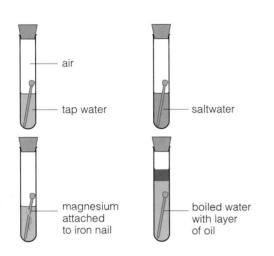

air

tap water

saltwater

magnesium
attached
to iron nail

boiled water
with layer
of oil

Figure 1 *Rusting experiments.*

11   Look at the following pairs of substances:
  i)   tin + silver nitrate
  ii) carbon + lead oxide
  iii) iron + zinc nitrate
  iv) copper oxide + zinc.
  a)   Which of the four pairs of substances would not
       normally react together? Briefly explain your
       choice.   *[3]*
  b)   Write a word equation for each of the pairs of
       substances that will react together.   *[3]*
                                              [Total 6]

12   Read the following passage then answer the
       questions which follow.

       Metals are among our most important resources. They
       are useful because of their valuable properties. Some
       metals, like gold, have been used for thousands of
       years, while others, like aluminium, have been used in
       large quantities only fairly recently.

  a)   Name four physical properties that are common
       to most metals.   *[4]*
  b)   Explain why gold has been known and used for
       thousands of years.   *[1]*
  c)   Explain why it took so long to discover
       aluminium, even though it is the most abundant
       metal in the Earth's crust.   *[2]*
  d)   Name the general products formed when metals
       react with the following:
       i)   oxygen
       ii) acids.   *[2]*
                                              [Total 9]

13   Write word equations for the following reactions:
  a)   heating nickel oxide with carbon   *[3]*
  b)   heating iron oxide with magnesium.   *[3]*
                                              [Total 6]

14   Millions of tin cans are used each year and most of
  R them end up on the rubbish dump. This is very
       wasteful and greater efforts are required to recycle
       more materials. Find out more about the methods,
       benefits and problems of recycling tin cans.

15   The English chemist, Humphrey Davy (1778–1829),
  R was credited with the discovery of several metals. Find
       out about these discoveries.

16   Magnesium reacts with acids to produce hydrogen
  P gas. What factors might affect how much hydrogen
       is produced in the reaction? For example, how would
       you investigate the effect of the length of the
       magnesium ribbon on the volume of gas produced?

17   A voltage is produced when two metals are dipped
  P into a solution of salt. What factors might affect
       the size of the voltage produced? For example, how
       would you investigate the effect of using different
       metals on the size of the voltage produced.

Further chemistry

6.1 Types of reactions

?

1 What is the difference between a chemical reaction and a physical change?   *[Total 2]*

2 Give three examples of everyday chemical reactions.   *[Total 3]*

How can we classify the many different reactions which take place? You will meet lots of chemical reactions, both in the laboratory and in the world around you. It is important to be able to work out the similarities and differences between the different reactions.

The importance of chemical reactions

A **chemical reaction** is a change in which one or more new substances are formed. This is different to a physical change in which no new substances are produced.

Chemical reactions take place all around us. Burning fuels, the ripening of fruit, cooking food, superglue setting, steel rusting and concrete setting are just a few examples. Chemical reactions are a vital part of life itself with growth, respiration, photosynthesis and digestion all involving chemical reactions. Even after plants and animals die, the decay of their remains involves chemical reactions.

Most of the substances around us are made by chemical reactions. Many are man-made such as plastics, medicines, toiletries, paints, detergents, fertilisers and cement. Others are made by chemical reactions that take place naturally, such as the oxygen in the air which is made by photosynthesis.

The different types of reactions can be classified under different headings. Some of the commonest ones are described here.

Oxidation

Oxidation occurs when a substance reacts with oxygen. For example:

zinc + oxygen → zinc oxide

Other examples of oxidation include rusting and some foods like butter and cooking oils going off. Respiration, which takes place in the cells of living organisms, is the oxidation of sugars.

Combustion

Combustion occurs when a substance burns in oxygen. Good examples of combustion reactions are the burning of fossil fuels and many rocket fuels. For example:

Figure 1.1 *Butter and cooking oils go rancid due to oxidation.*

methane (natural gas) + oxygen → carbon dioxide + water

hydrogen + oxygen → water

All combustion reactions are also oxidation reactions, because substances react with oxygen when they burn. However, some substances, such as copper, react with oxygen but do not burn. These are oxidation but not combustion reactions.

Reduction

Reduction occurs when a substance loses oxygen. This is the opposite of oxidation. Good examples include the extraction of metals from their ores. For example, iron is extracted from its ore haematite, which contains iron oxide, by reaction with carbon. The iron oxide loses its oxygen to form iron. The word equation is:

iron oxide + carbon → iron + carbon dioxide

Decomposition

Decomposition occurs when a compound breaks down into simpler substances. Not all compounds decompose easily, but some do and it can be brought about by heat, light or electricity.

Thermal decomposition

Thermal decomposition occurs when a substance is decomposed using heat. Some examples of substances that decompose on heating are:

heat energy
silver oxide → silver + oxygen

heat energy
calcium carbonate (limestone) → calcium oxide (lime) + carbon dioxide

Electrical decomposition (electrolysis)

Electrolysis occurs when a substance is decomposed using electricity. Those substances that can be decomposed by electricity have to be molten or dissolved first. Some metals, such as sodium, are extracted from their ores by electrical decomposition. The word equation is:

electrical energy
sodium chloride → sodium + chlorine

Figure 1.2 *The space shuttle engines use the reaction between hydrogen and oxygen.*

The phrase 'in the limelight' comes from the first stage spotlight (used in the 1800s). When limestone is heated, it glows very brightly as it forms lime. This glow was used to provide light for actors on the stage.

Bleach is made by the electrolysis of salt water.

Figure 1.3 *Substances on films decompose when exposed to light.*

Decomposition by light

This is much less common than thermal or electrical decomposition. One very important example is the decomposition of silver bromide. The word equation is:

$$\text{silver bromide} \xrightarrow{\text{light energy}} \text{silver} + \text{bromine}$$

This reaction is used in photography. Films are coated with silver bromide and other similar substances. On the parts of the film that are exposed to light, silver metal forms. In developing, the unexposed silver bromide is washed off leaving silver on parts of the film which were exposed to light. In this way the negative of the photograph is produced.

Neutralisation (acid–base)

Neutralisation is the reaction between an acid and a base producing a salt and water. Metal oxides, metal hydroxides and metal carbonates are all examples of bases.

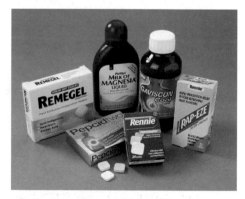

Figure 1.4 *Indigestion tablets contain bases that neutralise excess stomach acid.*

There are many everyday examples of neutralisation reactions, such as the reaction of indigestion tablets with acid in your stomach. Indigestion is caused by excess hydrochloric acid. It can be cured using indigestion tablets which contain the base calcium carbonate. The word equation is:

$$\begin{matrix}\text{hydrochloric}\\\text{acid}\\\text{(in your}\\\text{stomach)}\end{matrix} + \begin{matrix}\text{calcium}\\\text{carbonate}\\\text{(in indigestion}\\\text{tablet)}\end{matrix} \rightarrow \begin{matrix}\text{calcium}\\\text{chloride}\end{matrix} + \begin{matrix}\text{carbon}\\\text{dioxide}\end{matrix} + \text{water}$$

Precipitation

Precipitation occurs when a solid is produced from solutions that are mixed together. For example, when a solution of potassium iodide is added to a solution of lead nitrate, a yellow solid (precipitate) is formed. The word equation is:

$$\begin{matrix}\text{lead nitrate}\\\text{solution}\end{matrix} + \begin{matrix}\text{potassium iodide}\\\text{solution}\end{matrix} \rightarrow \begin{matrix}\text{lead iodide}\\\text{solid}\end{matrix} + \begin{matrix}\text{potassium nitrate}\\\text{solution}\end{matrix}$$

Hard water can be softened by adding washing soda. It removes the dissolved calcium particles that make the water hard as a precipitate of calcium carbonate.

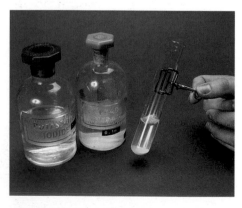

Figure 1.5 *A precipitate of yellow lead iodide.*

Displacement

In a **displacement** reaction, a more reactive element takes the place of a less reactive one in a compound. Displacement reactions can be used to extract metals from compounds. For example, chromium can be extracted from chromium oxide by heating it with aluminium. The word equation is:

chromium oxide + aluminium → chromium + aluminium oxide

Conservation of mass

During all chemical reactions, the total mass of all the reactants used up is the same as the mass of the products formed. This is because no new atoms are created or destroyed: they are just rearranged. Figure 1.6 shows the mass before and after the reaction between solutions of lead nitrate and potassium iodide.

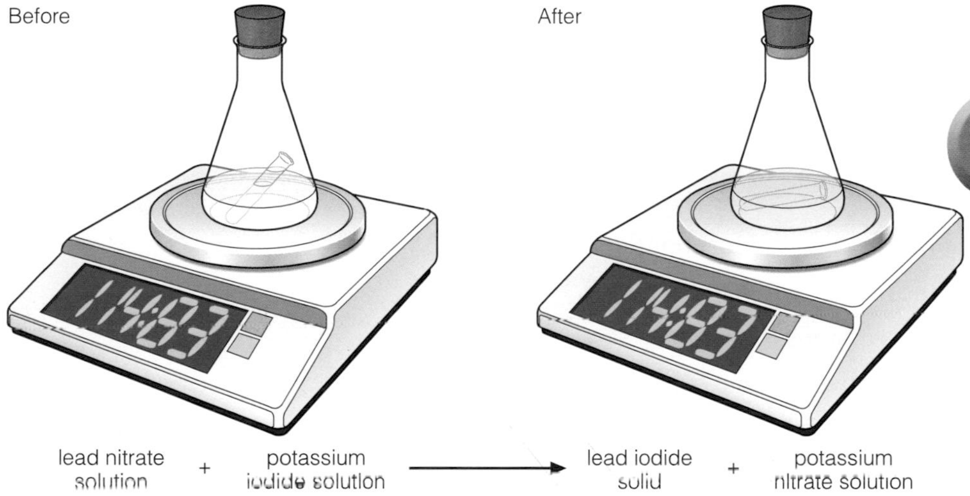

Before   After

| lead nitrate | + | potassium | → | lead iodide | + | potassium |
| solution | | iodide solution | | solid | | nitrate solution |

Figure 1.6 *Mass is conserved in chemical reactions.*

In some reactions, such as burning metals, the metal appears to get heavier. This is because it has combined with oxygen from the air. The total mass of the metal burned plus the oxygen used up from the air will equal the mass of the metal oxide produced.

In other reactions, such as metals reacting with acids or decomposition reactions, the mass appears to decrease. In this case it is because some of the products are gases which escape. The total mass of the gases plus the other products will equal the mass of the reactants.

3 For each of the following reactions, decide which type of reaction it is.
a) copper oxide + hydrogen → copper + water [1]
b) sulphuric acid + sodium hydroxide → sodium sulphate + water [1]
c) calcium carbonate → calcium oxide + carbon dioxide [1]
d) phosphorus + oxygen → phosphorus oxide [1]
e) aluminium + iron oxide → aluminium oxide + iron [1]
[Total 5]

4 Explain the principle of conservation of mass in your own words. [Total 2]

5 When magnesium reacts with hydrochloric acid in a flask on a balance, the mass decreases.
a) Explain why the mass decreases. [2]
b) Explain why this does not break the law of conservation of mass. [1]
[Total 3]

6 When magnesium is burned in air in a crucible, the mass of contents of the crucible increases.
a) Explain why the mass increases. [2]
b) Explain why this does not break the law of conservation of mass. [1]
[Total 3]

Energy changes during reactions

You will have noticed that heat is given out during many chemical reactions. You might have noticed some reactions where the opposite happens and the reaction mixture feels cold. Almost all reactions involve energy changes.

Exothermic reactions

These are reactions where the reaction mixture get hotter. In these reactions, chemical energy from the reactants is converted into heat energy and given out. Examples include combustion, respiration and neutralisation. Most reactions are **exothermic**, though the amount of heat given out may be small.

Endothermic reactions

These are reactions where the reaction mixture gets colder. In these reactions, heat energy is taken in and converted into chemical energy in the products. Examples include the decomposition of metal carbonates and the reaction of acids with baking powder. **Endothermic** reactions are less common.

?

7 a) What is the difference between an exothermic and an endothermic reaction? *[2]*
b) Give one example of each type of reaction. *[2]*
[Total 4]

Summary

○ New substances are always formed in chemical reactions.

○ Oxidation occurs when a substance reacts with oxygen.

○ Combustion occurs when a substance burns in oxygen.

○ Reduction occurs when oxygen is removed from a substance.

○ Decomposition occurs when a substance is broken up into simpler ones.

○ Decomposition can be caused by heat (thermal decomposition), electricity (electrolysis) or light.

○ Neutralisation occurs when an acid reacts with a base.

○ Precipitation occurs when solutions react to form a solid.

○ Displacement occurs when a more reactive element takes the place of a less reactive element in a compound.

○ The mass of the products in a reaction equals the mass of the reactants.

○ Almost all reactions involve energy changes. Most reactions are exothermic (the reaction mixture gets hotter), but some are endothermic (the reaction mixture gets colder).

Questions

1 Copy and complete the following sentences.
In a _____ reaction, new substances are formed. In a _____ change, no new substances are formed. _____ is conserved in both types of change. Examples of types of chemical reactions include _____, _____ and _____.
[Total 3]

2 Is each of the following a chemical reaction or a physical change:
a) burning petrol in an engine *[1]*
b) using indigestion tablets *[1]*
c) paint drying *[1]*
d) bacon frying *[1]*
e) a car rusting *[1]*
f) a dead leaf rotting *[1]*
g) dissolving nail varnish in nail varnish remover *[1]*
h) digesting food? *[1]*
[Total 8]

3 For each of the following reactions, write a word equation <u>and</u> name the type of reaction:
a) When copper oxide is heated with hydrogen, copper and steam are formed. *[2]*
b) When hydrochloric acid is mixed with sodium hydroxide, sodium chloride and water are formed. *[2]*
c) When chlorine is passed through a solution of potassium bromide, bromine and potassium chloride are formed. *[2]*
d) When light shines on silver chloride, silver and chlorine are formed. *[2]*
e) When solutions of sodium sulphate and barium nitrate are mixed, sodium nitrate solution and solid barium sulphate are formed. *[2]*
f) When nickel is heated in air, nickel oxide is formed, although the nickel does not burn. *[2]*
[Total 12]

4 Emily carried out an experiment to investigate how much heat was given out when different amounts of zinc react with copper sulphate solution. She mixed copper sulphate solution with zinc powder in a boiling tube in each experiment. Her results are shown in Table 1.1.
a) Copy the table and complete the final column. *[1]*
b) Is this reaction exothermic or endothermic? *[1]*
c) The reaction is a displacement reaction. Write a word equation for this reaction. *[1]*
d) What is the independent variable in this experiment? *[1]*
e) What is the dependent variable in this experiment? *[1]*
f) Plot a graph of temperature rise (*y*-axis) against mass of zinc (*x*-axis). *[4]*
g) Describe the relationship between the mass of zinc and the temperature rise. *[3]*
h) Try to explain this relationship. *[2]*
i) What must Emily have done to make this a fair test? *[2]*
j) If the copper sulphate solution had a mass of 20 g in each experiment, what would have been the total mass of the chemicals in the beaker at the end of the experiment if 1 g of zinc was added? *[1]*
(Total 17)

Table 1.1

Mass of zinc (g)	Starting temperature (°C)	Final temperature (°C)	Temperature rise (°C)
0	23	23	
0.25	23	31	
0.50	23	39	
0.75	23	46	
1.00	24	53	
1.25	23	58	
1.50	23	64	
1.75	22	64	
2.00	23	65	
2.25	23	65	
2.50	22	64	

6.2 The rate of chemical reactions

What affects the **rate** (speed) of chemical reactions and how can we speed them up or slow them down? Some reactions, like explosions, are very quick, but other reactions, like rusting, are very slow. To be able to control chemical reactions you need to understand the factors that affect their rate.

How reactions take place

For two substances to react, their particles must collide with each other. The particles in liquids and gases are constantly moving about and the particles in solids vibrate about fixed positions. Therefore, when different substances are mixed together, their particles are likely to collide with each other (except for mixtures of solids).

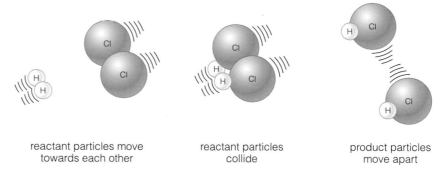

| reactant particles move towards each other | reactant particles collide | product particles move apart |

Figure 2.1 *Reaction of hydrogen and chlorine particles.*

Some of these collisions may result in reactions. The more frequent the collisions, the faster the reaction.

Activation energy

Particles need to have enough energy to react. This amount of energy is called the **activation energy**. Not all of the collisions between particles produce reactions because some of the particles do not have enough energy.

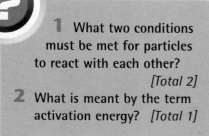

?

1 What two conditions must be met for particles to react with each other?
[Total 2]

2 What is meant by the term activation energy? *[Total 1]*

Reactions such as magnesium reacting with hydrochloric acid take place very easily because the reaction has a low activation energy. Other reactions do not take place unless extra energy is supplied. For example, methane and oxygen do not react with each other unless extra energy is supplied, usually from a spark or a flame. Once the reaction has started however, the heat energy the reaction gives out supplies the unreacted particles with enough energy to continue the reaction.

Speeding up reactions

Reactions occur when the reactant particles collide with enough energy to form new substances. The rate of a reaction can be changed by altering the energy of the particles or how often they collide. Therefore **temperature**, **concentration** of solutions and the **surface area** of solids affect the rate of reactions, as do substances called **catalysts**.

The effect of temperature

The higher the temperature, the faster the reaction. For example, if butter is not put in a fridge it goes rancid much faster (butter going rancid is a chemical reaction). In fact, the reason that all food is kept in a fridge is to slow down the reactions that make it go off.

There are two reasons why reactions are faster at higher temperatures. Firstly, the particles move faster and so collide more often. Secondly, the particles have more energy and so are more likely to react when they do collide. This combined effect means that temperature has a very big effect on the rate of a reaction. In fact, as a rough guide to some reactions, the rate is approximately doubled by an increase in temperature of 10 °C.

The effect of concentration

The higher the concentration of a solution, the faster the reaction. For example, if bleach is used to remove a stain, it will be removed faster by a more concentrated bleach.

In a more concentrated solution, the particles of the dissolved substance are closer together. This means that when another substance is added, collisions will take place more often.

Gas explosions in homes can be caused by switching on a light. If gas has been leaking, then a tiny spark from turning on a light can provide the activation energy to start the explosive reaction between the methane and the oxygen.

Figure 2.2 *Butter goes off more slowly if kept cool in a fridge.*

Figure 2.3 *Some bottles of bleach are more concentrated than others.*

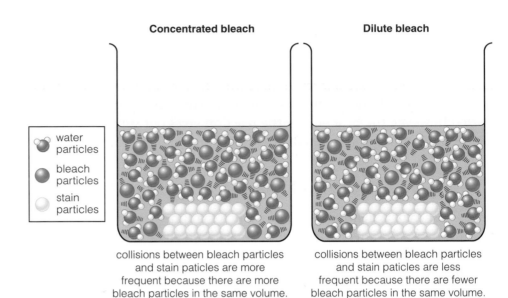

Figure 2.4 *The difference between concentrated and dilute solutions.*

collisions between bleach particles and stain paticles are more frequent because there are more bleach particles in the same volume.

collisions between bleach particles and stain paticles are less frequent because there are fewer bleach particles in the same volume.

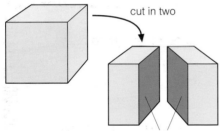

cut in two

more surface area

Figure 2.5 *Breaking up a solid to increase surface area.*

3 Why does each of the following increase the rate of chemical reactions:
a) increasing the temperature [4]
b) increasing the concentration of solutions [2]
c) increasing the surface area of solids [2]
d) adding a catalyst? [2]
[Total 10]

Increasing surface area

The smaller the pieces a solid is made into, the greater its surface area and so the faster it reacts. For example, indigestion tablets work faster if they are chewed rather than just swallowed. Chewing breaks them up into smaller pieces, increasing their surface area.

For example, if a cube is cut in half, there are two extra surfaces. So there is a larger surface area.

The more pieces a solid is broken up into, the more surface area it has and so more of its particles can be hit by the other reactant. This means the reaction is faster and explains why a powder reacts faster than lumps of a solid.

The effect of catalysts

Catalysts are substances that change the rate of reactions without being used up. Most catalysts speed up reactions and work by lowering the activation energy. Catalysts that slow reactions down are called **inhibitors**. They work by increasing the activation energy.

Margarine is made by reacting plant oils, such as sunflower oil, with hydrogen. The reaction is slow but is speeded up by a nickel catalyst. Once made, margarine is easily oxidised and goes off, so inhibitors called antioxidants are added to margarine to slow down the oxidation.

Enzymes are biological catalysts. Enzymes work best at specific temperatures and stop working at higher temperatures. For example, enzymes in the human body work best around 37 °C which is body temperature. There are specific enzymes for many chemical reactions in living creatures. For example, enzymes are used to break down food in digestion. The food industry also makes use of enzymes in the production of bread, beer, yoghurts and cheese.

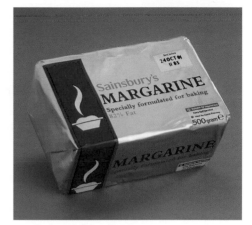

Figure 2.6 *A catalyst is used to make margarine and an inhibitor is used to stop it going off.*

Summary

- For substances to react with each other, their particles must collide and have enough energy to react.
- The minimum amount of energy that particles need to react is called the activation energy.
- Increasing the temperature of a reaction mixture makes it go faster because more particles have enough energy to react and the particles collide more often.
- Increasing the concentration of a solution makes a reaction go faster because the particles are closer together and so collide more often.
- Decreasing the size of pieces of a solid increases its surface area. This makes a reaction go faster because there are more particles at the surface for the other reactant to collide with.
- A catalyst is a substance that changes the rate of a reaction without being used up.
- An enzyme is a biological catalyst.

6 Further chemistry

Questions

1 Copy and complete the following sentences.
For particles to react with each other, they must have
enough _____ and _____ with each
other. The rate of a chemical reaction is changed by
_____, _____ of solutions and the
_____ _____ of solids. A
_____ is a substance that speeds up a
reaction but is not used up.   *[Total 3]*

2 Explain each of the following.
   a) Butter goes rancid (goes off) faster if it is not kept
      in a fridge.   *[1]*
   b) Carrots cook faster if they are sliced.   *[1]*
   c) Difficult stains can be removed more easily with
      neat cleaning solutions (i.e. taken straight from
      the bottle) rather than adding the solutions
      to water first.   *[1]*
   d) An aspirin tablet works faster if it is crushed
      rather than swallowed whole.   *[1]*
                                             [Total 4]

3 Imran did an experiment to see how changing the
surface area of limestone affected the rate at which
it reacts with hydrochloric acid. He timed how long it
took for the reaction to produce 50 cm³ of carbon
dioxide gas. His results are shown in Table 2.1.

Table 2.1

Size	large chips	small chips	powder
Time (s)	150	110	15

   a) What was the independent variable in this
      experiment ?   *[1]*
   b) What was the dependent variable in this
      experiment?   *[1]*
   c) Which had the biggest surface area large chips,
      small chips or powder?   *[1]*
   d) What is the relationship between the surface area
      and the time the reaction takes?   *[1]*
   e) What is the relationship between the surface area
      and the rate of the reaction?   *[1]*

   f) Explain why changing the surface area has the
      effect that it does.   *[2]*
   g) What must Imran have done to make this
      experiment a fair test?   *[4]*
   h) Write a word equation for this reaction (limestone
      is calcium carbonate).   *[2]*
                                            [Total 13]

4 When hydrochloric acid reacts with sodium
thiosulphate, the solution turns cloudy because of
the formation of sulphur. After a time you can no
longer see through it. Rebecca did some experiments
using this reaction and timed how long it took to
turn too cloudy to see through. Her results are
shown in Table 2.2.

Table 2.2

Experiment	A	B	C	D	E
Temperature (°C)	20	20	20	30	40
Volume of sodium thiosulphate (cm³)	50	50	25	50	50
Volume of hydrochloric acid (cm³)	5	10	5	10	10
Volume of water (cm³)	5	0	30	0	0
Time to become too cloudy to see through (s)	80	40	160	20	10

   a) Which experiment was the fastest?   *[1]*
   b) i) Which experiments can be used to see the
          effect of changing the concentration of the
          sodium thiosulphate?
      ii) What is its effect?   *[2]*
   c) i) Which experiments can be used to see the
          effect of changing the concentration of the
          hydrochloric acid?
      ii) What is its effect?   *[2]*
   d) i) Which experiments can be used to see the
          effect of changing the temperature?
      ii) What is its effect?   *[2]*
   e) Why was water added in experiments A and C? *[1]*
                                             [Total 8]

6.3 The structure of atoms

All substances are made of tiny particles called atoms, but what are atoms made of? We cannot see atoms, but an understanding of what atoms are and the differences between atoms is very important if we are to make sense of chemistry.

The size of atoms

Atoms are tiny. If 100 000 000 carbon atoms were placed in a line, the line would only be 7.7 mm long.

Atomic structure

Atoms are made up of three smaller particles called **protons**, **neutrons** and **electrons**. Table 3.1 shows the mass and electric charge of these particles. The mass is shown as relative mass, which is the mass of the particle compared to a proton.

At the centre of the atom is a tiny **nucleus**, which is far smaller than the atom. The nucleus contains protons and neutrons, and so most of the mass of the atom is in the nucleus. Outside the nucleus are the electrons which orbit the nucleus in **shells**.

> **!** The size of a carbon atom compared to the height of an adult is the same as the height of an adult compared to the distance from the Earth to Venus.

Table 3.1

	Relative mass	Electric charge
proton	1	+1
neutron	1	neutral
electron	0.0005	−1

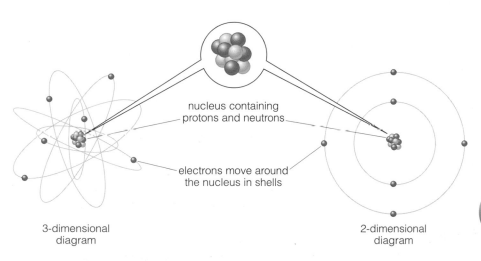

nucleus containing protons and neutrons

electrons move around the nucleus in shells

3-dimensional diagram

2-dimensional diagram

Figure 3.1 *The inside of an atom.*

Atoms are neutral because they contain the same number of electrons, which are negatively charged, and protons which are positively charged.

> **!** The nucleus is tiny compared to the size of the atom. If the nucleus was the size of a pea, then the atom would be the size of a football pitch.

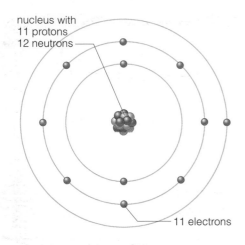

nucleus with
11 protons
12 neutrons

11 electrons

Figure 3.2 *Sodium atom.*

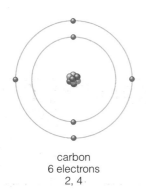

carbon
6 electrons
2, 4

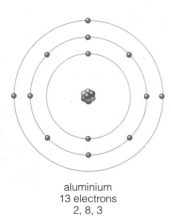

aluminium
13 electrons
2, 8, 3

Figure 3.3 *Electron shells of carbon and aluminium.*

Atomic number and mass number

Atoms of different elements have different numbers of protons, neutrons and electrons. Atoms are described by their **mass number** and **atomic number** (also called proton number):

> **atomic number = number of protons**
> **mass number = number of protons + number of neutrons**

These two numbers can be used to work out how many protons, neutrons and electrons there are in an atom. Remember that because atoms are neutral, the number of electrons always equals the number of protons:

- number of protons = atomic number
- number of neutrons = mass number – atomic number
- number of electrons = atomic number.

For example, for sodium atoms:

> atomic number = 11
> mass number = 23.

Therefore:

> number of protons = 11
> number of neutrons = 23 – 11 = 12
> number of electrons = 11.

The number of protons in the nucleus of an atom determines which element the atom is. For example, all atoms with eleven protons are sodium atoms. Atoms of different elements have different numbers of protons. The elements are placed in order of atomic number in the Periodic Table.

Electronic structure

The electrons are arranged in shells (energy levels). Two electrons can fit in the first shell, eight electrons in the second shell and eight electrons in the third shell (there are more shells after these three). Electrons fill the shells closest to the nucleus first.

Rather than drawing the shells, the electronic structure is often written out. For example, the electronic structure of carbon atoms is 2,4 which means there are two electrons in the first shell and four in the second shell. The electronic structure of aluminium atoms is 2,8,3 which means there are two electrons in the first shell, eight in the second shell and three in the third shell.

Summary

- Atoms contain protons, neutrons and electrons.
- The protons and neutrons are found in the nucleus which is very small compared to the size of the atom.
- The electrons orbit the nucleus in shells.
- Electrons occupy the shells closest to the nucleus, but only a limited number of electrons can fit in each shell.
- The atomic number is the number of protons in an atom.
- The mass number is the number of protons plus the number of neutrons in an atom.
- Atoms are neutral because they contain the same number of electrons and protons.

Questions

1 Copy and complete the following sentences.
Atoms contain smaller subatomic particles called
_____, _____ and _____.
At the centre of the atom is the _____
which contains the _____ and
_____. *[Total 3]*

2 a) Explain why atoms are neutral. *[3]*
b) Explain why the nucleus contains most of the mass of the atom. *[2]*
[Total 5]

3 a) What is meant by the atomic number of an atom? *[1]*
b) What is meant by the mass number of an atom? *[1]*
c) Copy and complete Table 3.2. *[8]*

Table 3.2

Atom	He	Cl	N	
Atomic number	2			18
Mass number	4			40
Number of protons		17		
Number of neutrons		18	7	
Number of electrons				18
Electronic structure			2,5	

[Total 10]

4 Look at Table 3.3.

Table 3.3

Atom	Atomic number	Mass number
potassium	19	39
aluminium	13	27
hydrogen	1	1
calcium	20	40
sulphur	16	32

a) Which atom has 13 electrons? *[1]*
b) Which atom has the electronic structure 2,8,6? *[1]*
c) Which atom has no neutrons? *[1]*
d) Which two atoms have the same number of neutrons? *[2]*
e) Which atoms have equal numbers of neutrons and protons? *[2]*
f) Which atoms have equal numbers of electrons and protons? *[1]*
[Total 8]

6.4 The Periodic Table

Why is the **Periodic Table** so important and why are the elements arranged in such an unusual way? The Periodic Table can be used to predict the chemical and physical properties of the elements.

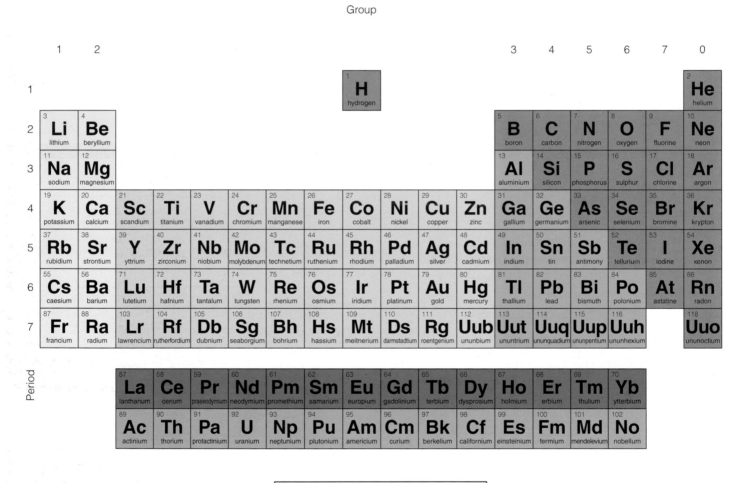

Figure 4.1 *The Periodic Table.*

How the Periodic Table is arranged

The elements are arranged in order of increasing atomic number (the atomic number is the number of protons in the nucleus). The vertical columns in the table are called **groups**, and the horizontal rows are called **periods**. The block in the middle is known as the **transition metals**. The blocks at the bottom are known as the **lanthanides and actinides**. This arrangement puts the metals towards the left and the non-metals on the right of the table.

The block at the bottom should actually be put between Group 2 and the transition metals as shown in Figure 4.2. However, it is usually placed below so that the table fits better onto a piece of paper.

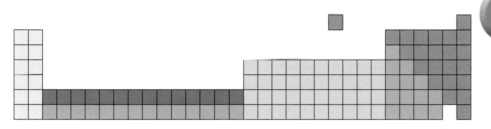

Figure 4.2 *The long form of the Periodic Table.*

Groups

All the elements in the same group have similar chemical properties. This is because they all have the same number of electrons in their outer shell.

For example, in Group 1 all the elements have one electron in their outer shell. The electronic structure of the first three elements in Group 1 are:

- lithium   2,1
- sodium   2,8,1
- potassium   2,8,8,1

The outer electrons are the most important because these are the electrons involved in chemical reactions.

Element 102 is called nobelium after Alfred Nobel, the man who founded the Nobel Peace Prize (and several other awards). He was also the inventor of dynamite! He hoped that his explosives would help to end wars and he worked for world peace.

1 What is the Periodic Table? [Total 1]

2 In what order are the elements in the Periodic Table? [Total 1]

3 Give the symbol of the element:
a) at the top of Group 7 [1]
b) in Group 3, Period 3 [1]
c) one of the transition metals. [1]
[Total 3]

4 How many electrons will each of the following elements have in its outer energy level:
a) magnesium (Mg) [1]
b) bromine (Br) [1]
c) phosphorus (P)? [1]
[Total 3]

Figure 4.3 *Caesium reacts explosively with water.*

Group 1 – the alkali metals

This group contains well known elements such as sodium and potassium. All the elements in Group 1:

○ have one electron in their outer shell of electrons
○ are soft metals
○ are solids with quite low melting points
○ have a relatively low density (some even float on water)
○ react with water forming hydrogen gas and an alkali.

Going down the group from lithium to francium, the elements become more reactive. For example, lithium fizzes when it reacts with water whereas caesium reacts explosively.

Group 7 – the halogens

This group contains well known elements such as fluorine, chlorine, bromine and iodine. All the elements in Group 7:

○ have seven electrons in their outer shell
○ are non-metals
○ are poisonous
○ are coloured
○ have fairly low melting points
○ are made up of particles that are molecules containing two atoms (e.g. chlorine molecules, Cl_2).

Going down the group from fluorine to astatine, the elements become less reactive.

> **!** Chlorine was used as a poison gas during World War I, killing thousands of soldiers.

Group 0 – the noble gases

This group contains well known elements such as helium, neon and argon. All the elements in Group 0:

○ have a full outer shell
○ are non-metals
○ are gases
○ are colourless
○ are made up of particles that are individual atoms
○ are very unreactive (most do not react with anything at all).

> **!** Air ships are filled with helium because it is very light and unreactive.

Figure 4.4 *A modern airship.*

The transition metals

The central block in the Periodic Table contains many common metals such as iron, copper, gold, silver and platinum. All of the elements in this block:

- are metals (and so conduct electricity and heat)
- have high melting points (with a few exceptions, e.g. mercury)
- generally form coloured compounds
- often act as catalysts.

> Platinum is more valuable than gold. However, in the sixteenth century, the Spanish Government dumped all their platinum in the sea because they thought it might be used to make false coins!

Summary

- The elements in the Periodic Table are arranged in order of increasing atomic number.
- The metals are on the left of the table, with non-metals on the right.
- The vertical columns are called groups.
- The horizontal rows are called periods.
- All the elements in the same group have similar chemical properties because they have the same number of electrons in their outer shell.
- The outer electrons are involved in chemical reactions.

Questions

1 Copy and complete the following sentences.
The Periodic Table lists all the _____ in order
of increasing _____ _____. The rows
are called _____ and the columns are called
_____. It is arranged so that elements in the
same _____ have similar chemical properties.
Non-metals are found on the _____ of
the table.   *[Total 3]*

2 Use the Periodic Table on page 190 to help you
answer the following questions.
a) Name the element at the top of Group 4.   *[1]*
b) Name the element in Group 7, Period 3.   *[1]*
c) Name a metal in Group 5.   *[1]*
d) Name a non-metal in Group 3.   *[1]*
e) In which group is the element with atomic
number 50?   *[1]*
                                              [Total 5]

3 a) Copy the outline of the main part of the Periodic
Table shown in Figure 4.5. Shade all the elements
that, at room temperature, are solids in one
colour, liquids in another and gases in a third
colour. Make a key for the three colours.   *[4]*
  ○ Elements that are gases: hydrogen, helium,
nitrogen, oxygen, fluorine, neon, chlorine,
argon, krypton, xenon and radon.
  ○ Elements that are liquids: mercury, bromine.
  ○ Elements that are solids: the rest.

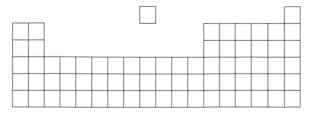

Figure 4.5

b) Is there a link between the state of an element
and its position in the table?   *[2]*
                                              [Total 6]

4 State which group of the Periodic Table the following
elements belong in.
a) Element X is a reactive non-metal solid consisting
of X_2 molecules.   *[1]*
b) Element Z is an unreactive gas.   *[1]*
                                              [Total 2]

5 This question is about francium, the element at the
bottom of Group 1.
a) What is the symbol of francium?   *[1]*
b) Is it a metal or a non-metal?   *[1]*
c) Will it be more or less reactive than caesium, the
element above it?   *[1]*
d) i)   Describe the reaction between water and
francium.
    ii) Name the gas formed in this reaction. *[2]*
e) i)   Use the data in the table below to plot a graph
of melting points down Group 1 (*y*-axis)
against atomic number (*x*-axis).
    ii) Use the graph to predict the melting point of
francium.   *[5]*

Element	Atomic number	Melting point (°C)
lithium	3	180
sodium	11	98
potassium	19	64
rubidium	37	39
caesium	55	29
francium	87	?

[Total 10]

6 Use the Periodic Table on page 190 to help you
answer the following questions.
a) In which block is uranium (U)?   *[1]*
b) In which block is platinum (Pt)?   *[1]*
c) Name the most reactive element in Group 7. *[1]*
d) Will element 117 be a metal or a non-metal? *[1]*
                                              [Total 4]

6.5 Formulas and equations

How can you work out the formula of a compound? What do the numbers in chemical equations mean? Chemists use formulas and equations to save writing the full names of substances. This chapter will explain how to write formulas and what the numbers in equations mean.

Valency

The **valency** of an atom can be used to work out the formula of a compound. The valencies of some common atoms are shown in Table 5.1.

Table 5.1

Valency			
1	**2**	**3**	**4**
Na sodium	Mg magnesium	Al aluminium	C carbon
K potassium	Ca calcium	Fe iron (III)	Si silicon
H hydrogen	Cu copper	N nitrogen	
F fluorine	Zn zinc		
Cl chlorine	Fe iron (II)		
Br bromine	O oxygen		
I iodine	S sulphur		

Transition metals can have more than one valency. For example, iron can have a valency of 2 or 3.

For compounds made of molecules, the valency is the number of bonds each atom forms. Some examples are given on the next page. The diagrams with these examples show the bonds in the molecules, but in the rest of the book these bonds have not been drawn because diagrams without bonds give a better impression of what the molecules look like.

1 What is meant by the term valency? *[Total 1]*

Further chemistry

Figure 5.1 *Water (H₂O).*

Figure 5.2 *Methane (CH₄).*

Figure 5.3 *Carbon dioxide (CO₂).*

?

2 Give the names of the following substances:

a) ZnO [1]

b) CuCl₂ [1]

c) Fe₂S₃ [1]

[Total 3]

3 Write the formula of the following compounds:

a) sodium iodide [1]

b) copper oxide [1]

c) calcium bromide [1]

d) aluminium oxide [1]

e) potassium sulphide [1]

[Total 5]

Water is a compound made up of hydrogen and oxygen. Oxygen has a valency of two and so forms two bonds. Hydrogen has a valency of one and so forms one bond. This means that two hydrogen atoms must join to one oxygen atom by single bonds, hence the formula H_2O.

Methane is a compound made up of carbon and hydrogen. Carbon has a valency of four and so forms four bonds. Hydrogen has a valency of one and so forms one bond. This means that four hydrogen atoms must join to one carbon atom by single bonds, hence the formula CH_4.

Carbon dioxide is a compound made up of carbon and oxygen. Carbon has a valency of four and so forms four bonds. Oxygen has a valency of two and so forms two bonds. This means that two oxygen atoms must join to one carbon atom by double bonds, hence the formula CO_2.

There is a quick way to work out formulas called the cross-over method. To do this, the symbols and valencies should be written and then the valency numbers swapped round to give the formula. The numbers should be cancelled down if possible. Remember that 1s are not usually written in formulas. For example:

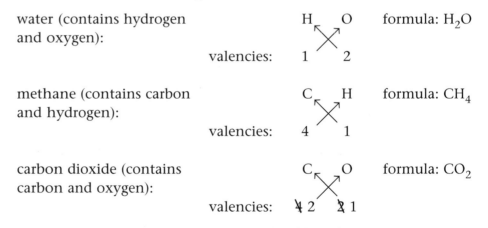

water (contains hydrogen and oxygen):   H   O   formula: H_2O
valencies: 1   2

methane (contains carbon and hydrogen):   C   H   formula: CH_4
valencies: 4   1

carbon dioxide (contains carbon and oxygen):   C   O   formula: CO_2
valencies: 4̶ 2   2̶ 1

Although many compounds are not made of molecules (they contain particles called ions), the formulas of most compounds can be worked out using the cross-over method.

Some atoms have two or more different valencies. For example, iron can have a valency of two or three, and so its compounds have the roman numerals (II) or (III) in their names to indicate the valency of the iron. For example:

iron(II) chloride (contains iron(II) and chlorine):   Fe   Cl   formula: $FeCl_2$
valencies: 2   1

iron(III) chloride (contains
iron(III) and chlorine):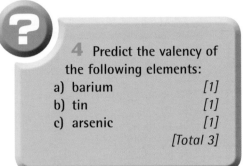

Predicting valencies

There is a link between the valency of an atom and its position in
the Periodic Table as shown in Table 5.2. The Periodic Table can be
used to predict the valency of atoms.

Table 5.2

Group	1	2	3	4	5	6	7
Valency	1	2	3	4	3	2	1

? **4** Predict the valency of
the following elements:
a) barium [1]
b) tin [1]
c) arsenic [1]
[Total 3]

Chemical equations

We often use word equations to describe what happens in a chemical
reaction. For example, the reaction of methane with oxygen is:

methane + oxygen → carbon dioxide + water

However, we often write equations with formulas rather than words.
There are numbers in front of the formulas to show how many atoms
or molecules react with each other. For example, in the reaction of
methane with oxygen, the equation is:

$CH_4 + 2O_2 \rightarrow CO_2 + 2H_2O$

This shows that one molecule of methane (made of one atom of
carbon and four atoms of hydrogen and written CH_4) reacts with two
molecules of oxygen (O_2) to produce one molecule of carbon dioxide
(CO_2) and two molecules of water (H_2O), as shown in Figure 5.4.

? **5** Balance the
following equations:
a) $C + O_2 \rightarrow CO$ [1]
b) $Fe + Cl_2 \rightarrow FeCl_3$ [1]
c) $C_3H_8 + O_2 \rightarrow$
$CO_2 + H_2O$ [1]
d) $Ag_2O \rightarrow Ag + O_2$ [1]
e) $Na + O_2 \rightarrow Na_2O$ [1]
f) $NH_3 + O_2 \rightarrow$
$NO + H_2O$ [1]
[Total 6]

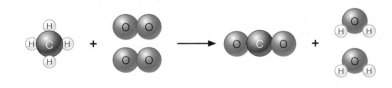

Figure 5.4

It can be seen that there are four hydrogen, one carbon and four oxygen atoms on both sides of the equation. We say that the equation is **balanced**. This has to be the case because we cannot make or destroy atoms in a chemical reaction.

Summary

- The valency of an atom helps you to work out the formula of a compound.
- In compounds made of molecules, the valency of an atom is the number of bonds the atom forms.
- Chemical equations are written with formulas to show us how many atoms or molecules of each substance react.
- Equations have to be balanced because atoms cannot be made or destroyed in chemical reactions.

Questions

1 Copy and complete the following sentences.
The formula of a molecule tells us how many
_____ of each kind are in a molecule. For
example, the formula of water is H_2O which means
that _____ hydrogen atoms are joined to
_____ oxygen atom. The formula of a
compound can be worked out using _____.

[Total 2]

2 Which elements do the following compounds contain:
a) nitrogen dioxide   *[1]*
b) calcium chloride   *[1]*
c) lead sulphide   *[1]*
d) iron(III) bromide?   *[1]*

[Total 4]

3 Write the formula of each of the following compounds:
a) potassium chloride   *[1]*
b) aluminium iodide   *[1]*
c) potassium oxide   *[1]*
d) calcium sulphide   *[1]*
e) iron(II) oxide   *[1]*
f) aluminium sulphide   *[1]*
g) copper bromide   *[1]*
h) zinc chloride   *[1]*
i) sodium nitride   *[1]*
j) hydrogen sulphide   *[1]*
k) hydrogen oxide   *[1]*
l) silane (containing silicon and hydrogen)   *[1]*
m) silica (containing silicon and oxygen).   *[1]*

[Total 13]

4 Name each of the following compounds:
a) NaBr   *[1]*
b) $MgCl_2$ *[1]*
c) FeF_2 *[1]*
d) CuS   *[1]*

[Total 4]

5 In each of the following equations, numbers are
required in the spaces to balance the equation. Copy
and complete the equations.
a) $Mg + \_\_\_ HCl \rightarrow MgCl_2 + H_2$ *[1]*
b) $N_2 + \_\_\_ H_2 \rightarrow \_\_\_ NH_3$ *[1]*
c) $C_2H_4 + \_\_\_ O_2 \rightarrow \_\_\_ CO_2 + \_\_\_ H_2O$ *[1]*
d) $\_\_\_ Na + O_2 \rightarrow \_\_\_ Na_2O$ *[1]*
e) $\_\_\_ Al + \_\_\_ Cl_2 \rightarrow \_\_\_ AlCl_3$ *[1]*

[Total 5]

6 Balance each of the following equations:
a) $H_2 + O_2 \rightarrow H_2O$ *[1]*
b) $H_2 + Cl_2 \rightarrow HCl$ *[1]*
c) $S + O_2 \rightarrow SO_2$ *[1]*
d) $SO_2 + O_2 \rightarrow SO_3$ *[1]*
e) $C_2H_6 + O_2 \rightarrow CO_2 + H_2O$ *[1]*

[Total 5]

7 Write an equation for each of the following reactions
(remember, equations must always be balanced):
a) magnesium + oxygen $\rightarrow$ magnesium oxide   *[2]*
b) aluminium + oxygen $\rightarrow$ aluminium oxide   *[2]*

[Total 4]

The uses of catalysts

Catalysts are substances that speed up chemical reactions without being used up. The product can be made in a shorter time if a catalyst is used. Using a catalyst also often means that reactions can be done at lower temperatures and pressures than they would otherwise. Overall, this uses less energy, saves time and saves money. Catalysts are used for many industrial processes. Some examples are shown in Table 6.1.

Enzymes are protein molecules, which are naturally occurring catalysts. Most biochemical processes (e.g. respiration, digestion) involve enzymes. We also use enzymes in some industrial reactions because they are highly efficient catalysts. Examples of such processes are given in Table 6.2.

Catalyst	Process
iron	making ammonia from nitrogen and hydrogen – ammonia is then used to make fertilisers
vanadium oxide	making sulphuric acid from sulphur dioxide and oxygen
nickel	making margarine from vegetable oils
Ziegler–Natta	making polythene from ethene

Table 6.1 *Some industrial catalysts.*

Type of process	Enzyme	Process
natural	protease	digesting protein molecules into amino acids
	lysozyme	found in tears in the eye – it kills bacteria, so protects the eye from infections
industrial	zymase	anaerobic respiration in yeast forming ethanol and carbon dioxide from sugars – used to make alcoholic drinks
	lactase	used in making yoghurt from milk

Table 6.2 *Some natural catalysts – enzymes.*

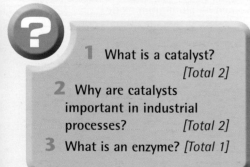

1 What is a catalyst? *[Total 2]*

2 Why are catalysts important in industrial processes? *[Total 2]*

3 What is an enzyme? *[Total 1]*

Catalytic converters

The combustion of petrol in car engines produces several substances that pollute the atmosphere. The polluting exhaust gases include:

- carbon dioxide – greenhouse gas causing **global warming**
- carbon monoxide – **toxic**
- nitrogen oxides – cause **acid rain**
- unburned petrol.

Since 1993, all petrol-engine cars have had to be built with catalytic converters to reduce pollution. Catalytic converters remove the polluting carbon monoxide and nitrogen oxides, along with the unburned hydrocarbons – but actually slightly increase the amount of carbon dioxide given out by cars.

Catalytic converters contain the catalysts platinum, rhodium and palladium. These all speed up the reactions to remove the pollutant gases.

These catalysts are very expensive metals. In the design of a catalytic converter, it is very important that the catalyst is as efficient as possible, while using as little of the metals as possible. In order to achieve this, the catalyst needs to have a very large surface area. The catalyst is spread very thinly on a ceramic honeycomb support (Figure 6.1). The converter is about the size of a shoe box, but there is a surface area of about three football pitches inside the converter. The catalyst layer is too thin to support itself, which is why it must be coated onto a stronger support.

Figure 6.1 *Inside a catalytic converter.*

When a catalytic converter is finished with, it is not thrown away. Firstly, the catalysts could cause damage to living creatures if they built up in the environment. Secondly, the metals are very valuable so they are removed and recycled to make new converters.

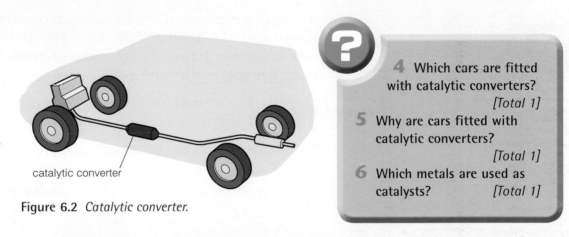

catalytic converter

Figure 6.2 *Catalytic converter.*

?

4 Which cars are fitted with catalytic converters?
[Total 1]

5 Why are cars fitted with catalytic converters?
[Total 1]

6 Which metals are used as catalysts? [Total 1]

Questions

1 a) List three pollutants removed from exhaust gases by catalytic converters. [3]
b) Give one pollutant that is not removed by catalytic converters. [1]
[Total 4]

2 a) Catalysts are usually made with a large surface area. Explain why. [1]
b) Explain, in terms of particles, why a large surface area has the effect it has. [2]
c) How is a large surface area achieved in a catalytic converter? [2]
[Total 5]

3 Give one economic and one environmental reason why we should not throw away old catalytic converters. [Total 2]

4 Catalytic converters do not work fully when they are cold. They only function properly when the car has been travelling for a few miles and the catalyst has warmed up. Give two reasons, in terms of particles, why catalytic converters work better at higher temperatures. [Total 4]

6 Further chemistry

Figure 6.3 *Methane burning.*

1 **What problems are associated with using fossil fuels?** *[Total 2]*

2 **Suggest some alternative fuels that could be used instead of fossil fuels.** *[Total 2]*

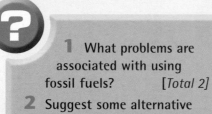

Some people suffering from angina, a heart condition, take small amounts of nitroglycerine as a medicine.

Useful energy changes

There is an energy change in all chemical reactions – these energy changes are put to use in many ways. Humans have always burned fuels to provide heat, starting with wood in the Stone Age. The burning of a fuel is a chemical reaction that releases a lot of heat. Fuels in use today include methane (natural gas), petrol, diesel, ethanol, biodiesel and hydrogen.

Explosions are very fast chemical reactions that give out a lot of heat and gases. Explosives have many uses – for example in mining, quarrying, demolition, air bags in cars and nail guns, as well as being used to cause death in wars and terrorism.

A common explosive is dynamite which contains nitrogylcerine – this is very unstable. It will explode if it is knocked too hard and so it is very dangerous. It is safer in the form of dynamite, which is made by mixing nitroglycerine with a clay.

Many explosives react with oxygen when they explode. Nitroglycerine is unusual in that no oxygen is needed:

nitroglycerine → carbon dioxide + steam + nitrogen + oxygen

Figure 6.4 *Dynamite is used to demolish tower blocks.*

The man who invented dynamite, Alfred Nobel, also founded the Nobel Peace prize. He worked for world peace and hoped that his explosives would help to end wars. He thought that people would be less likely to go to war knowing that their enemy could kill and destroy so much with explosives. He left the fortune that he made from explosives to set up the peace prize, along with several others, after his death.

Some special food cans are produced that will cook the food for you. There are two layers inside one of these cans – on the inside is the food, and around that is an outer layer containing lime (calcium oxide) and bags of water. When the water bags are punctured with a spike, an **exothermic** reaction is started. The heat released cooks the food in the can:

calcium oxide + water → calcium hydroxide

Ice packs are often used to treat injuries. Inside an ice pack there are crystals of ammonium nitrate and a bag of water. The ice pack is screwed up so that the bag of water bursts and mixes with the ammonium nitrate. The reaction between ammonium nitrate and water is **endothermic**, making the pack cold.

food

quicklime

foil separator

plastic button   water

Figure 6.5 *Self-heating can.*

Figure 6.6 *Ice pack in use on an injured knee.*

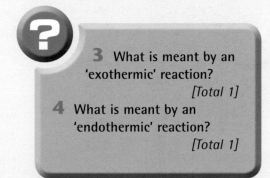

?

3 What is meant by an 'exothermic' reaction?
[Total 1]

4 What is meant by an 'endothermic' reaction?
[Total 1]

Questions

1 a) There are three essential features of a chemical reaction used in explosives. What are they? *[3]*
   b) Why is nitroglycerine a very dangerous explosive? *[1]*
   c) Give two peaceful uses for explosives. *[2]*
   d) In what way do you think Alfred Nobel believed that his explosives could be used to end wars? *[1]*
   [Total 7]

2 a) Where would self-heating cans be useful? *[1]*
   b) Describe, in your own words, how they work. *[4]*
   [Total 5]

3 a) In what circumstances would ice packs in first aid kits be useful? *[1]*
   b) Describe, in your own words, how they work. *[3]*
   [Total 4]

6 Further chemistry

The development of the Periodic Table

H	Li	Be	B	C	N	O
F	Na	Mg	Al	Si	P	S
Cl	K	Ca	Cr	Ti	Mn	Fe
Co Ni	Cu	Zn	Y	In	As	Se

Table 6.3 *Newlands' octaves.*

?

1 In what order did John Newlands arrange the elements? [Total 1]

2 What did he discover when he arranged them in this way? [Total 1]

Figure 6.8 *Dimitri Mendeleev.*

In the early 1800s, about 30 chemical elements were known. Several chemists had also spotted that groups of elements – such as lithium, sodium and potassium – had similar properties. However, no one had found an overall pattern in the behaviour of the elements.

In 1864, around 50 elements were known. The British chemist John Newlands spotted a pattern when he arranged these elements in order of **atomic mass**. He noticed that the properties of the elements seemed to repeat every eighth element – he called this the 'law of octaves' comparing it to musical scales. Lithium, sodium and potassium, for example, are all reactive metals that can be cut with a knife and react vigorously with water, and they were in the same column.

Newlands' ideas were not accepted at the time because the table did not work after calcium. For example, the very unreactive metal copper was in the same group as the highly reactive metals lithium, sodium and potassium.

Dimitri Mendeleev, a Russian chemist, devised a table in 1869 which is the basis of the Periodic Table as we know it. Although he did not know about Newlands' arrangement, his basic idea was the same. However, he realised that there were elements that had not been discovered yet and left gaps for them (shown by * in Table 6.4).

Mendeleev went further and used the patterns in his table to predict the properties of these elements that he thought had yet to be discovered. Three of these elements were discovered in the next few years and his predictions were very accurate. Table 6.5 shows his predictions about the properties of the element between silicon and tin – he called it 'eka-silicon'. It also shows the actual properties of the element when it was discovered in 1886 (called germanium).

In devising his table, Mendeleev did not stick completely to the atomic mass order. For example, he swapped iodine (I) and tellurium (Te) because iodine fitted much better with fluorine, chlorine and bromine than tellurium did. Mendeleev thought that he had to change the order because the atomic masses of some elements had been measured inaccurately. Mendeleev had actually placed the elements in order of

The development of the Periodic Table

6

Group I		Group II		Group III		Group IV		Group V		Group VI		Group VII		Group VIII
H														
Li		Be		B		C		N		O		F		
Na		Mg		Al		Si		P		S		Cl		
K		Ca		*		*		As		Se		Br		Fe Co Ni
	Cu		Zn		*		Tc*		V		Cr		Mn	
Rb		Sr		Y		Sw		Sb		Te		I		Ru Rh Pd
	Ag		Cd		In		Zr		Sb		Mo		*	

Table 6.4 *Mendeleev's periodic table.*

Table 6.5

	Appearance	Melting point	Atomic mass	Density	Formula of oxide	Formula of chloride
'eka-silicon' (Es)	grey metal	over 800°C	72	5.5 g/cm^3	EsO$_2$	EsCl$_4$
germanium (Ge)	grey-white metal	947°C	72.3	5.47 g/cm^3	GeO$_2$	GeCl$_4$

atomic number (the number of protons in each atom), even though he did not know it because **protons**, **neutrons** and **electrons** had not been discovered at the time.

Mendeleev's table was accepted because many of his remarkable predictions about undiscovered elements proved to be correct. His table has been modified as more elements, including the **noble gases**, have been discovered – but the modern table is based on his.

?

3 What key thing did Mendeleev do differently to Newlands? *[Total 1]*

Questions

1 a) Why were Newlands' ideas ignored at the time? *[1]*
   b) In what ways were Newlands' ideas useful and not useful? *[2]*
   [Total 3]

2 a) What convinced people that Mendeleev's table was useful? *[2]*
   b) Why did he not put the elements in strict atomic mass order? *[1]*
   c) In what order had Mendeleev placed the elements, even though he did not realise? *[1]*
   [Total 4]

6 Further chemistry

The development of atomic structure

The idea that substances are made of atoms was accepted in the early 1800s following work by Dalton. However, it is only more recently that scientists realised that atoms are made up of even smaller particles.

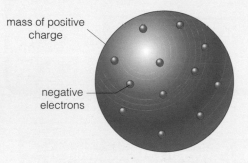

mass of positive charge

negative electrons

Figure 6.9 *Thomson's plum pudding model (1897).*

Thomson's plum pudding model

In 1897, the British scientist J. J. Thomson (1856–1940), working in Cambridge, discovered the **electron** while carrying out experiments on the conduction of electricity through gases. Thomson put forward the plum pudding model of the atom. He suggested that the atom was a tiny sphere of positive charge (the pudding) with negatively charged electrons (the plums) spread throughout the atom.

Rutherford and Bohr's model

Thomson's model was replaced in 1911 by new ideas from Ernest Rutherford (1871–1937), who had earlier worked for Thomson. Rutherford, who was born in New Zealand but working in Manchester, developed his new ideas following experiments by his fellow workers Geiger and Marsden.

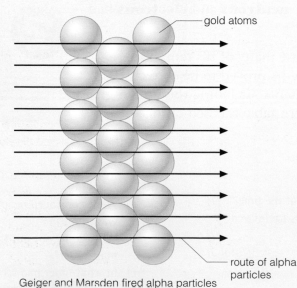

gold atoms

route of alpha particles

Geiger and Marsden fired alpha particles (helium atoms without any electrons) at a very thin piece of gold foil. It was expected that the alpha particles would pass straight through the foil or would only be slightly deflected (based on the *plum pudding* model).

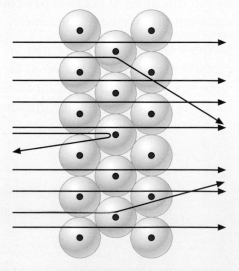

Some of the alpha particles were deflected at large angles or even bounced back. Rutherford realised that this was due to each atom's positive charge being in a tiny nucleus at the centre.

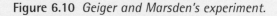

Figure 6.10 *Geiger and Marsden's experiment.*

The development of atomic structure

Rutherford realised that the results did not fit in with Thomson's model and proposed a new model to explain these results. He said that most of the mass and positive charge in an atom must be concentrated in a tiny **nucleus** which is much smaller than the atom itself. The electrons move in the space around the nucleus.

Rutherford realised that his model was not totally correct because the negative electrons would spiral into the nucleus, attracted by the positive charge. In 1913, Neils Bohr (1885–1962), a Danish scientist working with Rutherford, used the new 'quantum physics' to develop the model. He proposed that the electrons moved in stable orbits called shells.

Chadwick's model

In 1932, James Chadwick (1891–1974), who was working with Rutherford, developed the model further when he discovered the **neutron**. Scientists knew that there was some extra mass in atoms that could not be explained by the Rutherford–Bohr model. Chadwick proposed that neutrons were in the nucleus of atoms, that they had no electric charge and were of similar mass to **protons**.

These ideas have been developed further since then, but the basic idea of a tiny nucleus containing protons and neutrons surrounded by electrons remains. Science works by people proposing theories that fit and explain known facts. As more facts are discovered, theories have to be changed or replaced by new ones. When a scientist suggests a theory, it is only a proposed explanation and not a statement of fact.

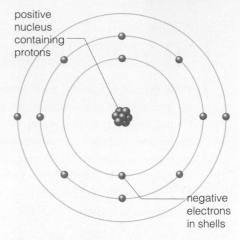

positive nucleus containing protons

negative electrons in shells

Figure 6.11 *Rutherford–Bohr model (1913).*

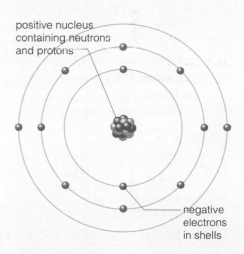

positive nucleus containing neutrons and protons

negative electrons in shells

Figure 6.12 *Chadwick model (1932).*

Questions

1 What significant contribution did each of the following people make to our present ideas about the structure of atoms?
   a) Thomson   [1]
   b) Rutherford   [3]
   c) Bohr   [1]
   d) Chadwick.   [2]
                            [Total 7]

2 Draw a time line to show how ideas about the structure of atoms developed.   [Total 5]

3 The development of ideas about atomic structure shows how science works.
   a) Explain, in simple terms, why Thomson's model was replaced by Rutherford's.   [1]
   b) Describe how scientific theories develop, are changed or replaced.   [2]
                            [Total 3]

6 Further chemistry

End of section questions

1 What type of reaction is each of the following:
  a) hydrochloric acid + potassium hydroxide →
     potassium chloride + water   *[1]*
  b) butane + oxygen → carbon dioxide + water   *[1]*
  c) copper + silver nitrate → copper nitrate + silver   *[1]*
  d) copper oxide + hydrogen → copper + water   *[1]*
  e) calcium hydrogencarbonate → water + calcium
     carbonate + carbon dioxide?   *[1]*
                                                [Total 5]

2 A series of experiments were carried out to see the effect
of acid concentration on the rate of the reaction between
calcium carbonate and hydrochloric acid. The rate was
measured in cm^3 of carbon dioxide produced per second
(by timing how long it took to collect 50 cm^3 and
calculating rate as volume ÷ time). The results are shown
in Table 1.
(M is a unit for concentration.)

Table 1

Concentration of acid (M)	0.50	1.00	1.50	2.00	2.50
Time to collect 50 cm^3 of CO_2 (s)	128	67	42	32	26
Rate (cm^3/s)	0.39	0.75	1.20	1.56	1.92

  a) What is the independent variable in this
     experiment?   *[1]*
  b) What is the dependent variable in this experiment? *[1]*
  c) i) Write a word equation for the reaction.
     ii) What type of reaction is this?   *[2]*
  d) Plot a graph of rate (*y*-axis) against concentration
     (*x*-axis).   *[4]*
  e) What happens to the reaction rate as the
     concentration of the acid increases?   *[1]*
  f) Explain, in terms of particles, why concentration
     affects the rate in this way.   *[2]*
  g) Give two other ways in which this reaction could be
     made to go faster (there are no catalysts for this
     reaction).   *[2]*
                                               [Total 13]

3 This question is about astatine (At), the element at the
bottom of Group 7. You will need the data in Table 2
about the other Group 7 elements to answer the
following questions. Note: the radius of atoms is
measured in nanometres (nm), where 1 nm is one
millionth of a millimetre.

Table 2

Element	Melting point (°C)	Boiling point (°C)	Radius of atom (nm)
fluorine	−219	−188	0.072
chlorine	−101	−35	0.099
bromine	−7	59	0.114
iodine	114	184	0.133

  a) Is astatine a metal or a non-metal?   *[1]*
  b) What will be the formula of astatine molecules?   *[2]*
  c) i) Predict the melting and boiling points of astatine
        using the data in Table 2.
     ii) Will astatine be a solid, liquid or gas at room
        temperature?   *[3]*
  d) Predict the radius of an astatine atom using the
     data in the table.   *[1]*
  e) Astatine is formed when chlorine reacts with sodium
     astatide.

     sodium astatide + chlorine → astatine + sodium chloride

     i) What type of reaction is this?
     ii) Which is more reactive, astatine or chlorine? *[2]*
                                                [Total 9]

4 Write the formula of each of the following compounds
(you will need to use the valencies in the Table 5.1 on
page 195):
  a) aluminium bromide   *[1]*
  b) calcium oxide   *[1]*
  c) iron(III) sulphide   *[1]*
  d) sodium hydride   *[1]*
  e) ammonia (containing nitrogen and hydrogen)   *[1]*
                                                [Total 5]

5 a) Balance each of the following equations:

i) $CaO + HCl \rightarrow CaCl_2 + H_2O$

ii) $Al + O_2 \rightarrow Al_2O_3$

iii) $C_3H_8 + O_2 \rightarrow CO_2 + H_2O$

iv) $CaCO_3 \rightarrow CaO + CO_2$

v) $C_6H_{12}O_6 + O_2 \rightarrow CO_2 + H_2O$ *[5]*

b) What type of reaction is each of the reactions in part a)? *[5]*

[Total 10]

6 a) Copy the outline Periodic Table shown in Figure 1. Draw it so that it fills about half a page. *[1]*

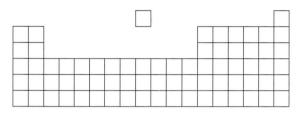

Figure 1

b) Use different colours to shade Groups 0, 1 and 7, and the transition metal block (make a key). *[5]*

c) Write the valency of each of the elements in Table 5.1 on page 195 in its box on your sketch (e.g. write '1' in the box for sodium). *[2]*

d) What trends do you notice in valency and position in the Periodic Table? *[2]*

e) Write the formula of each of the following compounds. The valencies of some of the elements are not in the Table 5.1 on page 195 but you may be able to work them out:

i) caesium bromide

ii) hydrogen selenide (contains selenium)

iii) strontium sulphide

iv) phosphine (contains phosphorus and hydrogen). *[4]*

f) i) What do you think is the valency of the Group 0 elements?

ii) Explain your answer. *[2]*

[Total 16]

7 Copy and complete Table 3. *[Total 11]*

Table 3

Atom	H	Li		Ne	
Atomic number	1	3			
Mass number	1				32
Number of protons			9		
Number of neutrons		4	10	10	
Number of electrons					16
Electronic structure				2,8	

8 Enzymes are used in the production of some foods and drinks. Find out about what they are used to make and how the processes are carried out.

R

9 Until 1894, none of the noble gases had been discovered. Find out about the discovery of argon by Lord Rayleigh and Sir William Ramsey. Find out about the contribution each scientist made and how the discovery of argon led to the discovery of other noble gases.

R

10 The reaction between sodium thiosulphate and hydrochloric acid produces a precipitate of sulphur, which makes the mixture cloudy. What factors might affect the rate of this reaction? For example, how would you investigate the effect of changing the temperature on the rate of this reaction?

P

11 The reaction between zinc and copper sulphate solution is exothermic. What factors might affect the temperature rise in this reaction? For example, how would you investigate the effect of changing the concentration of copper sulphate solution on the temperature rise?

P

Investigations

What are investigations?

A **hypothesis** is an idea about how something works. It can be used to make a **prediction**. The purpose of an **investigation** is to test a prediction and find the answer to a scientific question.

The **data** produced in an investigation can be used to show whether the hypothesis is correct or not. If the data from several investigations support a hypothesis, the hypothesis becomes a **theory**.

New ideas are being suggested and tested in science all the time. Eventually, if an idea is well tested it may be accepted by all scientists. However, even well-tested and established ideas can sometimes be proved wrong by further experiments or new ideas.

Many questions can be answered by doing experiments. These involve changing something and measuring the effects of changing it, such as in the example above. However, there are other scientific questions that cannot be answered in this way. These questions may involve surveys, or careful observations, without changing anything.

Scientists do not always have to carry out the investigations or observations themselves. A scientist with a new idea about rocks could look at observations that have already been made to see if they fit with the idea. Observations made and reported by someone else are called **secondary sources**.

Variables and values

A **variable** is a factor than can change. Each variable can be described in words or numbers (with units), which are called **values**. Variables can be of different types:

- A **continuous variable** is something that can be one of a continuous range of values, and can have any numerical value.

- A **categoric variable** is described in words, or in numbers that cannot be split into smaller values.

In most investigations you will choose a variable to change. This is called the **independent variable**. It is independent because its values don't depend on carrying out the investigation.

The **dependent variable** is what changes when the values of the independent variable are altered. This variable *depends* on the independent variable.

You might wonder what affects the pH of an acid solution. If you were a scientist, you would think up a hypothesis, such as 'the temperature of a solution affects its pH'. You would then use this hypothesis to make a prediction such as 'the higher the temperature the lower the pH', and then design a set of experiments to test the prediction by measuring the pH of the solution at different temperatures.

Chemists have studied how rock formations are made over many years. They do not make changes to the rocks themselves, but observe the changes that have occurred naturally, and then make predictions about what will happen in the future.

The volume of an acid solution is a continuous variable, but the type of acid is a categoric variable.
The atomic number of an element is also a categoric variable because, although it has a numeric value, it can only be 1, 2, 3, 4, etc. – it can never be 2.6 or 3.9.

Investigations involve finding out if there are **relationships** between different variables.

Fair testing

In most investigations there will be more than one variable that could be an independent variable. Since you only want to measure the effect of one independent variable, you need to stop all these other variables from changing. You need to try to control them. These are the control variables. Some **control variables** are very difficult to control.

Gathering data

The data you gather during an investigation needs to be valid, accurate and reliable.

- **Valid** data is data that is directly relevant to your investigation.

- **Accurate** data is data that is very close to the true value. You need to think about how accurate your data needs to be when choosing the measuring instruments for your investigation. When you choose a measuring device for measuring something, you need to think about the sensitivity of the device. Instruments that are more sensitive will allow you to take readings with more significant figures, which should therefore be more accurate. However, very sensitive instruments are not always needed

- **Reliable** data is data that will be the same if you repeat the experiment, or if someone else does the same experiment. You can make your results more reliable by taking each measurement several times and working out a mean or average value.

Suppose you are finding out how the concentration of an acid affects the speed of reaction between the acid and a metal.
- the independent variable is the concentration of an acid (and it is a continuous variable)
- the dependent variable is the speed of the reaction (this is also a continuous variable)
- the control variables are the volume of the acid, the temperature (both continuous variables), the type of acid, the type of metal and the form of the metal (all categoric variables).

When measuring volumes of solutions, a burette with scale divisions of 0.1 cm^3 is more sensitive and accurate than a measuring cylinder with 1.0 cm^3 divisions.

Presenting your results

The values of all variables should be recorded in a table, including the values of the control variables. If there is a **relationship** between the dependent variable and the independent variable in an investigation, there will be a pattern in the results. This is easiest to see by plotting a chart or graph. The independent variable is usually plotted on the horizontal axis. Draw a line graph if your independent variable is a continuous variable. Draw a bar chart if your independent variable is categoric.

If there is a relationship between the two variables, the points on the graph will form a line or a curve. Draw a line of best fit (or curve of best fit) through your points. The line or curve of best fit is the line you would get if all your measurements were perfectly accurate.

If you have gathered data using a datalogger and computer, you can use a spreadsheet program to produce graphs of your results.

The example investigation on the following pages shows you how to plan, carry out and report a typical investigation.

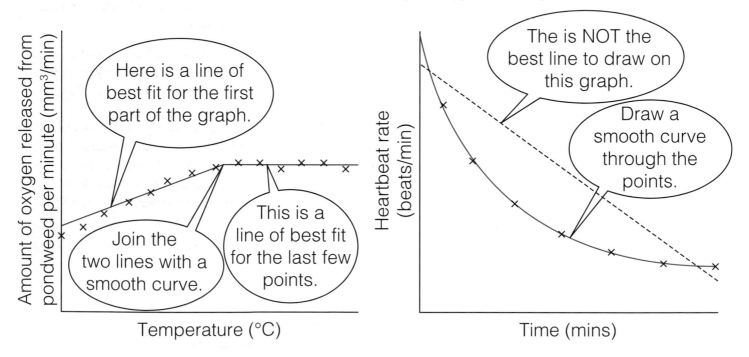

Figure 1.1 *Not all graphs form a straight line*

An example investigation

Consider an investigation to see what affects how much lather (foam) is produced when a detergent is shaken with water.

Plan

1 Make observations and think about the subject. Describe briefly what you are trying to find out. This is the aim.

When detergent is shaken with water, lather is produced. I want to find out if adding more detergent produces more lather.

2 Choose one variable to investigate – this is the independent variable.

Independent variable = the volume of detergent

I want to find out how changing the volume of detergent affects the volume of lather produced when a detergent is shaken with water. Dependent variable = the volume of lather produced

3 Make a prediction about the effect of the independent variable on the dependent variable. Try to explain why you think this will happen using your scientific knowledge.

I predict that the greater the volume of detergent used, the more lather will be produced.

Lather is produced by the reaction of water particles with detergent particles. This means that the more detergent particles there are, the more lather there is produced.

4 Plan how to carry out the investigation. Make it as accurate as possible.

I shall do the experiment in a boiling tube. I will put 5 cm³ of water into the tube and add different volumes of detergent (0, 0.2, 0.4, 0.6, 0.8 and 1.0 cm³). I will put a stopper in the tube and shake it three times. I will measure the height of the lather using a ruler.

Apparatus:
- *boiling tubes*
- *boiling tube rack*
- *1 cm³ syringe*
- *rubber bung*
- *water*
- *10 cm³ measuring cylinder*
- *detergent*
- *ruler*

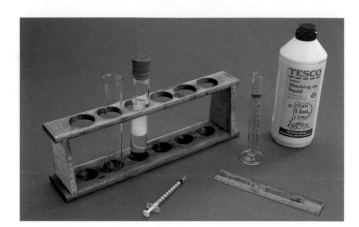

Figure 1.2

5 Describe how you will make it safe.

To make this experiment safe I will
- find a clear space away from other groups
- wear eye protection during the investigation
- hold my thumb over the stopper while shaking the boiling tube
- wash away any spillages with lots of water.

6 Show your plan to your teacher.

Obtain evidence

7 Do the experiment.

8 Record the results in a table.

Table 1.1

*This result was not included in the average because it clearly does not fit in with the others.

Lather height (cm)	Amount of detergent (cm³)					
	0.0	0.2	0.4	0.6	0.8	1.0
Experiment 1	0.0	3.0	5.1	7.7	8.6	9.9
Experiment 2	0.0	2.8	5.5	9.6*	8.6	9.3
Average	0.0	2.9	5.3	7.7	8.6	9.6

Analysis

9 Describe any pattern shown by the results (you may need to plot a graph first).

As more detergent is added, more lather is produced. However, as more and more detergent is used, adding extra detergent does not produce as much extra lather. It looks as though it might reach a point where adding more detergent produces no extra lather.

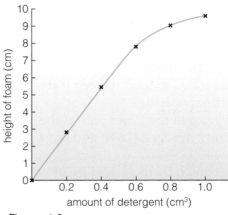

Figure 1.3

10 State the conclusion of the experiment and try to explain in scientific terms why this happened.

The greater the volume of detergent used, the more lather is produced, but as more detergent is used the effect gets smaller.

Lather is produced by the reaction of water particles with detergent particles. The more detergent particles there are, the more lather is produced. However, as more and more detergent particles are added, there is less water for each detergent particle to react with, so the effect gets smaller.

Evaluation

11 Consider the evidence obtained during the investigation and think about how the procedure could be improved. What could be done to test the conclusions more thoroughly? How could the practical techniques be changed to improve accuracy and reliability?

The accuracy of the results could be improved by using larger amounts of water and detergent, to reduce the errors involved in measuring volumes.

The reliability of the results could be improved if each measurement was repeated more often. This would also clearly highlight 'odd' results like the one in experiment 2, for 0.6 cm³ of detergent.

The results could be checked against secondary sources of data. In this experiment this would be the results obtained by other class groups.

Finally the investigation could be extended by carrying on beyond 1.0 cm³ of detergent to see if adding more and more detergent eventually stops producing extra lather.

Glossary

acid   A solution with a pH of less than 7.

acid rain   Rain that is more acidic than normal (pH less than 5.6) – the acidity is mainly due to dissolved sulphur dioxide and nitrogen dioxide from air pollution.

activation energy   The minimum amount of energy that particles need to react.

accurate   A measurement that is accurate is one that is close to the true value.

additive   Chemicals added to food to keep it fresh, improve its taste or appearance.

air   The mixture of gases in the lower part of the atmosphere–(mainly nitrogen (78%) and oxygen (21%)).

air pressure   Force caused by molecules in air hitting surfaces.

alchemy   An early form of chemistry and study of matter. Two of the main aims of alchemy were to change metals like lead into gold, and to find a potion which would let you live forever.

alkali   A solution with a pH greater than 7.

allergy   Unwanted reaction by the body to a chemical.

alloy   A metal with one or more other elements added to improve its properties.

antacid   A substance which will neutralise an acid (usually meaning a substance taken to reduce acidity in the stomach).

apparatus   Equipment used in experiments.

atmosphere   A mixture of gases that surrounds the Earth.

atom   A small particle from which all substances are made.

atomic mass   Average mass of an atom on a scale where $_{12}C$ atoms have mass of exactly 12.

atomic number   The number of protons in an atom.

barometer   An instrument used to measure air pressure.

base   A substance which will neutralise an acid forming a salt and water.

battery   Two or more cells joined together.

bimetallic strip   Two strips of different metals joined together that bend when heated as one metal expands more than the other.

biodegradable   Will decompose naturally over time.

biofuel   A fuel made from plants/crops.

blast furnace   Industrial equipment used for the extraction of iron.

boiling   The change of state which occurs when a liquid rapidly changes into a gas (at the liquid's boiling point).

boiling point   The temperature at which a liquid rapidly changes into a gas.

brittle   A material that breaks easily.

bronze   A strong, hard alloy of copper and tin.

Bronze Age   A period in history when bronze was the main material used for tools and weapons (started about 2000 BC in Europe).

Bunsen burner   Natural gas burner used as a source of heat in the laboratory.

burning   Combustion – a rapid reaction in which a substance combines with oxygen, catches fire and gives out energy.

carbon neutral   A fuel that releases the same amount of carbon dioxide when it burns as the crops from which it is made took in as they grew.

cast iron   Iron with high carbon content (it is very brittle).

categoric variable   A variable that has a set of fixed values. These can be words (e.g. iron, copper, tin) or a fixed set of values (e.g. shoe sizes).

catalyst   A substance that changes the speed of a chemical reaction without being used up.

cell (electrical)   Device which produces electricity from a chemical reaction.

Celsius scale   Standard temperature scale which sets the freezing point of water at 0 ˚C and its boiling point at 100 ˚C.

chalk   A mineral consisting mainly of calcium carbonate.

chemical   A pure substance which can be either an element or a compound.

chemical equation A way of writing out the changes which take place during a chemical reaction. A chemical equation shows the formulas of the reactants and products.

chemical industry Any business which changes raw materials into useful products by chemical processes.

chemical properties How a substance acts in chemical reactions.

chemical reaction A change in which one or more new substances are formed.

chemistry The science which studies the structure and properties of matter.

chlorination Addition of chlorine gas to water to kill germs.

chromatography A process in which substances are separated by their different solubility in a solvent, which is moving through a solid (e.g. paper).

coal A solid fossil fuel formed from the decay of plant material over millions of years under heat and pressure and in the absence of air.

coke An impure form of carbon, produced by heating coal in the absence of air.

colloid A mixture where the particles of one substance are spread evenly throughout another substance. The particles in a colloid are larger than the solute particles in a solution.

combustion Burning – a rapid reaction in which a substance combines with oxygen, catches fire and gives out energy.

compound A substance made from atoms of different kinds chemically joined together.

concentration A measure of how much solute is dissolved in a solvent.

condensation Change of state which occurs when a gas changes into a liquid.

conservation of mass The law which states that the total mass does not alter during chemical and physical changes.

Contact Process Industrial process used in manufacturing sulphuric acid.

continental crust The part of the Earth's crust that is not covered by sea water.

continuous variable A variable that can have any numerical value. Temperature is a continuous variable.

contraction When a substance gets smaller without any change in mass.

control variable A variable that must be kept the same to make an investigation a fair test.

cooling When a substance loses energy and its temperature falls.

cooling curve Graph of temperature against time as a substance is steadily cooled.

core The innermost part of the Earth, thought to be mainly iron and nickel.

corrosion Reaction which forms compounds on the surface of a metal.

cracking The breakdown of longer hydrocarbon molecules into shorter ones.

crude oil A liquid fossil fuel formed from the decay of sea creatures over millions of years under heat and pressure and in the absence of air.

crust The outer layer of the Earth.

crystal A solid with a regular shape and flat surfaces which reflect light.

crystallisation The formation of crystals as a solution cools.

data A collection of measurements.

decanting Separating an insoluble solid from a liquid by pouring off the liquid.

decomposition A reaction in which a compound is broken down into simpler substances.

dependent variable The variable that you measure in an investigation. For example, you might measure the current in a circuit when you change the voltage. The current is the dependent variable.

density The mass per unit volume of a substance (usually the mass of 1 cm^3, measured in g/cm^3) (density = mass ÷ volume).

dependent variable The variable that is affected by changes in the independent variable and measured in an investigation.

diffusion The movement of particles from an area of high concentration to an area of lower concentration.

displacement A reaction in which a more reactive element takes the place of a less reactive element in a compound.

distillation A process in which a solvent is separated from a solute by heating the solution. The solvent boils and then condenses and the solvent is collected.

ductility The ability of a substance to be stretched into a wire.

E numbers Food additives that have been approved by the European Food Safety Authority.

effervescence The production of a gas in a reaction in solution.

electrical conductivity The ability of a substance to allow electricity to pass through it.

electrolysis The breaking down of a substance using electricity.

electron A negatively charged particle inside an atom.

electron shells Regions in which electrons move around the nucleus in an atom.

electronic balance Instrument to measure mass accurately.

electroplating Putting a thin coating of a metal on another metal using electricity.

element A substance made up of only one kind of atom.

endothermic reaction A reaction in which heat energy is converted to chemical energy and so cools down.

enzyme A biological catalyst.

erosion The breaking up of pieces of rock as they are moved by the wind, by gravity, by the water in rivers, streams and the sea, and by ice in glaciers.

evaporation Change of state which happens when a liquid changes into a gas (below the boiling point).

exothermic reaction A reaction in which chemical energy is converted to heat energy, and so heats up.

expansion When a substance gets bigger in size without any change in mass.

experiment A practical investigation to gather information and improve our understanding of our world.

extrusive igneous rock A rock formed from the crystallisation of liquid rock at the Earth's surface.

filtrate The liquid that passes through a filter.

filtration Method to separate a mixture of a liquid and an insoluble solid by passing it through paper or other material which only allows the liquid through.

flammability How easily a substance catches fire.

flexibility The ability of a substance to bend without breaking.

fossil The remains or imprints of plants and animals that lived millions of years ago.

fossil fuels Fuels formed from the decay of the remains of living organisms over millions of years under heat and pressure in the absence of air.

fraction A mixture of substances with similar boiling points produced by fractional distillation.

fractional distillation A process in which a mixture of liquids with different boiling points is separated by distillation.

freezing Change of state which occurs when a liquid changes into a solid.

freezing point The temperature at which a liquid turns into a solid (this is the same temperature as the melting point of the substance).

fuel A source of energy (which is usually burned to release the energy).

fullerene Molecular form of the element carbon. The most common example called Buckminster fullerene consists of spherical molecules with the formula C_{60}.

galvanising Covering iron and steel by dipping it in molten zinc (the zinc coating helps prevent corrosion).

gas State in which substances have no fixed volume or shape, but spread out in all directions.

global warming The gradual increase in average global temperatures.

greenhouse effect Heat being trapped by gases in the atmosphere, thought to lead to global warming.

group A vertical column in the Periodic Table.

haematite An iron ore made mainly of iron oxide.

hazard symbols Standard symbols used to warn of specific dangers in dealing with a chemical.

heating When a substance gains energy and its temperature rises.

heating curve Graph of temperature against time as a substance is steadily heated.

humus Mixture of rotting plant and animal material found in soil.

hydrated Having water added or containing water.

hydrocarbon A compound containing hydrogen and carbon only.

hyperactivity Abnormally high level of activity or excitement by a person.

hypothesis An idea about why something happens but that does not have very much evidence to support it. If more evidence is found to support the hypothesis, it becomes a theory.

igneous rock A rock formed from the cooling and crystallisation of liquid rock.

immiscible Liquids that do not mix together but form two separate layers.

incomplete combustion The burning of a substance without enough oxygen present .

independent variable The variable that you change in an investigation. For example, you might measure the current in a circuit when you change the voltage. The voltage is the independent variable.

indicators Substances which change colour as the pH of a solution alters.

inhibitor A substance that slows down a chemical reaction without being used up itself.

insoluble A substance that does not dissolve in a solvent.

intrusive igneous rock A rock formed from the crystallisation of liquid rock under the Earth's surface.

investigation Trying to find the answer to a scientific question by making measurements and/ or observations.

Iron Age A period in history after the Bronze Age when iron was the main material used for tools and weapons (started about 1000 BC in Europe).

iron ore A rock which contains compounds of iron (e.g. iron oxide) and is used as a source of the metal.

labour intensive A process involving a lot of work by people.

lanthanides and actinides A block of rare metals in the Periodic Table.

lava Liquid rock on the Earth's surface.

law A description of what happens in certain situations based on observations and experiments.

lime Calcium oxide (made by roasting limestone or chalk).

limestone A mineral which is mainly calcium carbonate.

limewater A solution of calcium hydroxide in water, used to test for carbon dioxide which turns it cloudy.

liquid State in which substances have a fixed volume but no fixed shape – they take the shape of the container.

lithosphere The outer part of the Earth (the crust and some of the upper mantle).

litmus A natural substance obtained from lichen which is used as an indicator (red in acids and blue in alkalis).

magma Liquid rock beneath the Earth's surface.

malleability The ability of a substance to be hammered into shape.

mantle A layer of the Earth's structure between the crust and the core.

mass A measure of the amount of matter a substance contains (units – grams (g) and kilograms (kg)).

mass number The number of protons plus the number of neutrons in an atom.

matter All the substances and materials of the universe which are made up of atoms and molecules.

melting The change of state which occurs when a solid changes into a liquid.

melting point The temperature at which a solid turns into a liquid (and vice versa).

meniscus The curved surface of a liquid in a thin tube.

metal Elements which are generally hard, shiny and conduct electricity (found on the left-hand side of the Periodic Table).

metamorphic rock A rock formed from the action of heat and/or pressure on other rocks.

mineral An element or compound that is found naturally on, or within, the Earth.

Glossary

miscible Liquids that mix with each other.

mixture More than one substance – contains different types of particles that are not joined together.

molecule A particle made from atoms joined together.

nanobots Tiny particle programmed to do certain jobs at a molecular level.

nanocomposites Stronger and stiffer than ordinary plastics.

nanometres Unit of length equalling 1×10^{-9} metre (nm).

nanoparticles Particles and molecules whose sizes range from 10 to 100 nanometres.

nanotechnology The science that deals with particles whose sizes range from 10 to 100 nanometres.

native An element found uncombined in nature.

natural gas A gaseous fossil fuel formed from the decay of sea creatures over millions of years under heat and pressure in the absence of air.

neutral Neither acidic nor alkaline (pH = 7).

neutralisation A reaction in which an acid reacts with a base producing a salt and water.

neutron A neutral particle inside the nucleus of an atom.

non-ferrous Metals other than iron.

non-metal Elements which are generally not shiny and do not conduct electricity (found on the right-hand side of the Periodic Table).

non-renewable energy source A source of energy that cannot be replaced once used and will eventually run out.

nucleus The central part of an atom (made up of protons and neutrons).

oceanic crust The part of the Earth's crust that is covered by sea water.

oleum Very concentrated sulphuric acid formed during the Contact Process.

ore Rock or mineral from which a metal can be extracted.

oxidation A reaction in which a substance combines with oxygen.

particle theory Theory which explains the properties of matter by assuming that all substances are made up of tiny particles.

pascal Unit of pressure.

period A horizontal row in the Periodic Table.

Periodic Table A table showing all the elements in atomic number order.

petrochemical industry Industry which makes substances from crude oil.

pH scale Scale which usually runs from 0 to 14 and measures the acidity or alkalinity of solutions.

physical barrier Coating put on a metal to prevent corrosion.

physical change A change in which no new substances are formed.

physical properties A description of what a substance does or looks like, which does not involve chemical reactions.

plastic A man-made material which can be shaped or moulded (many common plastics are made from crude oil).

pollution Substance produced by human activity which when released into our environment can cause harm (e.g. into water or the atmosphere).

precipitate A solid formed by the reaction of two solutions.

precipitation A reaction in which a solid is produced when solutions are mixed together.

precise A measurement taken with a piece of apparatus with a high level of sensitivity (e.g. a balance that measures to the nearest 0.01 g rather than the?

prediction Saying what you think will happen in an investigation and why you think it will happen.

preservatives Chemicals added to food to keep it fresh longer.

products The new substances formed in a chemical reaction.

properties A description of what a substance does or looks like.

proton A positively charged particle found inside the nucleus of an atom.

pure A single substance (rather than a mixture of substances).

quarry Open-pit mine from which rock or minerals are extracted.

raw materials Naturally occurring materials from which useful products can be made or extracted.

reactants The substances that take part in a chemical reaction.

reaction rate The speed of a chemical reaction.

reactivity series A list of metals in order of how quickly they react.

recycling Collecting and reusing a material to save the natural resources.

reducing agent A substance which can be used to remove oxygen from a compound.

reduction A reaction in which a substance loses oxygen.

renewable energy source A source of energy that can be replaced once used.

relationship A link between two variables. If there is a relationship between two variables, one will change when the other changes.

reliable A measurement or observation that is reliable is one that will be the same when it is repeated.

reservoir Lake or loch which is used as a source of water for domestic or industrial use.

residue The solid that does not pass through a filter.

rock cycle A cycle showing how the three groups of rocks change from one to another.

rusting The corrosion of iron or steel (water and oxygen must be present for rusting to occur).

sacrificial protection Protecting a metal from corrosion by attaching it to a more reactive metal (which corrodes first).

salt Compound (other than water) formed during the neutralisation of an acid with a base.

saturated solution A solution in which no more solute will dissolve at that temperature.

scientific model An explanation put forward by scientists, that may or may not be correct, to help explain observations.

secondary sources A source that contains information that other people have gathered and written about.

sediment Broken up pieces of rock.

sedimentary rock Rock formed when sediments are deposited and cemented together.

seismic waves Waves that travel through the Earth.

sensitivity The more sensitive a measuring instrument is the more accurately it can measure something. A balance that can measure down to 1 g is less sensitive than one that can measure down to 0.001 g.

slag A waste substance formed during the extraction of iron. Made of the impurities from limestone and iron ore.

smart materials Materials that change in a consistent way with changes in their environment. The materials can be used to control and give information.

soil A mixture of rock fragments, humus, air, water and dissolved minerals that covers much of our land.

solid State in which substances have a fixed volume and a fixed shape.

solubility A measure of how much solute dissolves in a solvent.

solubility curve A graph showing how the solubility of a solute varies with temperature.

soluble When a substance can dissolve in a solvent.

solute The substance that dissolves in a solvent.

solution A mixture of a solute dissolved in a solvent.

solvent A liquid in which a solute dissolves.

states of matter The three different forms of matter:–solid, liquid and gas.

sublimation When a solid changes directly into a gas without melting first (and vice versa).

suspension A mixture of insoluble solid particles spread through a liquid.

sustainable A process that can be continued without running out of resources or damaging the Earth.

tectonic plates Separate, huge, slow moving slabs of rock that make up the lithosphere.

temperature A measurement of how hot or cold something is.

theory An idea about why something happens that has lots of evidence from investigations to support it.

thermal conductivity The ability of a substance to allow heat to pass through it.

thermal decomposition A reaction in which a substance is broken down by heat into simpler substances.

thermometer An instrument used to measure temperature.

thermostat A device which contains a bimetallic strip and is used to switch an electrical circuit on and off as the temperature changes.

time The measurement of how long something lasts or has existed (units – hours (hr), minutes (min) and seconds (s)).

tin plated Steel coated with tin (mainly used to make food containers).

titration A way of measuring the exact volume of acid and alkali needed for neutralisation.

toxicity A measure of how poisonous a substance is.

transition metals The central block of metals in the Periodic Table.

tsunami A large sea wave caused by earthquake or volcanic eruption.

universal indicator A mixture of dyes which display a range of different colours as the pH of a solution changes.

unsaturated solution A solution which can dissolve more solute at that temperature.

valency The number of bonds an atom forms in a molecule.

valid Valid data is data that is directly relevant to the question that is being answered.

values The numbers (or labels) that a variable can have.

vapour A substance in the gaseous state.

variable A factor that can change in an experiment.

voltage Measure of the amount of electrical energy supplied by a cell or battery (units – volts (V)).

volume The space taken up by an object (units – litres (l), cubic centimetres (cm^3) or cubic metres (m^3)).

water cycle The movement of water between land, sea and sky (usually as a liquid or gas).

weathering The breaking up of rocks into smaller pieces by natural processes.

word equation A way of writing out the changes which take place during a chemical reaction, showing the reactants and products in words.